Before Forever After

Before Forever After

When Conversations About Living
Meet Questions About Dying

HELENA DOLNY

STAGING
POST
The Stories We Tell

First published by Staging Post in 2017

10 Orange Street
Sunnyside
Auckland Park 2092
South Africa
+2711 628 3200
www.stagingpost.co.za

ISBN 978-0-9947079-8-7

Edited by Tanya Pampalone
Cover design by Palesa Motsomi
Set in Sabon 10.5/14pt
Printed by Digital Action, Cape Town
Job no. 003004

I dedicate this book to:

*My mother: known as Regie in Czechoslovakia and West Germany,
Regina in England, and Gina in South Africa. A migrant thrice over.
A survivor.*

*My father, Antoni, whose love and constancy gave
my mother and myself both roots and wings.*

*My daughters, Tessa and Kyla, with heartfelt gratitude
for making the best of the parenting I offered.*

*John, my love, my true partner
in our journey of a life with no deferment.*

*All those who so generously gave time and trusted me
with their stories and conversations in the service of learning
—without you I could not have written this book.*

I am that supreme and fiery force that sends forth all living sparks.
Death hath no part in me, yet I bestow death,
wherefore I am girt about with wisdom as with wings ...
I am the source of the thundered word by which all creatures were made,
I permeate all things that they may not die.
I am life.

—Hildegard of Bingen (1098–1179), medieval abbess and theologian, poet, artist, musician, scientist, and healer

Contents

PART THREE: Secrets

PART FOUR: Respecting Choices

PART FIVE: Ritual

PART TEN: New Beginnings

PART ELEVEN: Live the Questions

PROLOGUE
Pink Tulips

Pink tulips in a frosted glass vase; they stood erect at first, bending their heads only slightly. As their petals unfolded they gently filled with air, and as they swelled the intensity of their color faded, just a fraction of a shade. Days passed and they stretched their necks like swans towards the light that fell into the room from the bay window.

They leaned. They took a bow. I loved watching them change.

'Mama,' my younger daughter Kyla asked, 'when you buy tulips, why do you always buy the pink ones?'

Indeed, why always pink tulips?

A man pushed a bicycle up the steep hill, the last leg of his journey after his night shift at the factory. The headlamp cut through the fogginess of the icy winter morning. Number 5 Argyle Street, Accrington, Lancashire. It was the only house in the terrace with its lights on.

'Gina?' he called out softly. Their three-year-old must be fast asleep. 'Gina?' he called again, just a little louder.

'Toni, I think the baby is coming,' his wife answered, whispering loudly.

He washed, his muscular arms rubbing his sturdy body, toweling himself dry quickly. He put on his brown striped suit, the one from Burtons with two pairs of trousers—the suit lasted longer that way. He picked up his son and knocked on the neighbor's front door. They would look after him while he took his wife to the maternity home.

Rough Lee Maternity home, a Victorian structure, was a couple of miles away. The hours passed by and, just before midday, Gina pushed her baby into the world.

'It's a girl, healthy, 8 pounds 5 ounces,' the nurse told Toni. 'Visiting time: 4pm.'

A girl. He was happy. He wanted a girl. He walked back down the cobbled streets, past rows of terraced housing. People walked. Buses hardly ran on Sundays. Mill sheds, mine chimneys, church spires shaped the skyline; cotton, coal and religion crowded into this northern English Pennine Valley town surrounded by wilderness.

Sunday. The shops were closed. Flowers? February. If it were summer he could cut flowers from his own garden, but there was nothing there to cut now. The cemetery. That's it, on the other side of town, the only place you could buy flowers on a Sunday. He'd never been there.

He's an immigrant, a World War II displaced person living in the United Kingdom. His ancestors are buried in Poland and Gina's in Czechoslovakia. If he hurried he'd just make it, enough time to check in on his son, walk to the cemetery and get back to the maternity ward by 4pm.

The father of a newborn girl: will she have his brown flecked eyes, or the piercing blue eyes of Gina's family? He couldn't yet know. He looked at what was on sale, chose pink tulips and returned down into the valley, crossing the town center and up to the other side.

He entered the ward. Eight women, eight healthy babies. The mothers' faces shone with happiness, relief and mystery. It was the shadows under their eyes that told the tale of the strain of pregnancy and birth-giving.

'Toni. She's the only girl born here today. There are seven boys,' murmured Gina, 'and she's a Sunday's child of a Sunday's child.'

A nurse brought a vase filled with water, as well as sugar and salt. She pricked the base of the tulip heads with a needle, so they'd breathe more easily as they opened. Gina was the only woman in the ward who had fresh flowers that winter Sunday afternoon. She felt loved and special.

This is my mother's story of her giving birth to me, Helena Maria, and my father's thoughtfulness on that day. Pink tulips took on a special significance in our family.

I used to think it quirky that my dad walked to the cemetery immediately after my birth. Now I think of it as auspicious that his newborn child— me—would make several life choices, which meant that death and dying would become a consistent life-partner.

INTRODUCTION
The Hummingbird

Sitting on a slope in a lightly forested area of California, not far from San Francisco, I was preparing to die. I was 12,000 miles from Johannesburg, the place I now called home.

After sunrise, I went through the ritual I had planned. My daughter had gotten married just 10 days before and so, for the day's special occasion, I brought a candle in a red glass from the table décor of the wedding meal. I also had dried wild herbs, sage as my favorite, to burn and immerse myself in their smokiness—'snuffing' it's called in North America, so I had learned this week. We call these herbs *mpepo* in South Africa. The leaves lay withered and brittle on their stems in a small ceramic bowl which was damaged on my journey of many stopovers. The bowl, with its missing piece was perfect—the air would draw more easily when I lit the herbs. I had one small black stone, obsidian, carrying the energies of protection, the cleansing of negative attachments and grounding equilibrium. Yesterday, in the shadows of the late afternoon, as the sun lowered itself behind my back, I settled into the sitting place I'd chosen the day before. I placed these objects, each one with meaning for me, on a patch of flat earth and I added wild flowers.

I imagined I would prefer to die in the soft light of early morning. I didn't know if I would sleep during the night ahead of me or not. I'd never spent a night in the wild before, alone, without shelter. Would I find that I was still too scared?

I was attending a course in the Henry W. Coe State Park, which explored life, death and the rites of final passage. After four days of intense exploration and discussion we'd been asked to envisage our final hours of life. Each participant had chosen a solitary place to spend in the wilderness from mid-afternoon to late morning of the next day; a time to contemplate and imagine our own deaths.

I'd traveled far to spend this week in the wilderness. I wanted to learn to have conversations about living and dying more easily, and to be part of making those conversations become a normal occurrence which people have on any day, any month, any year. People who avoided talking about dying as part of their daily living seemed to create additional problems for themselves on top of the normal stress experienced when people face illness and death.

I had spent 15 years working as an agricultural economist, at first with rural African communities, and then 10 years as a banker working to create easier access to finance. I became more interested in people than finance, how they embrace change and what choices they make. I retrained to become a leadership coach. Many of my clients focused on life purpose and joy and their ability to inspire and lead others in the workplace. Now I wanted to add more strings to my bow and pursue conversations about dying interfaced with questions about how we choose to live. There's something about embracing mortality that helps clarify what's important to us. I set out to become more skilled at having such conversations, and that included getting closer to the practice of dying.

My training as a hospice lay counselor had been thorough and respectfully secular. There was more technical detail than I'd anticipated: products to moisten dry lips, egg shell mattresses to prevent bed sores and social mapping of family relationships to anticipate possible family dramas. There was an important emphasis on unconditional positive regard; compassion without judgment as mission-critical to the hospice offering.

But I wanted something more than this socio-technical knowledge. I wanted to learn how to best create and support the emotional environment that would serve the person dying and those around them. I wanted to embrace a universal spirituality which was distinct from the rituals of any specific religious denomination. I also questioned my own internal state of readiness to accept impermanence, and wanted to feel more solid and grounded within myself.

The week-long course was offered by the School of Lost Borders, an organization which focuses on the reintroduction of ritual into modern-day lifestyles. The conceptual underpinning of Dying as a Rite of Passage was that we, as participants, would only be able to offer the best version of ourselves in the service of others if we were 'at ease with our own dying.'

The online brochure indicated that we would work with two questions:

How do we live so we may fully become our dying?

How do we accept our dying, so we may fully embrace our living?

The facilitators anchored their teaching in the practices of Native Americans, whose array of cultures commonly share a community approach to dying. They have a structure, a 'death lodge' on the edge of a settlement where people visit and take their leave of the dying. The facilitators believed that time spent alone in nature, taking lessons from the natural world, would encourage participants to explore their 'own truth about living and dying' and 'bridge the growing wisdom of the modern hospice movement' with the 'ancient wisdom of indigenous peoples.'

On the second day of the course, as I sat in the forest clearing in our circle of 16 people (12 people closely cared for by 4 trainers), a hummingbird flew across our group and then hovered over me.

'Ah hah, the hummingbird is choosing you,' I was told. 'The humming bird is your totem, your guardian, your spirit guide. The qualities of the hummingbird are yours to connect with should you be open to the learning they offer.'

Later, I read about how hummingbirds fly huge distances, their wings moving in the shape of the infinity symbol indicative of their indefatigable energy and how they audaciously take on birds of prey in certain circumstances. Nothing is too big for them. They're associated with timelessness, healing, warrior energy, vitality, affection, joy, playfulness, and being a messenger—all of this in a bird that weighs less than 2 ounces!

My fellow participants spoke of totems with gravity, and conveyed I was being offered something precious from another culture. I felt honored by this possibility, joyful and encouraged.

We spent the first four days talking about mortality, beginning with our early childhood memories right through to adulthood and where we were at that point in our lives. Each day had a rhythm of group work, solo time in the forest—sitting or walking—and then a sharing of reflections. We began every morning formally with the snuffing ceremony. Each person would take a turn holding a bowl of burning herbs and move it up and down, in front and behind, so that the smoke would swirl and signal your readiness for sacred conversation. You took your turn to speak when holding the 'talking stick'—there was no interrupting, no speaking without the stick in your hand.

Those days were a preparation. From the afternoon of the fifth day until late morning on day six, we were to spend time alone in the forest, fasting and in contemplation of our own dying. We'd leave our tents at the campsite and travel lightly, being sure to be physically warm and carrying enough water. The fast/meditation was optional but no one opted out. Applicants for this course were vetted months ago, and every person had prepared psychologically.

I was fearful, not of death, but of being alone in the darkness of the night without walls and security systems between me and the rest of the world. So many of us in the modern world have learned to live in this way, far removed from childhoods of unlocked doors. I am a woman now living in Johannesburg, a city offering gritty, joyous, diverse relationships, but a place of such material disparity that the expectation of armed robberies is normal. At home, I sleep behind three locked doors in an apartment building that has guards at its gated entrance and its grounds surrounded by high fencing topped with barbed wire. At night security lamps illuminate the garden and building entrances and cameras relay footage to screens in the guardhouse.

I needed to quell my anxiety about being alone in the forest. A transition worked itself out in my head: 'chunking,' taking incremental steps towards a better frame of mind.

On the first night, I slept inside the tent and zipped up the entrance firmly—I didn't want bugs inside and I felt safe. On the second night, I slept with my head at the tent entrance and left the flap untied. On my third night, I slept alongside my tent leaving the entrance open just in case I got scared and wanted to crawl back inside.

I discovered the magic of sleeping in the open air. I lay on my mat and looked upwards at the beauty of the intricate dark silhouettes of the branches of the tree above, and then beyond to the kaleidoscope of stars filling the sky. I was enthralled. And I was now ready enough to spend my night in the forest alone.

The task for our solo meditation and fast was to contemplate our own death, and envisage it happening. As the evening darkened into night, the forest became quiet. I planned to die after dawn. I drifted into sleep easily and woke at 3:50am, 10 minutes before the alarm which I'd forgotten to put on. I wanted time to ready myself while watching the sky getting lighter as the morning sun crested over the distant hilltops.

I lit my *mpepo* herbs and sat immersed in the pleasure of thinking about each one of the people in my life who I love and have loved. Those still living knew just how much I loved them—I think I've always taken enough care to make sure of that. I didn't feel the need to write. I had no 'significant' last thoughts or messages to leave behind. As the sky brightened, I sat still, breathing deeply, then more deeply and then lost myself in my breathing, reaching a meditative place where my mind flooded with color that flowed and swirled and then stilled itself into a silken backdrop.

A whirr in the trees close by announced a hummingbird. My totem. This was my prompt, my time to depart from this earthly state of being.

The night in contemplation of my own death changed me. Something shifted in terms of my relationship with impermanence. The experience offered me a meaningful insight regarding my own end-of-earthly life. At the time of my dying, I would prefer solitude—having loved ones nearby will be too hard, distracting, conflicting, pulling me back and making departure more difficult.

My week in the wilderness was spiritually strengthening. I was ready to work with how we live and how we die in whatever form the opportunity might present itself in my future. I took the re-appearance of my totem, the hummingbird, as a confirmation of my choice.

As a coach, I wanted to master conversations that included death as a topic, as people explored how to live their lives better. I expected to do pro bono support work through hospice. I never planned to write a book!

That journey, this book, began as an impulsive response to a phone conversation. My eldest daughter, Tessa, who lives in Cape Town, phoned in a state of agitation.

'Candice's grandmother died on Friday night,' Tessa told me. 'She was only 69. She had a stroke.'

Tessa is an art therapist and Candice* was her nine-year-old client, a high-functioning autistic child. The previous Saturday morning Candice's mom phoned her to say, 'Granny died suddenly during the night. They will do an autopsy. We must go to the mortuary. We need your help. Please come and be with the kids.'

Just 69. Out of the blue.

'Sixty-nine years old. That's the same age as my dad!' Tessa exclaimed.

She was now anxious that she could wake up one morning to be told that her beloved father, Ed, had died during the night.

'Mama, don't you have something I can read?' she asked. 'Something that can help me think and be more ready for when something happens to Dad?'

I'm the one with the library. People gave me books on cancer when Tessa's stepfather, my husband Joe Slovo, was dying 15 years before. After his death, when I lost myself in sadness, people gave me books on grief, on dying, on ritual.

I scoured my bookshelves. As a coach, I have shelves overflowing with books in the living-your-life-to-your-full-potential genre. But I'd also kept many of the books from the time of my late husband Joe's four-year illness. But a book to help you be in a better state of readiness to face death? Your own or the death of a loved one? And at a time when you are living a normal, healthy, everyday life?

I selected several books and thumbed through them to remind myself of their content. Too esoteric. Very religious. That one is better for after a death has happened. Among my couple of hundred books, I could not find an appropriate one to offer to my daughter that would meet her need.

I woke up the next Saturday morning with no plans except to go to the wholesale flower market. As I drove, I thought again of Tessa. Back home I worked at the kitchen counter unbundling the flowers. The vibrantly colored gerberas would look stunning on the server that divides the lounge from the dining area. The roses could wilt quickly in the heat; I cut their stems and floated the blossoms in a shallow blue glass bowl placed on the coffee table. The St. Joseph's lilies were for my study; I love inhaling their delicate scent while sitting at my desk.

Flower arranging—my personal playtime—and all the while I thought of Tessa's request; neuroscience studies suggest that we're often most creative after play.

I sat down and began to write. I wrote until darkness fell and I slept. The next day I felt compelled to continue. I was driven by an internal force that energized me. By Sunday night I had the outline for a book. I love writing—this would be my third book—and a joy to have something I felt strongly motivated to write about.

I began the project by writing stories, my own at first. I also wrote an eight-week series *Let's Talk About Dying* for *City Press*, a South

African Sunday newspaper. Readers contacted me, some sending in their own stories. I encountered such generosity—people wanting others to learn from their experience, stories offered in service. I asked many of them if I could speak with them in more detail and then craft a short story based on the transcript.

I also took stories from my family: my mother Gina, my daughters Tessa and Kyla, my brother Roman, my niece Stefanie, my first husband Ed, my late husband Joe and his sister Renée, and my current husband John. Friends and clients shared stories, as did my fellow residents at the Rockefeller Foundation Bellagio Center in Italy, where I spent a month on a writing scholarship. Fellow members of the International Women's Federation also collaborated.

At times, I've used pseudonyms, indicated with an asterisk, when people wanted to retain their privacy; in other cases, I altered places or circumstances for the same reason. Privileged to listen to dozens of stories, I've selected those with an *Aesop's Fables* essence to them, the stories which make you sit upright and consider: is there a moral in this story that might be relevant to my life?

I grouped the stories in parts around nine themes which came up repeatedly:

- Living Life Alive
- Relationships
- Secrets
- Respecting Choices
- Ritual
- Bereavement
- Money. Planning. Emotion
- Winding Up
- Let's Talk—Towards The Tipping Point

As soon as I finished the outline, I sent it to my daughter Tessa and asked her what she thought. She replied emphatically: 'I don't want to talk about it. But I'll read it when it's finished.' She takes after my mum, her grandmother Gina, who also said: 'I don't want to talk about it.' My now-late mother-in-law, Ina, already in her mid-eighties and beginning to face health issues, deflected, 'When the right time comes…'

Therein lies the rub. It seems to me that when someone dies our inevitable suffering is made worse when we haven't had certain conversations. People—family, friends, business partners—all too often quarrel over differences and misunderstandings that might have been avoided if people talked more, and earlier.

So how do you get people to talk more readily about living with intention and joy while mindful of their mortality? I wanted to find a way and a place to do this.

In 2014 I joined DignitySA and soon after became the chairperson for a year. I saw it as an advocacy group that stimulates debate in society. There is the worldwide contentious issue of physician-assisted dying, but in South Africa, it's problematic that Advance Directives and Living Wills do not yet have the standing of being legal documents which oblige doctors to follow patient wishes. And we also do not yet have enduring power of attorney which would be helpful to those who are diagnosed with dementia.

My work with DignitySA brought me into contact with Archbishop Emeritus Desmond Tutu, who holds strong views on the right to die with dignity and choice. Whenever work or family visits took me to Cape Town, I attended Archbishop Tutu's Friday morning service and enjoyed the conviviality of the group breakfast that followed.

Lord Joel Joffe of the UK's Dignity in Dying and 'The Arch', as Tutu is affectionately known, supported my aspiration to write a book that would get people to talk more readily. They contributed funds for my travel and research and importantly stood as references when I applied to the Rockefeller Foundation for a residency scholarship in Bellagio on the shores of Lake Como in Italy. The scholarship's single most important criterion is that the work undertaken is for the good of humankind.

I interviewed some of the pioneers in this field, including experts at the Gundersen Health Institute in La Crosse, Wisconsin, The Conversation Project in Boston and spent time with one of the Miami-based drafters of the *Five Wishes* document, a conversational guide to help people make decisions about how they'd like to live out their last days, which is now used in 32 states. My research and story gathering also took me to Amsterdam, Chicago, Edinburgh, London and Washington and, of course, to many corners of South Africa.

The question foremost in my mind was this: what would contribute towards creating a 'tipping point' and a time when it would become commonplace for people to talk easily about death as they lived their normal day-to-day lives?

I had four beliefs as I wrote. First, if we regularly had more conversations about what matters to us, if we actively engaged with our certain mortality, then possibly we'd become more intentional about our choices and thereby enhance the very quality with which we live our lives—mindfully and with no regrets.

My second belief was that talking more might result in suffering less. We human beings have the gift, the capacity of being able to love. The potential power and beauty of this emotion is equaled by the deep sadness we experience when we lose someone or even when we allow ourselves to think about our own death and separation from those we love.

My third belief, supported by neuroscience, is that questions are generative. They can be likened to the ignition key which turns on the engine, starting up the workings of our minds. I have drawn up questions relating to each section of this book for people to reflect upon and/or use as potential conversation prompts. Many people reflect seriously on their lives when they face a hiccup, when the future feels threatened. My goal is for adults of any age to read this book when they are not sick, and when they are not sad. I want to encourage discussions. I want people to go to their edge, where conversations about living meet questions about dying. I hope the questions will catalyze people to have conversations and take decisions, write them down and ensure that others know and understand those decisions.

My fourth belief is that storytelling offers us the best opportunity to learn from others. Stories offer us the chance to vicariously travel the world and, through multi-layered descriptions, gain glimpses into the lives and souls of others. Our ancestors passed on wisdom through fables and legends. Some love to listen, others love to tell, but *all* of us are hard-wired to engage with stories and remember them.

I was halfway through my writing endeavor when an unwelcome guest, self-doubt, paid me a visit. We were on holiday, having breakfast outside with a beautiful vista of South Africa's Tsitsikamma Mountains. As I voiced my doubt, a friend shouted, 'Look! There's a hummingbird.'

It hovered. Its appearance noted, it flew up and away. My totem. My spirits lifted. It was a whole year later that I learned South Africa does not have hummingbirds—but by this time I'd almost finished writing.

I was further encouraged by watching on YouTube the late Nobel Peace Prize recipient Wangari Maathai's telling of a hummingbird tale:

> I like to tell this story of the hummingbird because quite often we feel overwhelmed. It's a story from Japan.
>
> The story is about a big fire in the forest—a huge fire—raging. Animals stood at the edge, overwhelmed, powerless, transfixed as they watched the forest burning. The animals felt there was nothing they could do, except for the hummingbird which went to the nearest stream and took up a drop of water in its tiny beak and flew into the forest and dropped the water. The hummingbird went up and down, up and down, up and down, as fast as it could.
>
> In the meantime, all the other animals were discouraging, laughing and mocking the hummingbird, including the elephant with its big trunk that could bring much more water. 'What do you think you're doing?' asked the animals. The hummingbird, without stopping her work, turned to the other animals, and said 'I am doing what I can.'
>
> And that is what it's about. Be a hummingbird in your community, wherever you are. It's all we're called to do—the best we can.

This book has been driven by conversations, hundreds of them, some formal and some by chance. This book is not meant to be the last word on anything but rather the opening engagement in a conversation still to be had. It is my hope that this book will contribute towards a worldwide tipping point of death-in-life conversations. More talking, less suffering. More living life alive with intention and joy.

PART ONE
Living Life Alive

The Summer Day

Who made the world?
Who made the swan, and the black bear?
Who made the grasshopper?
This grasshopper, I mean—
the one who has flung herself out of the grass,
the one who is eating sugar out of my hand,
who is moving her jaws back and forth instead of up and down—
who is gazing around with her enormous and complicated eyes.
Now she lifts her pale forearms and thoroughly washes her face.
Now she snaps her wings open, and floats away.
I don't know exactly what a prayer is.
I do know how to pay attention, how to fall down
into the grass, how to kneel down in the grass,
how to be idle and blessed, how to stroll through the fields,
which is what I have been doing all day.
Tell me, what else should I have done?
Doesn't everything die at last, and too soon?
Tell me, what is it you plan to do
with your one wild and precious life?

—Mary Oliver, *House of Light*

Boots Crunching on Gravel

One night in our home in Ibex Hill in Lusaka, Zambia, I was in bed with the lights out when I heard the crunch of boots on gravel becoming louder and closer. This is it, I thought, this is finally it—South Africa's assassins have found out where we live.

Palms sweating, shallow panic breathing, I crept toward the wardrobe and reached to get Joe's Russian AK-47 rifle at the ready. I moved to the lounge passage where a double-width brick-built room-dividing unit might offer protection.

The wearer of the boots approached the front veranda. One person's boots? The scout? Where were the others? Then the walking stopped. It was quiet except for the background night sounds: dogs barking and the continuous buzz of insects. Was the person listening out for movements in the house just as I was also listening? The boots crunched gravel again. Surely a man. He was close to the veranda, his clothing brushing against the cement wall as though he were lowering his body to squat.

Would he try and force the window open? I heard shuffling, grunting, a thud. Then silence again. I waited, trembling.

The deep breathing became deeper and then turned into snoring. I separated two slats of the blinds and peeped through. The wearer of the boots was the night watchman from the main house. For whatever reason, he'd decided to sleep in the shelter of our veranda. It never happened before and it never happened again. But for those few minutes I was convinced this was my last night on earth. It was 1988.

Fear of a violent death has been my constant companion since my late 20s. It happened over time. There was not one irrevocable decision, not one life-changing commitment. It was a slow creep as the implications of my choices accumulated. I came to live a life in which fear was a familiar emotion.

My childhood fears were ordinary; the normal fear of loss or separation. As a four-year-old I fell off my tricycle outside the candy shop behind the supply truck. The driver came out, jumped in the cab and started reversing. People shouted as they watched his back tire coming closer towards me as I lay sprawled on the ground beside my bike. The tire grazed my outstretched arm before the truck came to a complete halt. But it's the hospital I remember most, and my fear when the nurse told me, 'If you don't stop crying, we'll send your mummy away.'

I was born in Accrington, a northeastern English town where Irish Catholic priests were relentless fear-mongers.

'If you don't go to mass on Sundays you will go to hell when you die,' they told us seven-year-olds as we prepared for our first holy communion.

I prayed earnestly for my parents who missed services. Dad liked to go to Polish mass and sing in the choir when not working on Sunday. My Czech mum told me that the services were not like the ones she grew up with, that she and God had private conversations, and that he understood her choices. My young self remained fearful that I might get to heaven and find Mum and Dad had not been allowed in.

After high school, I took a gap year to be a teaching assistant on a mission station, the Lwitikila Girls' Secondary School in Mpika, Zambia. At the end of that year, I made the most of the chance to travel, and headed to South Africa.

Three of us, 19-year-old British girls, flew in from Zambia, met up in Durban and then hitched along the Garden Route to Cape Town. It was 1973 and only white salesmen in large cars gave us lifts, except for the time a police officer stopped to offer us a ride from East London to Port Elizabeth.

He asked where we were coming from, and when we told him Zambia, it prompted a venomous declaration: 'Black bastard kaffir Kaunda [Zambian president Kenneth Kaunda]. Give me a gun and a chance and I'll shoot him any day.'

His casual predisposition to violence and the snuffing out of black lives shocked me. Politics suddenly had real meaning for me. This was three years before the 1976 Soweto uprising—the widespread student protests sparked by the apartheid government's insistence that Afrikaans be used as the medium of instruction.

Now more than ever I wanted work that would offer the possibility of changing lives. I grew up as working class in the United Kingdom and money was scarce, but I never went to bed hungry. In my gap year, I saw serious poverty. I gave up my place at the university where I had been accepted to study English literature and philosophy, and switched to study agricultural economics at the University of Reading in Berkshire.

Those three weeks in South Africa, the blood-thirsty policeman and the in-your-face-apartheid rules—public signs that read 'No Blacks' and 'Whites Only'—lit my interest in Southern African liberation struggles. Back in the United Kingdom, I joined the Angola Solidarity Committee and the Committee for Freedom for Mozambique, Angola and Guinea Bissau. I donated blood for Mozambican 'freedom fighters,' watching the bag fill up with my O-type blood and thinking about the concept of a 'just war' which Nelson Mandela spoke about in his inspirational speech from the dock:

> The ANC has spent half a century fighting against racialism. …When it triumphs as it certainly must it will not change their policy. … It is a struggle for the right to live. During my lifetime, I have dedicated myself to this struggle of the African people. I have fought against white domination, and I have fought against black domination.
>
> Fifty years of non-violence had brought the African people nothing but more and more repressive legislation and fewer and fewer rights. At the beginning of June 1961 after a long and anxious assessment, I and some colleagues came to the conclusion that it would be unrealistic and wrong for African leaders to continue preaching peace and non-violence at a time when the government met our peaceful demands with force.

During my first year in Reading I met Ed Wethli. Ed was a poultry specialist doing research. He'd grown up in Johannesburg but chose not to continue living there under apartheid. I fell head over heels in love with a man, a country, a history, and my future. Ed and I got married, and by the time I graduated in 1976, we'd already submitted our papers to work in newly independent Mozambique and moved there later that year. My job in the Ministry of Agriculture was creative. I designed a simplified accounting system for agricultural cooperatives, geared for people who had just finished literacy classes. Happiness amplified with the birth of my daughter, Tessa Josina, in 1980.

Things began to change. There had been more than one group organizing support against Portuguese colonial government. Frelimo, the principal opposition group who'd waged an armed struggle and occupied areas in the north of Mozambique, negotiated independence on a winner-takes-all basis. Renamo, the smaller, less radical opposition group who had been excluded from any share of power was hostile to Frelimo. They began attacks in the rural areas, supported by the South African government. They targeted development projects' infrastructure and the government employees who worked in them, including technicians like myself, were considered in danger. Our agricultural cooperative training centers closed.

In 1981, Ruth First, journalist, academic and anti-apartheid activist invited me to work at Maputo's Eduardo Mondlane University in the Centre of African Studies as a researcher and to teach on a course about the rural economy.

Ruth's husband, Joe Slovo, was the head of Special Operations, a unit within the armed wing of the ANC. He dropped by our home regularly. Joe was on a recruitment mission and Ed and I were valuable: we both had British passports. It was easy for us to be couriers driving cars through to ANC operatives in Swaziland. Sometimes the cars had cash concealed behind the door paneling; other times it was small munitions, guns, and detonators.

In early 1981 we were asked to take a 'family holiday.' The so-called holiday was geographically planned to disguise the real purpose of our travel which was to undertake the reconnaissance of power stations in the area which was then called the Eastern Transvaal. Ed and I, along with one-year-old Tessa, first traveled to Lesotho to spend a week with friends, and then we caught a train to Cape Town. There, we hired a car and over several days we drove a couple of thousand miles back to Mozambique doing touristy things, but with carefully planned meandering through the coal areas where the power stations were located.

Tessa and I spent hours in the back seat of a car. I knew as little as possible. If arrested, I was to act unaware. We figured that way our child would still have one parent.

Nelson Mandela's words from the dock continued to be present and relevant:

I do not, however, deny that I planned sabotage. I did not plan it in a spirit of recklessness, nor because I have any love of violence. I planned it as a result of a calm and sober assessment of the political situation that had arisen after many years of tyranny, exploitation and oppression of my people by the whites.

I have cherished the ideal of a democratic and free society in which all persons live together in harmony and with equal opportunities. It is an ideal which I hope to live for and to achieve. But, if needs be, it is an ideal for which I am prepared to die.

For our next 'holiday,' Ed and I were asked to go to Swaziland to source a second-hand vehicle, specifically a Ford Ranchero truck. The plan was to modify this vehicle to transport a Grad-P rocket launcher and five 48-pound shells. The target? Pretoria's Voortrekkerhoogte military base.

In July 1981, a team planted six limpet mines at Arnot Power Station and another team planted mines at the Delmas sub-station. In August, a third team successfully shelled Voortrekkerhoogte. The commander, on his return, gave Joe the screw cap of one of the shells—a memento I still have.

I felt quietly proud that Ed and I contributed to these acts of sabotage. The South Africa regime, aware that the ANC unit planning the sabotage was located in Mozambique, simultaneously carried out raids. In 1981, a South African hit squad attacked three ANC residences in Matola, a Maputo suburb. Months later, in my own neighborhood, a Mozambican family was killed by mistake. The hit squad burst through the front door shooting. But it was the wrong apartment; the ANC people lived next door.

Fear became part of daily living. Ed and I slept with passports and running shoes next to our beds. The papers of the Ford Ranchero were still in the glove box. The vehicle, abandoned in South Africa after the Voortrekkerhoogte raid, named Ed as the registered owner. Ed sawed through the bedroom floorboards of Tessa's bedroom and made a trapdoor so we could hide in our basement.

One night, an ANC comrade called with the pre-arranged warning message: 'There are unwelcome visitors in town.' I felt sick to my stomach and paralyzed by fear.

In 1982, our university department hosted an international social science conference. Ruth was the organizing dynamo. A couple of days later people were to gather in Ruth's office to toast the departure of a colleague. She passed my office with Aquino de Braganza, the Center's Director, together with a conference guest. Aquino called to me. 'Come Helena, come join us.' I was busy typing and said, 'I'll come just now.'

The explosion made the whole building shake. As I stepped into the corridor, smoke mingled with cement dust from a blown-out wall. Three figures, shadows in the dust emerged, covered in blood and shards of glass. Ruth had opened a letter bomb and was killed instantly.

Mozambican security officials closed off the building for days as they completed their forensic investigation. Afterwards, three of us organized water, buckets and disinfectant, and cleaned the walls splashed with blood. Ruth's poster of Mandela and Walter Sisulu on Robben Island lay on the floor, only slightly torn at the edges. Somehow its survival felt symbolic and comforting

I gave birth to Ruth Kyla as my marriage ended. Two years later, in 1986, Ed and I left Mozambique separately. Ed went to work with the cooperative movement in Bulawayo, Zimbabwe. I wanted to work with the ANC research department in Lusaka, Zambia. I'd written a PhD proposal on post-apartheid land reform in South Africa and I had also become involved in a serious relationship with Joe, Ruth's widower.

Joy competed with heartache. Since Ruth's death four years earlier there had been more assassinations of activists. I was scared that Tessa and Kyla and I could be caught in the crossfire. I traveled to Dublin at the end of 1984 to visit a friend of mine and found he was offering shelter to South African anti-apartheid activist Marius Schoon and his son Fritz. A few months earlier in Angola, Fritz had been in the same room when his mother Jeanette opened a letter bomb that killed her and his sister Katryn.

It seemed reasonable to consider that my children, if they were to live with me and Joe, would be in danger. Ed was a great dad and he could offer more safety, so we decided Tessa and Kyla would live with Ed in Bulawayo for school terms and with me during holidays. Tessa was just seven and Kyla was little more than two-and-a-half years old.

From 1987 to 1989, twice a term, I drove the 600 miles from Lusaka to Bulawayo to visit. I'd return to find Joe had prepared a special meal of welcome. I couldn't eat; I'd sit and cry. I wanted my children's safety but missing them felt too hard. I'd tell myself how lucky I was that I got to see them, unlike other comrades who had not seen their children for years. But knowing others were worse off made no difference to my pain. The crèche report from Kyla's nursery school described my child's distress at our separation. I still tried to reassure myself that this was a better option than their living in Lusaka with their fear-filled mother and their on-the-hit-list stepfather.

We all returned to Johannesburg in 1990, when the ANC was unbanned and Mandela finally freed. Danger still lurked—assassination plots were uncovered—but it would be cancer that ultimately claimed Joe's life. Death changed the form of its visitation, but not its constancy as a life companion.

Twenty years later I still live very much on the alert. I'm no longer frightened that assassins will burst through a door or send a letter bomb. There was one tense year, 1999, when I was CEO of the Land Bank; someone fired a bullet, meant to intimidate me, which broke through the skylight and landed in the kitchen where I was cooking an evening meal with my family. But now I live a very normal middle-class suburban Johannesburg life. Apartheid, however, dehumanized people and a legacy of violence is our daily norm. Death hovers as an ongoing possibility with the challenge not to take it too lightly, but also not to become incapacitated by fear.

I've been mugged on the downtown street outside my office. My car window was smashed in when I stopped at the traffic lights, and my cellphone was taken. On another occasion, Tessa and I were the only ones sleeping in the house when I realized that the noise that just woke me up, coming from the other side of the wall, was the sound of the hi-fi equipment being removed.

The worst experience was when my mum was visiting me from the UK and I drove with her and a friend's mother to Avalon Cemetery in Soweto on a Saturday afternoon. We had cleaned Joe's grave and were about to set off home. I had the key in the ignition and was waiting for Mum to close her door and put on her seat belt. I glanced over and saw a man lean in and thrust the jagged edges of a broken beer bottle close to her neck. He looked thin and hungry. I got out of the car and walked away with the keys to try to negotiate. Eventually he left with my watch and we drove home calmly. Later that evening, my delayed reaction set in, and I crashed my car.

These kinds of incidents, except perhaps the cemetery, make up daily life for all South Africans. I've been lucky, others less so. While living ordinary lives in South Africa, people often get killed, sometimes brutally—the legacy of apartheid remains imprinted on our national psyche.

This is home. It's the longest I've lived in one place—a quarter of a century—and I can't think of anywhere I'd rather be. This is where I'm anchored, where I have love and work and can immerse myself in the beauty of the African wilderness. But like everyone else, I'd prefer to live a little less warily.

But the upside of fear is that I've never taken living for granted. I've lived very much in the moment and cherished every catching of happiness as it's come my way.

I spend time reflecting on how I'm living. Is the work I'm doing worthwhile? Does it make a difference? What's next? What's giving me joy? Are there relationships that I want more of or that need more care?

Our world has changed. My earlier fear, like listening to the sound of boots crunching gravel, was a consequence of my conscious choice to be part of the ANC's liberation struggle. People now meet their death randomly. War is not confined to soldiers in war zones. There's a strategy of creating terror among civilians. New York's skyline changed; the site of the twin towers now hosts a memorial to the thousands who died there. If I must travel by plane, I try to remember to wear slip-on shoes; the rigor of security checks at airports requires the removal of our shoes and belts reminding us of the expectation of the next airport or airplane horror—location unknown. The school, the university, the hotel, the nightclub, the mall, the beach; acts of terror in public places like these are increasing worldwide. At the end of World War II, my parents were among the millions of displaced people who lived on with a sense of 'never again.' Seventy decades later, there is a new tidal wave of war and disruption; according to the United Nations one in every 122 people is a refugee.

Mostly, we don't get to choose how we die. What we do get to choose is how we live, how we shape our lives from the circumstances of our birth. What I am most sure of is that if we can live in a way that accepts and engages with the uncertain timing of our inevitable death at any age, there are some serious potential benefits. We can more consciously create for ourselves, and for those we love, the possibility of making and shaping the best outcome of life and what we'll leave behind.

Pulane: Life was Good and About to Get Better

Pulane* and I met each other professionally. Once she was a client of mine and during our sessions I'd come to understand what drove her. When I began to write she agreed to contribute her experience under an assumed name, wanting to take care not to hurt those dear to her, while still wanting others to learn from her experience.

She composed herself to tell her story, sitting on the sofa with her slender legs stretched out sideways on the soft antelope leather. Her fashion choice varied. Some days she wore a chic, sharply tailored, West African print dress and jacket. But today it was Armani. Style matters. Aesthetics matter. The hair extensions favored a few months ago were now discarded; Pulane's head was shaved and polished. A personal statement, a bold invitation to accept her however it was that she chose to present herself to the world. With attention to every detail, the porcelain platters of fruit she'd prepared for us looked like those in Johannes Vermeer's *Girl with a Pearl Earring*.

We had the whole afternoon ahead of us. Pulane had thought carefully about what she wanted to share of her story, what she'd like to offer for others to reflect on.

I was 23. Life was very good and about to get even better. I was part of the cool set, and lived with my boyfriend Mpho* in an apartment in Sandton, the glossy high-rise area of Johannesburg. I'd made it into a prestigious graduate program in one of the most respected global corporates. I was doing articles and was about to take my final chartered accountant exams. Once I passed those exams then my salary would double instantly, and a year later I'd get a nice fancy job. Money would roll in. I'd be able to spend like I'd never spent before.

I just needed to sort out one thing.

I knew something was wrong because I started gaining weight, inexplicably. I was feeling tired in a way that felt like exhaustion. It was not the normal tiredness of work-hard, play-hard simply put right by a long lie-in on a Sunday morning. After sleeping 16 hours I would wake up still feeling exhausted. I could feel something was wrong, but didn't know what it was. Diabetes or thyroid problems crossed my mind as possibilities.

Blood tests round one: no conclusion. Round two: something abnormal was showing up against the liver function. Round three: a biopsy, a colonoscopy and then a call from my doctor proposing that I see a certain specialist, an appointment secured for later that week.

I parked my car and walked into the specialist's waiting room. Marble, granite and wood: high-class finishes for high-class patients paying for private practice expertise. I filled in the forms at reception. I did a double take when I discovered the charge would be R2,000 for the 10-minute appointment, that was about half a month's wage for a factory worker. And this was Johannesburg in 2007. I remember thinking, that's a shitload of money! I couldn't imagine I'd ever be able to charge that kind of money even when fully qualified with years of experience. But I told myself, well maybe he's The One. The Magic Doctor who's going to fix me, and then he's worth every cent.

I went in and the specialist told me, 'You've got sclerosing cholangitis. It's odd that you have it. It's a disease most commonly found in white men over the age of 65. You probably have six months to live at most—unless you can get a liver transplant, but that's unlikely.'

Then he tapped his pen on the prescription pad on his desk.

'I could put you on some medication which costs R4,000 per month but it says here that you are doing articles. So, it's probably too expensive for you. And it's probably not going to work anyway. Come back and see me in another couple of weeks.'

And that was it. His whole demeanor said, 'Next patient please.' He started looking at his watch.

I sat like a gazelle caught in the glare of headlights. Astonished. I took a deep breath and gathered myself sufficiently to ask. 'Excuse me. What did you say my disease is?'

He said it again, 'Sclerosing cholangitis.'

I tried to repeat what he said out loud but I stumbled. I was shocked and I couldn't pronounce the two words, much less write them down for myself. I asked him to write down the name of the disease, thinking that if at least I had the right name, I could go home and look it up on the internet.

I tried asking another question. He started to get annoyed with me wanting to ask questions, impatient that I was delaying him from seeing his next patient.

I sat alone in the car in the car park. If the specialist knew he was going to tell me that I have six months to live, shouldn't there be a team on hand to counsel and educate me? I wondered if I was okay to drive. Should I find a therapist? I phoned my parents. I phoned Mpho. He was devastated, completely devastated. He'd been thinking, we're going to get married and have kids and we have forever and what do you mean we have six months? How did this happen? He went into devastation mode.

I went into project management mode, thinking I had to get as much information as possible. I surfed the internet and began my research.

I decided I was not going back to the guy who charged me R2,000 for 10 minutes to tell me about my death sentence. But I did take the decision to get the prescription for the expensive medication even though the specialist said he didn't think it would work. That decision was a big thing for me, not because of the money, but because I hate taking pills.

I started phoning around, trying to figure out who might be the best doctor for me to consult with further. I tried phoning one who commented, 'Sweetie, that's really odd,' and another said, 'Never heard of that disease.'

I made appointments with a cardiologist, and my gynecologist. I wanted to make sure everything else in my body was fine. My gynecologist is the one who helped the most. He was appalled by my experience. It turned out he had a friend at the state hospital who was head of the organ transplant clinic. He got on the phone immediately and explained my situation. Dr. S. agreed to see me—the 23-year-old African female with the autoimmune disease generally only found in elderly white males.

Dr. S. has serious expertise and is married to his work. But the downside is that he has zero social skills. He greeted me saying, 'Oh My God. You are so obese. If we are even going to have a chance at this whole thing we've got to figure out how you can lose the weight. But as your liver doesn't work, you are never going to lose weight. That's interesting. Now that's challenging.'

Another strange doctor, but this time not only knowledgeable but also professionally curious about my case. I realized that if I had any chance at all it would be to get over myself reacting to his lack of social skills and to work with him. He told me about the transplant preparation process I'd have to go through.

'They determine that everything else is fine, and then work out how sick you are due to the malfunctioning organ and determine whether you merit being pushed up the waiting list,' he said.

Within a fortnight my whole life had changed. I'd been a carefree articled clerk making good money, living in a great apartment, going out every single night, part of an in-crowd of upcoming black professionals. All of a sudden I had to think about life and whether I want to live, and what to choose to eat that might make a difference to whether I would live longer or not. I could not take for granted waking up in the morning. Suddenly I would wake up and be like 'Oh jeez, okay. I'm grateful I'm awake. I'm not jaundiced. It hasn't progressed.'

I became a lot more conscious of being alive. And that's when I realized that being alive is a choice every day.

And then?

Dr. S. was waiting for me to get to the dying stage so that he could do the transplant and save me. But I didn't want to get to that stage. I started believing that perhaps the doctors were wrong about this because they all expected me to be much more sick and dying and I wasn't.

I started reading up about alternative healing. I tried Body Talk. I tried Reiki. I tried energy balancing. I tried a range of things. I'd notice my body responding, improving and then think about what specifically I was doing at that time, like I'm eating better and I'm trying this Chinese treatment.

I talked with my parents about what was going on, but they were also just kind of waiting for me to die. They were scared. I found myself being the one who managed everyone around me. I found a way to be lighter because I needed to. I was living on hope and I needed to believe that I was going to be okay. I would actively imagine my liver and enzymes getting better, normalizing.

There were some bonuses. It was a good excuse to justify what my conservative parents would consider adventurous behavior, like traveling alone. I'd say, 'Can you imagine if this was my last year to live, wouldn't you want me to have experienced this?'

As a family, we started to talk about death. We grew up Christian and cosmopolitan, and at 23 I did not even know what my African rituals were. It was interesting figuring out how traditional my parents were about African rituals but I had never seen this aspect of them in my childhood. When I suggested a very simple funeral and light snacks, my father was so offended.

'What will people say? They would think we do not care for you, that we just wanted you to die. That's not how we do things.'

I think my father had not even thought about his own death and now he was confronting his child's death. Since then we've had many conversations and reached an understanding.

Pulane started a list of what she wanted to do with whatever time she would have. She wanted to study further and do an MBA, be clear about what jobs would be interesting, list what experiences to have— including getting married to Mpho—and what countries she wanted to visit.

Sclerosing cholangitis continues to be very present ten years later. Maybe youth is on her side in responding to treatments. Her doctor would say, 'I don't know why the disease is not progressing, but as long as you are feeling better that's the most important thing.'

Pulane's disease has become the barometer of her personal well-being.

I learned that my illness is also linked to my emotions, because at the unhappiest point in my marriage, when I didn't even know that I was so unhappy that I needed to go, my liver suddenly started deteriorating even though I was taking my medication and doing everything I was supposed to be doing. I started panicking and going back to my doctor regularly whereas I had been only checking in with him twice a year. He couldn't figure out what had gone wrong. Once I got divorced in 2014 my liver enzymes normalized again. It's made me a lot more connected with what goes on in my mind, heart, and body, and to listen to my body a lot more.

Now 33, she reflected on the eight challenging years she has lived with her life-threatening liver disease. She was philosophical about the consequences. Yes, she enjoys beautiful things and works hard to afford them, but that's not what drives her. She has assessed everything against exacting standards of quality and meaning.

Is this work worth doing? Is this relationship good enough? How do I want to spend my time this weekend? Where's my next travel destination? She's been impatient, and this impatience came with a price. It's been hard for her to play the longer game when faced with corporate politics or rough patches in relationships.

> It's meant I don't take life for granted. I live life fully every day. I don't live with the concepts of when I'm 25, when I'm 50, when I'm 64! I think about what I want my life to stand for.
>
> What would I like people to remember? What's my legacy? You know, if I'd never had the disease, would I have done half the things I have done by now? In a way, somehow, my disease has been a positive experience.

Stefanie: When Nick Became Nicholas

There's a photograph on the mantelpiece of Nick. The blond-haired, blue-eyed boy all dressed up for the wedding in a toddler-size black suit with a white shirt and bowtie—waistcoat and all. He's thrilled to be sitting behind the wheel of a posh car, pretending that he's about to drive. As his Aunt Anna said, 'Just as well he couldn't yet release the handbrake!'

On that sunny July day, Nick was just one month short of turning two, the much-adored first grandchild and first nephew, born to my niece Stefanie who's the oldest of four siblings, herself followed by Gareth, Anna and James. Since her relationship with Nick's father broke down for good not long after his birth, Stefanie lived at home with her mum, Sandra, and stepfather John.

Besotted. That's how everyone acted around Nick. His curiosity and the way he enjoyed doing things captivated them. He treated everything as an adventure, whether it was splashing in puddles, looking at a flower, or his pleasure in reciting full verses of nursery rhymes. Sitting on the local bus on the circular route all afternoon was Nick's idea of an exciting outing. A gift to this family, a rainmaker, his birth created possibilities for healing fractured relationships.

Stefanie was about to become a student again to get a post-graduate social work qualification at Lancaster University in the north of England. She was a single parent, fiercely motivated by what she wanted to be able to offer Nick as he grew up.

'I remember having a couple of days of deep thinking, I'm a mum, I'm responsible,' Stefanie said. 'This is not the life I want for my child; I need to take action. I need to think about how I want my life to be, and go for it and take it.'

Nick settled easily at the university nursery school; he quickly learned everyone's names and made friends. Stefanie's student family accommodation was comfortable, and as summer became autumn the next two years looked promising. Her decisions were turning out well.

In October, Stefanie, Nick and Dave—the promising new man in Stefanie's life—visited her dad and stepmother who lived in Blackpool, an hour's drive away. It was a full-on family weekend. Nick's grandad, my elder brother Roman, brought out the train set. The two of them played ball in the garden and then, through the bay window of the lounge, they watched people laughing and shouting as they rode the roller coaster in the nearby theme park. Nick chased the cat which ended up hiding in the wardrobe. Once darkness fell, the whole extended family took a tram to the far end of Blackpool's famous illuminations. Strings of brightly lit images hung across the wide carriageway that runs for miles along the seashore. They walked back wheeling Nick in his pram, and easy conversation mingled with laughter and candy floss. A snapshot of happiness.

Back at home in the student flat in Lancaster, the northern hemisphere winter set in. Nick became unwell the following Sunday, the last of October, when Britain turned its clocks back. In the middle of the night, Stefanie woke to use the bathroom and checked on Nick. He wasn't breathing. She immediately phoned for an ambulance and then phoned her mum.

That was when the seizures started. My brother raced to the hospital and remembers this:

It was just seizure after seizure after seizure and they were pumping all sorts of drugs into him to try and keep the seizures down. To watch that child totally wired up was incredible—monitors going like nobody's business, for his heart, for his breathing, for everything. You could see all the activity going on and you felt totally helpless. You couldn't even pick that child up and cuddle him. There was absolutely nothing you could do.

Their whole life, and Nick as they'd known him, evaporated. Stefanie told me:

It's as though I knew immediately. One day he was Nick, and then after that first night I started calling him Nicholas. The Nick I knew was gone, almost completely gone. From the moment he first went to the Lancaster hospital to the time of dying there were no words. He never walked again from the day he came down with the illness. Within 24 hours he was on a ventilator and placed into an induced coma which he remained in for almost two months. By the time he came off that ventilator, the devastation to his brain was enormous.

During this time, Nicholas was transferred to a specialist children's hospital at Pendlebury near Manchester. His seizures appeared to be under control and Nicholas was moved out of intensive care to the high dependency unit. The family congregated to spend Christmas together. Stefanie said they thought Nicholas might still be recognizing people; he seemed to smile now and again.

During Christmas time there was still something of him there. He always used to stroke my hair, and he tried to reach for it the way he used to. And he was refusing to eat, refusing very purposefully. And then he became less and less aware—when you look over the photographs from this time until his dying you can really notice the changes. He became a lot like a newborn with natural reflexes.

I was lucky that when Nicholas went to Pendlebury, there were family counselors on site. I got on well with one of them who was very understanding. I had this conversation with her about Nicholas, that I wanted him to be better.

She asked, 'What does that look like for you?'

What it looked like was Nicholas not having all the seizures. I recognized what 'better' realistically meant and came to an acceptance of my situation. Okay, he's unwell. I'm his mum but then also who else am I? How am I going to provide for him? What's our life going to be like?

It took another two months to get to a diagnosis.

I trusted those people. I remember coming in one morning and finding the consultant was there, he'd just popped in. A staff member told me he came in before and after every shift to see Nicholas and check if the medication they were trying was making any difference. It was partly the relationships that you built with them as well. Some parents question, some lose their temper. That was never my approach. We got compliments back, how highly thought of we were as a family, that they tried for us. Knowing that they had tried everything they could helped. By the time they came to the diagnosis, enough time had passed, and I'd seen enough to realize we were dealing with something very serious.

I could sense the doctor was having a hard time preparing to have a conversation with me. I remember saying to him, 'I'm not silly. I can see that my son is not getting any better. I can see other children coming in, making progress, getting better and going home. I'm very much aware of the path we're going down. In some respects, I would welcome a conversation.' My concern was, would Nicholas be like this for the rest of his life?

When it eventually came, the diagnosis was Alpers' disease, a rare condition which causes the brain to atrophy. Roman said the impact of learning of this diagnosis was like 'the hammer ball.'

On the MRI scan you can see the brain matter shrinking and there's a very distinct EEG pattern associated with it. Once we read up about it, we knew. Your hopes and your dreams for that child evaporated. The things you thought you'd be doing with your grandchild are gone. It's over. You're not ever going to walk in the sand on the beach together again. He is going to die.

After the diagnosis, Stefanie, fully supported by her doctor, put a Do Not Resuscitate—a DNR—in place, a legal order to withhold CPR if Nicholas's heart were to stop or he stopped breathing. Roman told me, 'I watched my daughter in awe and admiration become a remarkable young woman, making this difficult decision.'

Released from hospital, Stefanie and Nicholas moved back to Great Harwood to stay with her mum. For months they watched Nicholas deteriorate. They were helped by people at the Rainbow Trust, an organization which supports families caring for a terminally ill child. Now a quadriplegic with no control of his limbs, Nicholas needed a special wheelchair to go on outings or to the park.

When seizures happened, it was back to the hospital and then home again.

Nicholas's swallowing reflex had gone; he had to be fed though a feeding tube which went straight into his stomach. Roman told me he sometimes thought to himself, why are we letting him suffer like this?

'The Nick we knew had gone a long time before,' he told me. 'With Alpers, his identity was taken. We literally had a shell of him there that we were caring for and keeping going. No mom should ever watch her child die. It's the hardest thing in the world.'

Stefanie was appreciative of their doctor who, in the last few weeks on 'false alarm' visits, asked her: 'Do you want memories of him dying in this house?'

He was right to ask. I didn't want memories of him dying there. It was good to have had that conversation. I wanted him to die at Derrian House, the children's hospice. When Nicholas died not long after, I remember being grateful to this doctor. Thank goodness he had that conversation with me. Thank goodness Nicholas didn't die at home.

I asked Stefanie if, in retrospect, she wished Nicolas had died on that very first night. Might that have happened if she hadn't woken to go the toilet, checked on him and found he wasn't breathing? Stefanie was unequivocal in her response.

I've pondered over that. If he'd gone that night I would have always wondered. There would have been nothing showing up on the post-mortem to indicate that what had happened was the start of a catastrophic illness.

There still would have been the grief and trauma to go through, but there would also have been the not knowing, the wondering about what could I have done? They might have thought it was cot death. There would have always been that question of what was it? And I'd have been left without any of the strength that came from the experience. I wouldn't have gotten any of the positives.

The positives?

My relationship with my dad got better and better. My dad getting back in touch with grandma, his own mother—that's a big one. Nicholas's illness was the instigator for getting back into that relationship. The people I met through it. People would say how it also changed their lives, like the man in church who apparently was feeling quite lost about his vocation, not clear about what he should be doing. One day he took Nicholas to the altar for the blessing and said that Nicholas looked at him and he knew in that moment he was going to become a vicar. And he did.

What I went through stands me in good stead for the social work I do now and what I bring to it. There's a real difference in approach, the way that I view the world, what I learned about myself and what I learned about other people. I no longer work full-time, partly because my job can be really stressful, but I feel I probably take things to heart more because of what happened with Nick. It's hard when I see a family and the son or daughter is unwell and I see they're end-of-lifers. I try not to do those cases, but inevitably now and again I have to.

The impact on my relationship with Dave was postive. I discovered his patience and know now that I could go through anything with him. Our relationship is a better relationship. We're more giving with each other. I have perspective on what matters. When I listen to friends complaining about things that irritate them about their partner or hear about the tiffs my friends get into, I want to tell them, it doesn't matter. In the bigger scheme of things, it's not actually about whether the toilet seat is up or down, or whether there is a wet towel on the floor. And if it doesn't matter, drop it. So when there actually is a crisis you can be there together.

It has been eight years since Nick died, and in the meantime Stefanie and Dave married. They waited to have children until they felt they were emotionally ready. Cerys is now five and Kayla nearly two. I asked them both if Nick's death had any other effects on the way she and Dave now choose to live their life.

'We are conscious of what can be taken from you,' Dave said. 'We're nervous when the girls get sick because we realize that bad things can happen with kids. We know realistically that there are things that will take a child down and you won't get it back. A lot of other parents are oblivious. They always think that there'll be another drug that'll fix whatever's ailing a child.'

Stefanie works part-time, recognizing that one never knows what's going to happen in the future, trying to make the most of the now.

It's not only about work-life balance. It's about recognizing that life is precious. Time goes very quickly. Children grow and change very quickly. It's about having the time to fully appreciate what you have. I consciously try to remember some of the things we've just done, and how it feels particularly when I've enjoyed something. I want to hang onto that memory so I write in the books.

I leafed through the two 'keepsake journals' that Stefanie regularly fills in for Cerys and Kayla. She regrets she didn't do one with Nick when he was alive. After he died it was too hard to write things down, and over time, she realizes there are things she's forgotten.

But no one in the family has forgotten how Nick lit up their lives. Kayla bears some resemblance, and in her keepsake journal there's a specific page for describing siblings. Stefanie has written:

Nicholas Alexander Robinson. Born August 3, 2003, died May 10, 2007. He was three and a half when he died. He would have been 10 when you were born! I like to think he would have been a good big brother to you. You remind me of him—you have a very sunny disposition, and when I see him in you, it feels like a gift.

Kee: Sculpting Mortality

Villa Serbelloni, an elegant 15th-century villa, a philanthropic gift to the Rockefeller Foundation, now houses the Bellagio Center and offers working residences to up to 12 people at any one time: artists, scientists, writers, thought leaders from all over the world. I was fortunate to have such a residency from mid-August to mid-September 2015 for the specific purpose of making progress on this book.

The ochre-painted villa with its tiled roof sits high up, perched on two sides of the Bellagio promontory overlooking Lake Como. Breathtaking is not a clichéd adjective. Your eyes feast on an ever-changing canvas of sky, water and mountains, light, color, clouds on the move from dawn to night, impacted by varying weather. The extensive gardens are a mix of both manicured avenues and forest, with 15 miles of pathways to explore; there is even a series of caves, one of which can be accessed from five different entrances.

A commitment to engage with fellow residents and present your work is one of the conditions of accepting the Rockefeller award. One evening it was sculptor Siu Kee Ho's scheduled turn to talk about his work in the conference room where we congregated before our formal dinner.

The first image Kee projected onto the screen was of himself on the grounds of the Center, standing inside the cave with the five points of entry.

Dressed in a white cotton three-quarter-length robe with kaftan sleeves, he wore a leather harness around his head, fashioned to accommodate two attachments. A large metal circle, beaten, burnished and polished, was bolted to the harness on the crown of his head. Sunlight entered the cave, bouncing between rock-wall and metal circle, creating the effect of a shimmering halo, the symbol of divinity, of mind-spirit energy.

Kee was bent forward. A substantial rock, tethered to the head harness under the chin, hung in front of him and the weight of it awkwardly pulled him down. For Kee, the discomfort of the rock symbolized life's inescapable constraint—mortality. The halo and the rock: the juxtaposition of the divine and mortality.

Each one of us had been invited to leave any writing about our work in the library for others to peruse at leisure. From his book *The*

Constrained Body, I had learned that Kee's sculptures have consistently explored the limitations of the body to remind his audience of their mortality. Each sculpture has one feature of limitation that symbolizes mortality and then a second feature which symbolizes divinity as infinite mind-spirit energy.

Kee's next projected image was of Pan Gu, the ancient Chinese myth about the origin of the universe. Kee read the myth to us:

> It was said that in time immemorial, heaven and earth were not separated, and all the universe was in chaos. Pan Gu was born in this void. As Pan Gu grew, heaven and earth were pushed apart. Each day he grew by the length of one Zhang. After 18,000 years, heaven became incredibly high, earth immeasurably deep and Pan Gu unimaginably tall. That was how the world began.
>
> When Pan Gu cried, the tears made the Yellow River and the Yangtze River. When he breathed, the wind rose, when he spoke thunder loosened, and when he looked around lightning flashed. When he died, he fell apart, and the five mountains of China sprang into existence from his body. His eyes became the sun and the moon.

Different geographies and cultures have all created their parallel mythologies of the origins of the universe and for Kee they provoke the same existential questions. Who brings us into this world? Why do I have to live here for some decades of time?

> Mortality is the constant reminder of our limitations. We don't exist forever. It makes a lot of people frustrated. If you are doing well in your life, you will want to keep it forever. If you are not doing so well in your life, you are looking forward to the afterlife.
>
> Many religions hold that life is a cycle and there is afterlife, or transformation into another being; for some the afterlife holds the promise of looking forward to a higher state of existence. But no matter if it is good or bad, you know your life as a human will come to an end.

I met with Kee after the presentation and he explained further. For him living with an awareness of mortality means he's especially careful about two aspects of living. The first is his recognition of his need to create legacy. The second is a self-awareness of human limitations—both generally and what's specific to him.

'As humans we do not have the same sense of smell as a dog,' he told me, 'or the same visual ability of the eagle. We cannot fly. We can't run as far or fast as tigers and lions.'

But the limitation that Kee has worked most with is communication; behavioral not physical.

I'm a quiet person. I prefer to be an observer rather than actively participating. Before I was 30, I hardly spoke. As an artist, I was so in my own world, very concentrated on my artistic practice. I could easily be silent for four to five days at a time just like my father. I had a problem to speak with people, not just physically, but mentally. I'm still learning.

Three relationships challenged his preference for silence. Firstly, when he was 30, he got married. Even though he loved his wife a lot, living with another person every day was a great challenge. Secondly, his son was born.

You see this life coming from you and your wife, and you see him growing up day by day. I thought more about how I grew up and started to notice more about human relationships, starting with the very close relationships with members of my family. My son is bigger now, he's 13, starting to develop his own identity, his own thinking, his own taste of fashion. We are at a new stage of communication.

And, finally, Kee started to teach.

They are all young people interested in art just as I was at the age of 18. Most of my students trust me. They come to talk to me about very personal things, not just about their art and their studies. Some boys come to me and tell me that they find themselves gay or girls tell me they find themselves lesbian. I never thought I would have this kind of personal dialogue, but they want to have someone older to give them advice, even though I don't think I can give it. But they don't get support from their families, and they can't get the acceptance of their parents. I am now learning more about how to communicate through real in-depth conversation, with trust.

Creating legacy, for Kee, includes being a role model as to how he lives with integrity in his daily life.

> I think I fulfilled most of my responsibility at work. I've nurtured quite a number of young people who were interested in art and I gave them opportunity.
>
> I have a very good relationship with my parents. We recently started to visit them regularly on Sundays and have breakfast together, the Chinese yam cha and dim sum, and we enjoy it a lot.
>
> My wife is my greatest gift. She is the person who changed me quite a lot. She was not directly wanting to change me, but I changed because of the relationship with her. It's very satisfying.
>
> And my son? I had a vacation with him recently in Europe before coming here. I am satisfied that he is 13 and has started to have his own thinking. I can expect that he will find his way. I talked to him about mortality. I asked him what he would do if I passed away suddenly, and he said, 'Don't talk about it.'

I asked Kee that if this was his last day on earth, how does he look upon the way he's been living in the world? He answered with gentle and joyous reflection.

'Well, if today is my last day in the world, I think it's okay. With my family, with my work, I feel satisfied. I think it doesn't matter if I don't live another day.'

'So what happens for you then when you die?'

'I believe in an afterlife, but not a specific form of afterlife. I believe in the energy of the person. I think of it as an ongoing energy, rather than having a life as another kind of being. We feel this energy even in our existing life, in our bodies.'

'So it's not personified? It passes into the universe?'

'Yes. Yes.'

'Stardust?'

'Right. Right.'

Kee has selected what is important to him and acted with intention to fulfill those outcomes. He decided to role-model a way of being in his family relationships, in the way he engages as a teacher and to create a sculptural philosophical legacy that will outlive him. An ordinary life? How many of us can look at our own lives and say we've lived with such care, authenticity and integrity?

Sam: What if I Have Only 30 Years to Live?

The first time I saw Sam was on YouTube. Smartly dressed in a button-up shirt and jacket, he was speaking to his fellow students at Harvard University. Students are encouraged and mentored to practice public speaking, and they are free to choose any topic. Sam's choice was an odd one for a 23-year-old, but there it was: *A Practical Guide to Mortality*. His talk was about the decision he made as a freshman, where he undertook a 'thought experiment' in which he imagined he would be dead at 30.

> I try to be comfortable with my own death and remember my own mortality as often as possible. Instead of thinking that I would have my 20s to 'figure myself out,' with my real contributions to the world and my loved ones starting later, I wanted to push myself to do the important things now. Complacency is fine if you have an infinite amount of time to get over yourself. But when you have a finite amount of time and, even worse, an uncertain amount of finite time, death is a pretty good incentive to get moving.

Sam talked about the things he's tackled which he thinks he would not have pushed himself to do if it were not for the time pressure he put himself under. This applied to both doing things and tackling issues that arose in his relationships.

> When I was a sophomore I roomed in a double with my best friend but he decided that he wanted to room with someone else the next year, one week before the housing deadline. I thought we had agreed the month before to room together again and I was livid. After not speaking for a few days, we talked about it in the dining hall and couldn't reconcile. Afterwards we ran into each other outside and

I yelled at him, with what I felt was a righteous anger. I was very hurt. Thankfully, as I walked away, I ran into another close friend. She and I walked to the river, sat on a bench and talked it over, with tears in my eyes the whole time. I trusted someone, I cared about my buddy, I trusted him and I got screwed.

The reality is that complacency can happen in relationships too, just like it can for your aspirations. Knowing that I'm going to die, possibly soon, made it easier to forgive my friend faster. I'm still close to him today because I was able to appreciate that there were so many other great things about our friendship other than that incident.

If I knew I had only a little time left, I would make myself vulnerable with the people I care about. I would notice them more, care enough to give them the criticisms and compliments they can't see about themselves. And since I know that I don't know when I'm going to die, maybe today is the day that you and I and all of us need to do that.

I tracked Sam down, and we agreed to meet each other on Skype. He's now working in Mumbai for the Mahindra & Mahindra conglomerate, a Harvard graduate groomed for success.

I was curious to learn what led him, as a young student, to choose his 30-years-of-life framework. Sam told me it was after watching a video of a Steve Jobs's 2005 Stanford University commencement address, where Jobs had said: 'For the past 33 years, I have looked in the mirror every morning and asked myself, "If today were the last day of my life, would I want to do what I am about to do today?" And whenever the answer has been no for too many days in a row, I know I need to change something.'

It was this that gave Sam the idea for what he called the '30-frame.'

The idea is that I try to reframe every triumph and tribulation in the context of the expectation that I will die at 30, rather than framing it in the context of today, or this week or my seemingly infinite life stretching forward ahead for the next 80 years. It tends to clarify what really matters, what makes me excited, what I find indispensable about the idea of a 'good life.' How else can I possibly hope to make good choices when planning and living my endless numbered days?

But Jobs was not Sam's only influence. He's immersed in popular culture and draws from it. He shared some of his favorites:

'Live Like You Were Dying,' a song by the American pop country star Tim McGraw: https://www.youtube.com/watch?v=_9TShlMkQnc

The lyrics from '525,600 minutes' from *Rent*, the musical about a bunch of bohemian types from New York, most of whom have Aids and know they are going to die: https://www.youtube.com/watch?v=s1c3MARlJ0Q

The Last Lecture: Really Achieving Your Childhood Dreams, a talk by the late Randy Pausch, a computer science professor from Carnegie Mellon University: https://www.youtube.com/watch?v=ji5_MqicxSo

> The speakers in these talks get to the heart of this issue of what life is about and on what basis we should go about narrowing the infinite possible approaches. The great thing is everyone has different answers! Tim values experiences and family, *Rent* values love and being there for others, and Randy values the fulfilment and enablement of childhood dreams.
>
> It's great that there are so many answers, but I also think it's shocking that the answers are so far away from what most people spend most of their time working on. It just shows how easy it is to get distracted from what matters. That's why this heuristic, the 30-frame, is so important, valuable and useful. The goal of the 30-frame is to help me to have no significant regrets in my life, to make sure I never have a midlife crisis. Please understand that this is different to never making mistakes.

Sam started a bucket list when he was a senior, which he shared with me:

- I'd like to work at the Defense Advance Research Project Association. It's like the defense laboratory of the United States, their fundamental research arm. It's a cool research organization, the most well-funded lab in the world.
- I'd like to go to Burning Man, the big art festival in Nevada.
- I'd like to save someone's life. I'll do my Emergency Medical Training at some point, so I'll have the ability to be there for someone.
- I'd like to help a slave to freedom through purchase or escape.

- I'd like to swim with whales.
- I'm really into cooking. I want to be a master chef at home.

I asked about the absence of romance on his bucket list.

'Yeah, I guess getting married is probably on there. But I don't know. It's kind of outside of my control at this point. I'm not going to put something on the list that I can't control.'

I asked about his Advanced Directive.

'What's that?' he asked.

I explained that the AD is a document where you specify what kind of medical intervention you want in a situation when your life is in danger and are unable to speak for yourself and various care decisions need to be taken. Supposing, for example, tomorrow he were to be in a car accident and be unconscious. You can give guidelines and officially name someone who you trust to speak for you.

'What are your thoughts about actually dying?' I asked.

He told me he doesn't think about death very much; although he accepts it *will* happen he knows he has very little control about *when* it will happen.

'I can take preventative steps but an act of chance could happen at any time. I try to think about how to do best with the time that is given to me.'

Sam has put huge effort into how he lives his life and how he spends his time. While he called his speech, *A Practical Guide to Mortality*, his intense focus is on how he lives his life in the seven years left to him of his 30-frame. I mentally renamed his speech: *Living the Finite Life*.

I thought those were the final lines of my writing of Sam's story. When I finished the final draft of the manuscript I sent the stories back to the contributors. I wanted to be sure of their level of comfort and my accuracy. Sam responded.

Thanks for getting back in touch to check in.

The thoughts I would like to share with you now are that my thinking around this idea of the 30-frame has really changed a lot after leaving the womb of college and being in the working world for the past two years. I have experienced first hand how hard it is to make a meaningful contribution as an inexperienced person who is lacking skills appropriate to the job at hand. It can even be harmful to whatever goal you are pursuing to approach it with an egoistic mindset of 'I am going to solve this where others have failed because I know better.' It shows a lack of respect and empathy for the fact that others who may be just as capable as you have been trying for many years without clear success. I understand the importance and value of patience and practice more now.

I also feel like as I imagine my future growing and learning, I also imagine my relationships with others maturing and deepening, continuing to bear fruit (for both parties) for many years to come. The idea of this potential being unrealized is very sad to me now, making the idea of dying at 30 deeply unappealing. I think that it would be extremely unlikely or even impossible for me to not feel cheated out the many decades I might be able to enjoy with friends and family otherwise were I to die at 30.

Instead of feeling motivated by the 30-frame now, I imagine it and it makes me a bit sick at the prospect. It just doesn't feel like enough time for me to grow into the kind of contributor I want to be! And I want to be a part of my loved ones' lives for as long as I can. No matter how many accomplishments could possibly come before 30, I will never be able to feel good about missing out on the opportunity to enjoy the company of those I care for and to be there for them when they are in need. I feel I have been given so much, and it would be a real shame for me not to give as much as possible. How much I am able to give is clearly a function of how much time I am alive for, so the idea of that being cut shorter than the average lifespan is now more painful for me than motivating. I used to think that people didn't use their time as well as they could because they thought they had the luxury of time. I still think that's true, but I no longer think that imagining you will die young is the answer.

Feel free to include or not include these thoughts as you see fit . . .

Best,
Sam

Gina: The Joy Factor

It was Sunday evening and we'd arrived back at the Kruger Park lodge after our game drive. John, my husband, and my good friend Mapi, picked up on supper preparations while I went to find a quiet place to call my 88-year-old mother, Gina, who had been bedridden for the last three years.

Ring-ring. Ring-ring. I knew it would take my mum a while to roll over, stretch out for her phone and find and press the answer button. Ring-ring. Ring-ring. I sat patiently.

'Allo? Allo?' she said when she finally spoke, her English overlaid with an Eastern European accent, the result of her having grown up in Czechoslovakia.

'Hi, Mum. How are you?'

'Vell. I'm still trying to get better from zis cold. I've been in bed all day today. I didn't feel like getting up.'

In the last three years, my mum had on average been in bed 355 days per year. I could see her in my mind's eye as we spoke, lying like a queen—she is after all named Regina—under the peach-colored damask cotton duvet which she insists on using even when it's high summer and extremely hot.

'I'm svetting,' she said.

'I too would be sweating if I were under your duvet.'

Meeting her where she's at, not confronting and not contesting, is where I most tried to be with my mum as she embarked on the slowest fade I'd ever known, towards the end of her life.

'Mmm, that cold is lingering. Let me know if you want me to call Dr. Connell.'

'I'm okay. I know how to look after myself. Vat's news?'

'We spent the last hour watching a pride of 12 lions, adult females with their cubs. We watched through sunset until it got too dark. What's your news?'

I knew my friend Getti had planned to visit my mum that afternoon. Getti was a dear friend who I came to know through my husband John. Getti's partner Alan, who had died of cancer 18 months earlier, was John's oldest and closest friend. A month before I left for my Bellagio residency, an absence of 43 days, Getti asked to see me.

'I don't want you to worry about your mother while you're away,' he said. 'You must be able to enjoy the place and writing time. I'm proposing to visit your mother every day in your absence. I'd like keys and a list of people to contact in case of emergency.'

And that's indeed what Getti did. Friend extraordinaire, he's a gifted conversationalist; sometimes I think he now knows more than I do about my mother's family history.

'Getti came.'

'How is he?'

'He vasn't so bright as he usually is. His son has gone to university in London. He seemed a bit down. It's hard ven your children leave home. I felt like that ven you left.'

'We all leave, Mum, that's how it goes. You left your mum. I left you and Dad. Now Tessa and Kyla have left me. What else did Getti say? Did he bring anything this time?'

Getti is a fabulous cook and sometimes brings my mum cake, or cottage pie—something thoughtful that can be eaten by a very old bedridden lady who only puts her dentures in for special occasions.

'He brought chocolates,' she said. I could hear her fumbling under the pillow next to her for the packet. 'Lindt.'

Then she began to stumble. 'I don't vant...' She's searching for words, and I'm wondering if she's going to say she doesn't want visitors, she had said that in the past. She began again. 'I don't vant anyone...'

I listened to her silence as she searched for her words.

'He's a good man, Getti. He's a good-looking man. But I don't vant... I'm too old.' Another pause.

'I'm too old to get involved.'

Gob-smacked. Flabbergasted. I could not believe what my mother was saying to me. She was entertaining the notion of romance! I inhaled deeply to stymie the laughter that wanted to burst out. Obviously, Mum had forgotten that Getti is gay.

'I think maybe you're right, Mum. But it's nice for you to have a visitor, especially when I'm not around. He's a good friend.'

'Yes, he's a good friend.'

'Let me say goodnight, Mum. See you on Wednesday.'

I returned to the kitchen and John poured me a glass of wine. I told him about the conversation and he chuckled.

'So where do you think your mum and Getti would go on their first date? From the bedroom to the lounge? Watch a movie?'

I laughed, but I was also delighted. My mum was alive.

'Wick' is the old-fashioned Lancashire word of my childhood for life force. My mother still had it.

Even if Gina had given up on her body, her free-range capacity to contemplate romantic possibilities from the confines of her bed made me smile. She still had people, conversations and memories that gave her joy.

There is no reason to pity old people. Instead, young people should envy them. It is true that the old have no opportunities, no possibilities in the future. But they have more than that. Instead of possibilities in the future, they have realities in the past – the potentialities they have actualized, the meanings they have fulfilled, the values they have realized – and nothing and nobody can ever remove these assets from the past.

—Viktor Frankl, *Man's Search for Meaning*

Postscript One

In the last decade, I've worked with many people as an executive and life coach. A former client called recently and asked if I could see him once a month. It would be a private arrangement, not the leadership coaching his company had paid for several years earlier.

'You ask questions that make me think,' he told me. 'You make me uncomfortable. I spend time between sessions provoked into thinking outside my comfort zone. I appreciate this ability of yours.'

Roderick* is an extremely well-paid executive. When I met him 10 years before, he told me about his great performance reviews, but said what bothered him was that his boss didn't see him as a live, personable human being. He felt disregarded, appreciated only for being the super-efficient accountant who got the job done well.

After World War II, when the mining industry in the United Kingdom was re-thinking how to reorganize jobs, Fred Emery of London's Tavistock Institute of Human Relations came up with the six criteria of satisfactory work. The aim was to create jobs and a working environment which paid attention to these criteria. Robert Rehm, an organizational development specialist who I'd worked with in my time as CEO of the Land Bank, wrote up these criteria in his book *People in Charge*:

- a learning opportunity;
- variety;
- elbow room for making decisions and taking initiatives;
- ongoing support, recognition and feedback from colleagues;
- understanding where your job fits into the bigger picture and its being socially meaningful;
- a desirable future in terms of career progression in the company or the experience being accumulated.

Roderick scored well on five of them, but the deal breaker for him was the recognition factor. He ended up leaving that company.

About a third of my clients arrive with the intention to clarify what's next in their lives. I have the tools of my trade to facilitate their arriving at decisions for themselves. I've enjoyed clients borrowing from my library *A Life at Work* and *Care of the Soul* by modern philosopher Thomas Moore. I give out copies of Nancy Kline's *Time to Think* on creating a thinking environment and exploring limiting assumptions. Esoteric life coach, Martha Beck's *The Joy Diet* and *Finding Your Own North Star* are also popular.

I also sometimes ask clients to write their obituaries which they respond to with surprise but then the exercise illuminates. I do this because several years ago, I attended a weekend workshop run by Dorian Haarhoff, author of *The Writer's Voice*. He asked us to do two things I found unusual but unlocking. To start with he asked us to write a story using the hand we didn't normally write with! To get the *whole* brain working. Then he asked us to write *two* obituaries about ourselves. The first obituary was to be for if we died now and the other for in ten years' time. I still have the ones I wrote. For me it provoked clarification of what was important to me and what I wanted to pay attention to in my life going forward.

I've learned a lot from my clients. Their situations challenge me to reflect. But some of my most important learning has been right on my doorstep—learning from my mum. I received an email from an acquaintance who wrote that she'd heard my mother was in decline and she wished me well. She added that as my mother's quality of life had been compromised for quite some time, she expected that I'd also experience relief, eventually, on her passing.

I thought about this long and hard. I read an implicit judgment in the mail, an assessment of what constitutes a 'life worth living.' I realized that my journeying with my mother through her declining years was offering me the gift to see that mobility and being able to do the physical things many people consider as essential to 'quality of life' can become secondary.

My observation is that the continuing presence of joy is what matters most. I realized many of my clients are not only seeking purpose and living life with intention, but they are also in search of joy, both in their work and their personal lives.

PART TWO

Relationships

We are told that people stay in love because of chemistry or because they remain intrigued with each other, because of many kindnesses, because of luck. ... But part of it has got to be forgiveness and gratefulness.

—Ellen Goodman, *Wisdom Quotes*

Your Defects

An empty mirror and your worst destructive habits,
when they are held up to each other,
that's when the real making begins.
That's what art and crafting are.
. . .
Your doctor must have a broken leg to doctor.
Your defects are the ways that glory gets manifested.

—Rumi

Richard: Light Meets Shadow

There's a joke about two elderly brothers who haven't spoken for 30 years. They pass each other in the street. One glances the other way. The other goes as far as to crudely spit on the sidewalk—his personal way of indicating his dislike for someone. By now, the two brothers are not only elderly but they're becoming forgetful.

A friend asks one of them, 'What is it that you quarreled about so fiercely that you haven't spoken for 30 years?'

The reply was, 'Do you know what? I can't even remember.'

How often do we take a decision in the heat of the moment to close a relationship, and then when the temper has cooled and with the passage of time, we might, in a quiet moment, find ourselves wondering—what was it that we were so heated up about?

There's a childhood friend of mine from the same small northern English town, and we've kept in touch over the years, and used to meet up whenever I was in London. We enjoyed going to art exhibitions and sharing thoughts on books we'd read.

Richard* hadn't been speaking to his parents for several years. But I sometimes saw them when I was visiting my own parents.

Richard harbors grudges. He had a list of grievances from childhood to adulthood about what his parents had done to him. He couldn't seem to shake them off or philosophically accept them and find his place of peace.

We don't get training in parenthood. His sister Rowena* once made a point that seems relevant to me: so far Richard has chosen not to father a child and perhaps he doesn't understand how hard it can be to be a parent. Maybe that's why he's so relentlessly unforgiving?

His parents had a reputation for being harsh with their children. I was the teenage babysitter for young parents on our block and people

39

would gossip and make comments. I overheard what they said about Richard and Rowena's parents. We lived in row houses and sometimes people would put a glass to the wall to overhear what their neighbors were raising their voices about. Lots of people knew a lot about everybody else's business.

I remember Richard telling me on our school bus rides how his father had a temper and a heavy hand with a rubber hose that he used to discipline his children. Richard showed me the tips of red stripes peeking out above the elastic of his underpants. He told me the color would change to purple and blue in a day or two.

I always got Richard's blow-by-blow account of exactly how unreasonable his parents were as it was happening. In his teenage years, he seemed intent on rebelling and goading his parents, which just made things worse.

His dad was a Manchester United supporter, and from Richard's earliest childhood, he and his dad watched many football games cheering for Bobby Charlton, a world-famous iconic player in this era. At 14, Richard decided to stake out his right to independence: he started supporting United's bitter rivals Manchester City. Even I, who wasn't interested in sport, but grew up sandwiched between Roman and Martin, my two football-playing brothers, understood that this switch is like displaying a red rag to a bull. The foulest, most aggressive language I've ever heard, including gender invectives, has been when watching football. People die in fights that break out over football.

What was wrong with Richard that he didn't seem to get just how vexed his dad was by the switch in his support from United to City— not just any other team in the top division, but the other local team? Or maybe that was the point. He did get it.

At 16, Richard decided to further mark his independent identity by switching churches, from Methodist to Anglican. I couldn't understand him in this phase. I was into exploring eastern religions and existentialism, reading Kahlil Gibran and Samuel Beckett. I couldn't empathize—what was it that Richard found so seductive that he wanted to switch from one Christian church to another?

His dad went ballistic. He told Richard that when he was 18 and left home after high school he could do what he liked, but that as long as he was sleeping and eating under his roof, then this change in religion was unacceptable. So unacceptable that if he wanted to go through with it, he needed to pack his things and leave home. The only reason Richard did not leave home was because the school headmaster interceded, wrote his parents a letter, invited them for a discussion and requested more tolerance from them.

In his 20s, I heard Richard arrived home to introduce his fiancée. She was wearing a lapel badge supporting the right to choose to terminate a pregnancy—a hot topic in the United Kingdom at the time—possibly not the wisest choice of adornment on the first occasion of meeting your conservative religious future parents-in-law.

This time it was Richard's mom who went ballistic. His sister told me their mom overheard Richard and his wife-to-be talking, referring to her as a 'silly bitch.' Richard's dad stood by his wife, and asked his son and fiancée to leave. They never attended the wedding.

But anything you might try to say to Richard about how unresolved anger with others can eat away at your own soul and well-being was met by a stony silence. It's not a conversation between us that ever bore fruit.

As his parents got older, his father developed angina. They changed their lifestyle, ate differently and took long walks along the canal after supper. I had a concern that should his father die with things as they were between them and Richard, might there be regret?

Earlier in my life I had a colleague who'd tell me stories about how she was aggressively at odds with her mother. But they were talking, trying to create new ways of being, as adults in a relationship. My colleague wrote a long letter to her mother as her contribution, setting out her thoughts. This was not a letter to settle scores, but one with good intention, a foundation for a new way forward. Her mother died suddenly, unexpectedly, with the letter never read—it had been delayed in a postal strike. My colleague's grief was compounded by the thought that her mother died without ever having read her special letter.

One day while chatting on the phone to my own parents, I learned that Richard's mother was about to travel for 10 days. I called Richard to let him know. If he wanted time alone with his dad, this could be his chance. There was a non-committal grunt in response and our conversation continued with the catching up on other things happening in our lives. Two weeks later he called me.

'I went.'

'Went?'

I went to see my dad. I just woke up on the Saturday morning and started driving up the motorway. I got there mid-Saturday afternoon and found my dad in his garden. He was shocked to see me, as shocked as I was to see him. He's aged.

First we made some tea. It was a bit awkward. Then we went down to the chippy and got some take-away Holland's steak pudding, chips and mushy peas and settled down with a pint of beer. We started to talk and talk and talk. We refilled our glasses, talked some more, and refilled our glasses again. We even cried as each of us shared how the things that happened had made us feel, and how our misunderstandings had mushroomed. I couldn't believe it was two in the morning when we went to bed.

On Sunday, we cooked breakfast together. Dad gave me a tour of what he's busy with in his workshop and garden: the fishpond with its frogs, the greenhouse with early tomatoes, his glass box frames with different kinds of lettuces growing protected from the cold. It was good between us. And then I drove the five-hour journey home again. It was a long way to drive for a few hours but I'm glad I did it.

Four weeks later, his father unexpectedly died.

When I was next in London Richard and I met for a coffee at the National Portrait Gallery café. Richard said, 'Before we start talking I just want to say thanks properly. If it weren't for you, I wouldn't have seen my dad in his last weeks, and I would have felt completely different about his dying. I'm glad to have seen him. I'm glad we had those few hours of talking together.'

After Richard's dad died I wondered what would happen to the relationship with his mother? When we met for coffee he'd seemed so very grateful that he spent time with his father just a few weeks before his death, and that after many years of not talking to one another, they'd found a place of peace and acceptance to let bygones be bygones.

Would this same forgiveness extend to his mom?

It didn't. Instead there was a total freeze out.

The last time I saw Richard was in London in 2012. It was a bit awkward meeting up. I wasn't sure what we still had in common apart from reminiscing over childhood memories. I asked after his mom and he said he hadn't seen her for years.

'She's a waste of space,' he said. 'I don't have time in my life for her.'

I wondered what happened to provoke such an outburst and outcome. In contrast, he spoke about his father with such warmth. It was as though he'd re-scripted his childhood, and that anything bad that happened was his mum's fault.

I was on holiday with my husband John, and after meeting Richard in London we traveled north. I wanted to show John the landmarks of my childhood and the wild beauty of the Pennine Valley. I dropped in for a cup of tea with Richard's mom, now 20 years into her widowhood.

She had Chorley cakes ready, a Lancashire specialty: raisins cooked in a short crust pastry. She'd remembered them as my favorite when I was a child. We chatted about my life, what my daughters were doing —now both married but no grandchildren yet. She told me news about Rowena, how well she was doing professionally in the county education department and the joy she got from Rowena's children.

I asked about Richard and her face fell. She said she didn't understand. She told me that the last time she'd seen him was when she turned 80, three years earlier. To celebrate her birthday, she rented a large cottage in the Lake District and invited Richard and Rowena, their spouses and her three grandchildren. Richard came along with his second wife, Elspeth, a quiet, friendly woman who kept to herself at family gatherings.

Richard's mom said it was the hardest family weekend she'd ever had. And it's not even that a harsh word was spoken. Richard apparently turned up empty-handed. Rowena arrived with a huge Black Forest cake and sparklers for Saturday night, and salmon and trimmings for a Sunday champagne breakfast. Richard brought nothing.

> He didn't even bring me a birthday card. Everyone gave me presents at Sunday breakfast time and he just sat there reading the newspaper. Then he walked out of the cottage and down into the village with his wife. He'd booked in for a massage at the spa. When he came back he packed up his things and drove back to London. I don't know why he even came. Was it just to hurt me?
>
> He was always a difficult boy, sulky as a child. I know you were friends but I'm telling you, it was difficult to be his mother. His father

and I didn't know how to handle him. We probably made mistakes. But we tried to do the best we could. The worst disagreements we had in our marriage were over our children. Richard's dad had a hard childhood himself. I never knew my father-in-law—he was already late when we married. By all accounts he was strict and a bit too free with using a stick on his children.

She didn't understand why Richard suddenly cut her out of his life. She didn't even have a phone number for him, and besides she'd be afraid to phone him. Afraid he'd find a way of inflicting even more hurt. She had spent the last three years praying to come to a place of acceptance.

'It is what it is. I'm at peace with knowing that as a mother I tried my best.'

I asked how Rowena got on with her brother nowadays? His mom told me she no longer talks to her brother. 'She says she can't come to terms with the way he's chosen to close off his relationship with me. She's advised him she'll contact him and let him know when I die.'

When Richard gets the news of his mother's passing, might he have any regrets?

Darian Leader, psychoanalyst and author of *The New Black: Mourning, Melancholia and Depression*, mentions the Austrian-British psychoanalyst Melanie Klein who was known for her therapeutic work with children on the clinical phenomenon of 'splitting.'

Leader writes, 'Klein notes the way that good and bad can be absolutely polarized in mourning states. After a loss, for example, memories or dreams of the lost loved one can represent them as either all good, completely idealized and positive or, on the contrary, all bad, the incarnation of evil itself.'

Is this what's happened with Richard? Could it be that in his bereavement his father became the embodiment of all that was good and his mother the repository of all that was bad?

Isn't it true that, for all of us, our light and our shadow are always at play?

Holding Up the Mirror

Richard's story made me reflect on my own life and relationships—which ones did I have that were unresolved and might cause me regret if a death were to occur in this situation. Mostly all is well, but a couple of my relationships have scratches on their vinyl. I've heard my voice go up in pitch and volume when there's reference to those people in conversations. My internal barometer of well-being alerts me that I am not entirely at peace with these relationships.

In July 2014, I attended Archbishop Emeritus Desmond Tutu's service at St. George's Cathedral in Cape Town. Afterwards I chose one of his books and asked The Arch—the name by which he is fondly referred to by his parishioners and staff—to autograph it for me.

I chose *The Book of Forgiving*, which he co-authored with his daughter Mpho. He signed, 'Helena. Go for it. God bless you. Desmond.' He was his consistent encouraging self. I was thrilled.

I find the book so pertinent to the world I live in, the macro landscape of my country and the microcosm of my personal relationships. The Arch set out his own challenge to forgive his father for beating his gentle mother, knowing that his father hurt his mother because he himself was hurting. He wrote:

> There is nothing that cannot be forgiven and no one undeserving of forgiveness... I have often said that in South Africa there would have been no future without forgiveness. Our rage and quest for revenge would have been our destruction. This is as true for us individually as it is for us globally.
>
> In our own ways, we are all broken... Forgiveness is the journey we take toward healing the broken parts. Until we can forgive, we remain locked in our pain and locked out of the possibility of experiencing healing and freedom, locked out of the possibility of being at peace. Without forgiveness, we remain tethered to the person who harmed us. When we forgive, we take back control of our own fate and our own feelings. We become our own liberators.

Fine words. But I was still hankering for an apology; the person in question does not own the hurt they inflicted on me. And Eleanor

Roosevelt's words about your feeling hurt being a choice you make for yourself weren't helping me either.

The Arch, however, challenged my perspective of conditional forgiveness. 'Forgiveness,' he writes, 'is not dependent on the actions of others… The problem is that the strings we attach to the gift of forgiveness become the chains that bind us to the person who harmed us.'

In *The Book of Joy*, the Dalai Lama, in conversation with Archbishop Tutu, adds about forgiveness:

> There is an important distinction between forgiveness and simply allowing others' wrongdoing. Sometimes people misunderstand and think forgiveness means you accept or approve of wrongdoing. No, this is not the case. We must make an important distinction. The actor and action, or the person and what he has done. Where wrong action is concerned, it may be appropriate to take counteraction to stop it. Towards the actor, or the person, however, you can choose not to develop anger and hatred. This is where the power of forgiveness lies – not losing sight of the humanity of the person while responding to the wrongdoing with clarity and firmness.

I sit reading these books, taking stock of my flaws. I have not yet reached my place of unconditional forgiveness. I want acknowledgment that hurt was inflicted and the person was morally remiss. Meanwhile I feel protected by my lack of engagement—that in not engaging I cannot be hurt any more deeply. Forgiving, and therefore readiness to reengage, would be a big step back into the vulnerability that is an essential element of being in a relationship.

I've used Ron Kraybill's seven-step Cycle of Reconciliation when working as a coach with fractured relationships within teams in the workplace. Kraybill, a United Nations peace and development advisor, worked in South Africa on the National Peace Accord during the turbulent, violent early 1990s.

His cycle posits that when we are in (1) a relationship, we're vulnerable to (2) injury. A normal response is (3) withdrawal and a period of time in which we nurse our wounds and (4) reclaim our identity. The shift in the heart is the next step, and (5) internal commitment to reconciliation and acting upon this requires (6) restoration of risk. Kraybill then proposes (7) negotiation to meet present needs. After all, who would want to step back into a relationship feeling vulnerable to the possibility of the same hurt happening again? It seems worth the effort to negotiate for a shift in behaviors even though ultimately you are only in control of your own.

I am somewhere between step four and five. I've reclaimed my identity, but I haven't quite arrived at the shift in the heart.

The Arch suggests a prayer for the non-ready like me:

I want to be willing to forgive.
I am not yet ready for my heart to soften.
I am not yet ready to be vulnerable again.
I am not yet ready.
Grant me the will to want to forgive.
Grant it to me not yet but soon.

And in the meanwhile? What might I do so that I don't stay stuck in the same place? I could easily go back into the mindlessness of my daily busyness. But if I want to eventually reach a place of peace, I needed to commit to a process that might lead to healing.

Mpho and The Arch offer a series of meditations, activities, rituals and journal exercises. They call it the four-fold path: telling the story, naming the hurt, granting forgiveness, renewing or releasing the relationship.

Perhaps I'll work my way through the four-fold path and give it a chance to work on me. I read through *The Book of Forgiving* and started to make a list of the materials required for the reflective exercises, including:

- a palm-size stone;
- a journal;
- a list of people I need to forgive;
- a list of those who I would like to forgive me;
- a sheet of paper;
- a bowl of water;
- paints to decorate the stone;
- a breakable item;
- glue;
- markers;

- colored paper;
- fabric;
- a place where you can write with your finger in the sand for the wind to then blow the words away.

At the end of the year I'll spend my holidays in Nature's Valley, where the Tsitsikamma Mountains meet the sea on South Africa's southern coastline. There is sand enough to write on. Just one thing to be added to the list: a person with clear intention and an open heart.

Renée: Did She Know How Much She Meant to Me?

Readiness to die at any age, knowing there's always the possibility of the unexpected happening is not only about wanting to feel at peace in relationships. There's more. People have told me that they've sometimes had regrets that someone died and they were not sure whether they'd ever conveyed strongly enough to the deceased the special place they held in their heart.

Do the people we love really know we love them? How long ago is it that you or I last acknowledged our feelings for a special friend or family member? If we knew our time was limited, is there anything to consider putting in place that will tenderly acknowledge the special relationship? I heard of a grandfather who left a letter to be given to his granddaughter on her 21st birthday. She did not know he'd done this. She was thrilled; the letter, she said, was the most precious gift she received that day—even more so because it was unexpected.

The film *Mum's List* is based on the true story of Kate Greene. When her breast cancer took a turn for the worse, she realized she would not be part of her young sons' lives as they grew up. In her last weeks, she started writing a bucket list of what she'd like them to do on Post-It notes. The list included things like search for four-leaved clovers and go on holiday to the beach of her childhood. Kate added to the bucket list with text messages sent from her hospital bed. One such message read, 'Would be good if you settled down sooner rather than later, so you get to see grandchildren.' Finding happiness in a new family was what she wanted for her husband and the father of her children; she wanted him to find love again and remarry.

I admired Kate's creativity, her forward caring for relationships, thoughtful and inspirational.

Mum's List is about how Kate made suggestions that will manifest her love for her family and keep her present in their lives.

But what about the other way around? Our being careful enough to be sure those who are dying know of our love for them. When my sister-in-law Renée died, I created quiet time to think of my cherished memories of her, then wrote them down to share.

I first met Renée Ephron, née Slovo, in 1990 when Joe and I moved to Johannesburg following the release of Nelson Mandela and the unbanning of various political parties, including the African National Congress and the South African Communist Party. By then, I'd lived in southern Africa for more than 20 years, with blood relatives far away in England, Germany, and Poland. My first husband's family was mostly in Canada.

Renée welcomed us. At last she had a brother in the same city, and now he was acknowledged as someone to be proud of, rather than someone to be embarrassed about because of his politics.

By then, Tessa was almost 11 years old and Kyla six-and-a-half. Renée helped me set up our home. Tessa and Kyla arrived in Johannesburg from Bulawayo for their first Christmas. It was Renée who helped, who ran me around to show me the shopping areas. And it was her husband Sammy, who ran a second-hand car sales and body shop repair business, who sold me a car so that I had my own wheels quickly.

Renée acted with consistent generosity. For Tessa's birthday on January 4, 1991, she turned up with birthday gifts and treats for a kid who'd just landed in a gigantic city without friends, after living her first decade in much smaller urban settings in Maputo, Bulawayo, and Lusaka.

When I got a job that needed better clothes than I had, Renée raided her wardrobe to deck me out. I still have one beige linen embroidered waistcoat which I can't throw out because it brings to life my memories of Renée at that time.

I liked Renée a lot. We liked each other, and found it easy to be with one another. When I went to look at a house at 15 Urania Street, Observatory in 1991 and wanted a second opinion, but Joe was caught up in political meetings, it was Renée who came to look and gave her stamp of approval saying she was sure that her brother would like it and that the asking price was reasonable. It proved to be a lovely and secure place to live.

Renée introduced me to the calendar of Jewish festivities, and I began to enjoy Pesach and Rosh Hashanah and learn about the meaning of the rituals. When Kyla expressed interest, Renée took her to the shul in Doornfontein. We'd be invited to Observatory, Linksfield, Highlands North, wherever the next Ephron extended family gathering was to take place. I had to learn that on some of these occasions, even though there would eventually be more food than you could ever imagine, it would be wise to eat something before going—otherwise you'd have hunger pangs sitting through the long reading of the Haggadah.

When I turned 40 and celebrated it with a Saturday night party, Sammy cooked a huge pot of delicious calamari stew. Renée turned up early with a hundred plates and said, 'No paper plates! Not classy and the gravy makes the paper plates soggy!'

It was cruel that she only had five years of her brother before he died in January 1995. You might have thought that our relationship would wane after he died. But it didn't. Renée, joined by her niece Janine and Janine's husband Gary, kept an eye on me in my widowhood. They still remembered children's birthdays, and offered us continued inclusion in family gatherings, including the bar and bat mitzvahs, and big birthdays. When Renée and Sammy declared bankruptcy and moved to Cape Town, I'd see her when we were on our family holiday at the end of the year. She and I would go for extended walks on Muizenberg beach, and I joined them for Friday night Shabbat.

Later, after Renée and Sammy's three children all emigrated to Australia with their spouses and children, Sammy persuaded Renée to follow. He wanted his family close by. Gary and Janine also emigrated after an armed robbery which left Janine traumatized.

When I married John in October 2008, Renée and Gary came to our wedding. It was lovely that she joined the celebration, welcoming John as my new life partner. She was gracious about our wedding being held at Villa Arcadia. Now a venue occasionally rented out for special occasions, it was once the Jewish orphanage where she spent her childhood after her mother died in childbirth, when her brother Joe was 10 and she was just a toddler. Being on those premises, a huge mansion converted into dormitories upstairs and dining and living downstairs, brought back memories for her, many of which were not pleasant.

On her last visit to South Africa years ago, Sammy and Renée came for dinner. John had never met Sammy so it was an evening of discovery, the best evening I ever spent with them in 20 years. The three of them all knew the Johannesburg of decades ago and went down memory lane talking about visits to the Turffontein Racecourse. Renée and Sammy spoke about their life as it had unfolded, and the different businesses they had run: second-hand car sales, the body shop, importing tiles from Italy (with boxes of wine hidden in the middle of the tiles), a restaurant, a mobile knife-sharpening business. We laughed so much over dinner. The evening made me understand there are different ways of hearing the same story. I used to think of it as a story of serial business failure, of their sometimes starting a business and seeing the promise of its success through rose-colored glasses. That evening of retrospection gave me a different point of view, and left me with admiration for their huge resilience to take a fall and get up and try again, fall and try again, and then again.

It's impossible to think of Renée without remembering how she grumbled about Sammy *all the time*, how he irritated her, how she said he got on her nerves. And sometimes she'd laugh at her own grumpiness. But they lived a long life together while riding a roller coaster. They rubbed along, often abrasively. But her grief when Sammy died revealed the tender place he'd held in her heart for so many decades.

I'm glad she died when she did, because she was suffering. But I'm sorry I didn't get to see her one more time. Just weeks before, we had a long catching-up conversation and we spoke of me flying over for a visit early in the new year. It was not to be. She died on December 26, 2016.

Renée Ephron, née Slovo, my dear sister-in-law. You will always have a very special place in my heart. I'm so glad you came into my life. I will always think of you with gratitude.

After writing these thoughts down, I emailed them to join the flow of the many mails that warmly connected extended family members after her death, in a family diaspora that spanned three continents.

A few days later I sat quietly at dawn, my favorite time of watching the sky lighten, and listened to birdsong. I felt a sudden rush of sadness and a head full of questions. Did Renée know just how special the place was that I held for her in my heart? Why hadn't I thought of composing and sending her a letter when she was still alive when it was clear that cancer was getting the better of her? I wish I'd thought this through sooner. I began thinking about other people in my life I cared for, those who I'd like to be sure knew my feelings now, not posthumously.

Postscript Two

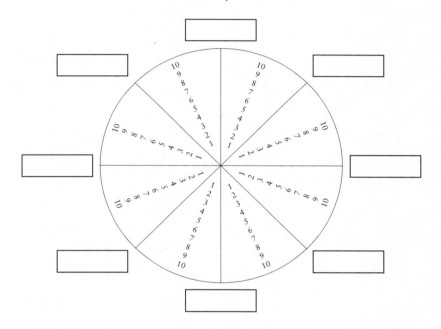

This Wheel of Life tool has worked effectively for me and for my clients in assessing important roles and relationships. For this exercise, you'll need three pens of different colors. In the rectangular boxes, fill in the relationships you want to think about. Then score each using the three different measures below with 10, the outside of the ring, being highest, and 1, towards the center of the wheel, being the lowest.

1st color: How important is this relationship to you?

2nd color: How much effort do you make in this relationship? Rate yourself.

3rd color: How satisfied are you? What is the quality of the engagement? What joy does it generate for you?

After scoring, evaluate what you've found. For example, perhaps for each relationship, each of the three scores are the same. Is that okay? Where is it that there are differences? What thoughts come to mind? What changes, if any, would you like to pursue?

PART THREE
Secrets

The reason people keep secrets is to prevent the breaking of relationships when those secrets are revealed. Why risk this before you die?

—Gonda Perez, In conversation with the author, November 2016

Secrets, silent, stony sit in the dark places of both our hearts: secrets weary of their tyranny, tyrants willing to be dethroned.

—James Joyce, *Ulysses*

The man who can keep a secret may be wise, but he is not half as wise as the man with no secrets to keep.

—Edgar Watson Howe, *Country Town Sayings*

Do nothing secretly; for Time sees and hears all things, and discloses all.

—Sophocles

Samuel: The Man in the Shadows

My colleague Samuel* is the sixth-born son of Ezekiel*, who had two families in the same neighborhood of Katlehong in Germiston, a town south-east of Johannesburg. Samuel's father took up with another woman and had two children with her while maintaining his marital relationship. Samuel and his mother, his siblings, the neighbors, they all knew about his second family and second home on the other side of the railway tracks.

When Samuel was eight, his father started to trust him with money. At first, Ezekiel sent him to buy the weekly train ticket that he needed to go to work on Monday morning, as well as tasking him to care for his lunch money. After high school Samuel managed his father's bank account, his insurance and funeral polices. His father named Samuel as the executor of his estate to manage the family affairs once he'd passed on.

For decades, his father had a steady job as a maintenance technician for a lift company, and a reputation for being reliable. But on weekends Ezekiel became an entertainer; he played his accordion at weddings and other social gatherings. Alcohol was his weekend indulgence—his giving his son part of his wages on Friday was his security that come Monday morning he would have his train ticket and lunch money for the week ahead.

Samuel's father was mostly not at home, especially not on weekends. Samuel had one etched-in memory of a Saturday afternoon when his father drew up outside the house in a fancy red car and brought in boxes. He'd been paid well and arrived with a once-off abundance of toys for this household of children. At the end of the afternoon he drove off again. His mother's attitude was enduring and forgiving. She said simply, 'Your father has a good heart.'

As the years progressed, the fancy cars became less fancy; juke boxes or disc jockeys replaced Ezekiel and his accordion, who in his elder years, spent more time with Samuel's family.

Samuel had fun in his childhood and teenage years. There was real neighborliness in Katlehong—there were always many other boys to play football with, all children whose parents had come from different rural areas. Samuel's father was Zulu, while the neighbors next door were Xhosa from the Eastern Cape. Everyone socialized freely.

Sometimes Samuel was asked, 'When will *you* be going to the mountains to become a man?'

The children were referring to the circumcision ceremony, a Xhosa tradition marking the rite of passage from boyhood to manhood. Samuel told his mother he also wanted to be circumcised. When she asked him why, he gave her all the scientific health reasons he'd heard mentioned, but basically he wanted to be like the boys next door. But no mountain retreat for Samuel, his mother sent him to the hospital for the surgery and it was done.

There was a man who visited his Eastern Cape neighbors frequently and took a shine to young Samuel. Sometimes Samuel would notice him standing on the sidelines of the community football field watching, and at the end of the game the man often complimented him on how well he played and offered him a coin. Samuel did well at school and got a place at a university near Durban. When he would return home for the holidays, sometimes he would bump into the neighbor's friend. The man always asked with genuine interest, 'How are your studies going? And your sister, how is she?' And just as when Samuel was a little boy, the man pressed money into his palm.

When Samuel was 23 his mother became ill and died. She, like her husband, also favored Samuel above all her other children. Before passing, she spelled out her wishes to him and everyone else: he, the level-headed one, the cleverest of her children, must take on the mantle of leadership in the family. This was extraordinary. Customarily social practice bestowed inheritance and head-of-household responsibilities on the eldest son.

In his last year at university, Samuel became sick but doctors could not diagnose the cause. When he returned home, his second-born brother offered help.

'No man, let me take you to this traditional healer. Don't tell anybody you know.'

Traditional medicine is often frowned upon but at the same time, it is commonly sought out. The healer started his African rituals, the throwing of the bones, the shaman's way of divining his circumstances and discerning the cause of illness.

The healer suddenly asked him, 'Who are you?'

'I'm Zwane*, Samuel Zwahke Zwane.'

'No, no, no, you are not a Zwane,' the healer said. 'Who are you?"

The healer then gave Samuel advice on what he needed to do to become healthy again. He gave him a packet of dried herbs, ground to a powder, to be mixed into water and taken daily for one month.

From the time of this encounter, something clicked into place in Samuel's mind. Aged 26, he started to ask questions.

I picked up that the wife of my second brother knew that my father who raised me was not my biological father and that she knew who he was. And that my mother's sister also knew my biological father. I wanted to talk with my father about it.

I confronted him. 'Are you my father, my biological father?'

My aunt, the one who knew, was also present. My father was silent. He never answered that question.

I asked further, 'Some say Madonsela*, the man who visited our neighbor, is my biological father.'

Then my father burst out, 'Who told you that? And whosoever told you that, that is a lie.' And I could see that he was hurt. He was deeply hurt.

But my aunt intervened. 'You must tell him the truth. He should know who his real father is.'

His father looked at his late wife's sister, stony-faced, and then looked at Samuel and insisted, 'I am your father.'

The aunt exploded and said she would not be silenced; she would speak the truth out loud. She told Samuel that the man from the Eastern Cape, the man who regularly visited their neighbors, was his father. It was Madonsela who fathered both Samuel and his younger sister.

Samuel's father remained stony-faced. He left the room and father and son never spoke of the matter again.

His aunt's declaration made sense to him. Madonsela, the man on the sidelines at the football games, his interest in his studies and his sister, the insinuating comments he overheard, the neighbors' questions about his becoming circumcised.

Samuel tussled with two responses, firstly his thoughts about his mother's morality, and secondly his thoughts about his biological family and the question of lineage and identity.

He shared with me that the older he became, the longer he lived his own adult life, the more he understood his mother. He does not judge her badly but he wished he would have been able to talk through all of this with her before she died. After death, there are no more conversations possible.

> There was a stage where I sat down and asked myself, what kind of a mother did I have? I found resolution when I started to consider the circumstances surrounding her. You know, this woman pulled everything together for the good of her family and I tend to think she was very successful. If it was not for her that house and our family would not be in existence.
>
> This is one of those things that I talk to my kids about. I try to get them to understand what's important for a marriage to work. My father used to drink a lot. When Friday came, he started to binge drink, as though that confirmed that he was in the entertainment business. You can't believe how he would drink. But come Monday he would go to work as if there had been no partying over the weekend.
>
> I sit now with my own experience and understanding of a marriage. I think that his drinking and being an entertainer created a gap in his marriage. He neglected his wife. Why was he drinking? I can't answer that, but it had a huge impact on his relationship.
>
> Now I see young guys who are married and drinking and their wives are in misery and want a shoulder to cry on. It's human nature. I've reached a better understanding of the circumstances that surrounded my mother and my family.

What was more complex for Samuel was his coming to terms with the fact that there's another blood lineage in his veins, another family history with its own culture and traditions. He never considered DNA testing; the circumstantial evidence supporting his biological paternity was strong.

Years after his mother's death, two men bearing a family likeness visited Samuel. They informed him they were his half-brothers born in the Eastern Cape working on a mine in the west of Johannesburg. Their father had passed away. They wanted him to join a family gathering the following Sunday.

Samuel went, and found his half-brothers' grandmother was also present. She exclaimed when she saw Samuel and called out for a young grandchild to come over. Samuel found himself facing a replica of himself as a small boy.

'What do you want of me?' Samuel asked the family. He had been wrestling with questions of identity since his aunt's revelation and reached his conclusion.

'I told them I've been raised Samuel Zwakhe Zwane. That was the family I was born into and grew up in. I know the problems of the Zwane family. I promised my mother that I would be a leader in this family. I don't know you. I don't want to know you further. I have grown up with the Zwane Zulu family traditions. I don't now want to change and adopt your different traditions.'

Samuel assured me he succeeded in saying this gently but firmly, ensuring an amicable parting and no pressure for further contact. I can imagine it. He has a deep, soft, but strong voice and can deliver a tough message without wavering.

At the time Samuel told me this story he was in his late 40s. I asked him if his own family was in the know. He answered that he'd shared the story with his boys. His elder son wanted to ask for a girl's hand in marriage, and traditionally in the letter of request to be written to the girl's family, it is customary for the line of ancestry to be set out. Samuel felt his son should know that their family surname Zwane, the son's grandfather, was not the surname of the biological lineage.

My son asked me, 'So who are you?'

'I was made to understand my surname is Madonsela and my father is originally from the Eastern Cape. He came here to work for the railways company and worked there for 42 years.'

'Did you know him?'

'You won't believe this. Yes, I knew this man in passing, but I never knew that he was my father.'

I asked Samuel what he learned from his experience that he would want others to take on board. He shared his view that secrets are mostly corrosive with complex ramifications. Neighbors talk, relatives talk. He always felt there was a whispering in the backdrop of his childhood. He favors having no secrets, and that people would work out how to live with the truth.

I thought we'd reached the end of Samuel's story-telling as we sat in comfortable silence, but then Samuel continued with a surprise addendum.

> Several years ago, I had an affair. It ended. Two years ago, the woman contacted me and told me, 'You have a daughter who is six years old.' I did the DNA testing. The child is mine.
>
> I spent two months thinking about what to do. My wife and I had been married for more than 20 years. I have never spent a night away from home. My wife trusted me completely. How would she respond to this betrayal? Should I take the risk of telling her? Would she find it possible to forgive me? How would this change our relationship?
>
> I spoke with my wife's best friend, who is married to my brother. She advised me not to say anything before Christmas, to wait for the New Year, and to arrange some leave time to be around after breaking the news as well as identify possibilities for counseling. I followed her advice.
>
> That was almost two years ago. We're still taking things slowly. My wife met the child's mother, satisfied herself that there's no relationship between us anymore. I see my daughter once a month. My boys met their half-sister. My wife has not yet met her. But recently she mentioned that, one of these months ahead, she'd like to come with me when I visit my daughter.
>
> It has been very difficult. We talked a lot about what was happening in our marriage in that year I had my extramarital affair. The pain of my wife's hurt also cut into me deeply. It was hard to see her so hurt. But my hurt at the hurt I'd caused—her seeing that, helped her to forgive me.

I asked what made him take the risk of sharing his secret. He answered poignantly. 'I didn't want to be the man in the shadows, watching my child play sport, and pressing a coin into her hand at the end of the game.'

Elsa: My Family's Subterfuge

This is not a story about death or loss in the physical, bodily sense of loss. But my friend Elsa* mourns the subterfuge which has so deeply impacted on how her family lives out their life and their lie. Unless something happens the deceit will be engraved on Elsa's tombstone in perpetuity, 'Here lies Elsa … beloved daughter of … sister to …'

I involuntarily became part of a long-term family subterfuge.

I'd become an extended member of the family of my friend Elsa. I got invited to many of the big family gatherings like significant birthdays, weddings, and funerals. On this particular occasion, a 50th birthday party, I sat with Elsa, her elder sister Julia* and her parents.

Julia and Elsa are born 14 years apart. It reminded me of my own family. My mother was 14 when her youngest brother was born and 17 when her younger sister Inge arrived. Inge, only 10 years older than me, has often felt like a cousin rather than an aunt. At least this was the way I'd always thought about Elsa and her family.

But later that night when Elsa and I were sitting alone, she said she was going to tell me a family secret that she wanted me to write about, but that I must disguise the names and promise not to let her parents or sister become aware that I was now in the know.

When my sister Julia was 14, Mom and Dad announced to the extended family that they were unexpectedly pregnant. The family story as it's told comments that my sister felt very awkward about the news. I guess it's hard as a teenager to think of your parents having sex, especially when your mom's as old as 40 and your dad is 42.

My mom gave up work early in her pregnancy. She told people she had problems with a pregnancy so late in life. She and my sister went off to stay with, and be cared for, by my granny and I was born on my granny's farm. We returned home for my christening and our relatives oohed and aahed over me as the new family member.

I don't remember a lot about my sister as I was growing up and I haven't become close to her over time. She left home when I was three and she was 17. She got married and started her own family, so as a child I became an aunt to nephews and nieces who are only a bit younger than me. When we had our family gatherings, people would comment how alike my sister and I looked, and sometimes there would be a kind of laugh and a whisper, which always made me feel uncomfortable.

When I was 18 my mom and dad sat me down and told me that they were not my parents after all—they were my grandparents. Julia, my sister, was my birth mother, and my biological dad was the boyfriend she'd had when she was 14. He never knew that he'd got his girlfriend pregnant. They were staunch Catholics and their daughter Julia becoming pregnant as a teenager was difficult to handle; the anticipated embarrassment, condemnation, and social shame in their neighborhood and church community.

Marriage to the father, terminating the pregnancy, or Julia's carrying the baby to term and giving me up for adoption were not options they wanted to consider. Their pretending they had a late pregnancy, and bringing me up as their child seemed like the best way forward for all concerned.

I was angry when they told me and I am still angry. I don't know why. Ma and Pa loved me as their child and brought me up as caring, attentive parents and I lacked for nothing. I suppose it's the deceit, my being central to a big lie. And I have a sort of retro-resentment of having always felt a bit lonely, the last born who felt like an only child without brothers and sisters as playmates whereas at my so-called sister's house my supposed nephew and niece had each other and had great fun.

It's strange now between my sister and me, my sister who it turns out is my birth mother, and my nephew and niece, who are actually my half-sister and half-brother. At family gatherings, we still act out the lie, I'm not sure why. That's the thing about secrets—they take on a life of their own and sometimes it's all too complex and too twisted to unravel and straighten things out.

Elsa wanted to share her story because she hopes that in the next generation there'll be more tolerance, that the depth of shame that her grandparents felt when their teenage daughter fell pregnant will no longer happen.

How many people know this story? Ten, 20, 30? I'm one more person now in the know. I'm one additional person complicit as I pledge to continue to act out the secret when we're together on future social occasions.

Joe: The Blue Aerogramme

My husband Joe Slovo, a popular liberation struggle hero in South Africa, died before dawn on Friday, January 6, 1995. Though we lived very privately, once Joe left the house he became a public figure: apartheid struggle hero; widower of Ruth First, his first wife assassinated by a letter bomb; member of Nelson Mandela's inner circle; and a member of Cabinet since the first-ever democratic elections in 1994, just eight months before he died.

His state funeral would take place in a football stadium seating 80,000, a stage-managed event. I held onto the possibility of organizing a wake, a memorial evening of just 100 people, family and friends more closely connected, which might allow us a more intimate remembrance. Thank goodness this happened as it made being on public display in front of 80,000 the next day, under the incessant click and flash of the photographers, a little more bearable.

At 8am, just five hours after Joe's death, there were people all over the house, the African National Congress in action. Urns arrived in the kitchen. The dining room server filled with cakes, scones, sandwiches. I took up the couple of Persian rugs we owned—the foot traffic would be heavy this week. People collected every chair they could find and brought them all into the lounge. Someone put a book on a table in the entrance hall for people to write their messages. Someone else found a box for people to put money into—it's a tradition among some black African cultures to contribute money to funerals. Everywhere I looked there were people: kitchen, dining room, lounge, study, veranda, and garden. Conversations were in full flow; people sharing their memories.

It was high summer and the purple blossoms of the jacaranda trees had fallen, their leaves thickened, providing welcome shade in the lower garden. This was the coolest place, the place where Joe chose to sit the most in those last days as his friends visited him for what they knew was the last time: family friends and anti-apartheid activists Harold Wolpe and Hillary Hamburger, playwright Barney Simon, ANC chief negotiator Cyril Ramaphosa and President Nelson Mandela. This prime spot now hosted a meeting of the funeral planning committee resolving how to combine differing needs and cultures into a state funeral.

I couldn't contemplate the African tradition of sitting on a mattress receiving people, day after day, for several days until the burial service. Maybe it would have been grounding? I would never know as I didn't give it a try. Instead I sat on chairs and drifted from room to room, from one cluster of people to another. I had only one responsibility: to be present and gracious all day long as scores of people arrived to offer their condolences.

My bedroom, Joe's dying room, was the only place not full of people. It became my place to take an occasional break from what felt like overexposure, and a place for private conversation.

The entire last month of Joe's dying was crowded. I craved solo time whilst feeling acutely lonesome. Joe and I knew one another for almost 20 years and were married for the last eight, politically challenging years. We loved with ease, warmth and joy. Intense companionship supported us through our four-year journey towards his dying. At a time when the personal lives of many politicians suffered, we took the personal time we needed. We lived together on the high wire. His last breath ended our dyad.

During the afternoon of the second day, Joe's colleague and friend Ronnie Kasrils asked to talk to me privately, and we went to my bedroom. He told me about a distraught young man in the street outside who would like to come in but felt unsure, ambivalent. Michael Sachs, he said, was dismayed about Joe's death. He wished he'd spoken with his father and now it was too late for any conversation. His biological father had died without ever acknowledging their relationship. Emotion side-swiped Michael; he was not able to figure out his place in this circumstance.

I was puzzled. Nothing Ronnie said held any meaning for me.

Michael Sachs? Joe's son?

Joe, as I would learn, was the biological father of Michael, born to Stephanie and Albie Sachs in London in the 1970s. I also came to know that many of my friends knew this story; they chose never to refer to it out of respect for my privacy. My close friend Gill said, 'Well. If you weren't going to bring up the subject, then I certainly wasn't.'

I had lived for almost 20 years with a different Michael Sachs birth story. In Maputo, I had my professional work, but I was also a hairdresser to several people in a city where hair salons had closed. My clientele included the exiled Albie Sachs who had come from London to Mozambique to work on a family law project. We had become close. When Ed and I divorced, it was Albie—who went on to be a Constitutional Court judge in the new South Africa—who acted as our lawyer and drafted our amicable separation agreement.

At that time in Mozambique, Albie told me how much he missed his sons who remained in London with their mother as part of a trial separation. He shared that fatherhood had not happened easily; there were fertility issues. Eventually, he and Stephanie decided to adopt. They were offered a baby boy, and then discovered Stephanie was pregnant. It often happens this way that people, having decided on adoption, relax and pregnancy ensues. Michael was born and the two brothers grew up together. That was my Michael Sachs story as told to me by his father.

Michael, now in his early 20s, was apparently pacing the street outside my house. Ronnie told me he was the spitting image of the young Joe Slovo. 'Just look at the photographs from the treason trial,' he said. 'There's no mistaking his paternity.'

I felt for the young man and his predicament. As for myself I felt ambushed. Why had Joe dissembled? Why did he not tell me about Michael? We'd spoken often of his long-term affair with Stephanie. Did he think I would judge him? Think less of him? Now I wondered, just how well did I know him?

Joe's relationship with Stephanie, and Michael's birth, long preceded our marriage. We arrived at second marriages with history. We were selective about what we shared about our younger selves. But this was an omission of magnitude. This hurt.

Several weeks after the funeral, I began paper sorting. We had three olive-green metal filing cabinets in my study, each with four drawers. Most of them contained my PhD research papers arranged by author, library-style. Then Joe and I each had a drawer that was personal. I was not familiar with his files. It was a Tuesday, late in the evening, when I took out a file labelled 'current correspondence,' but it was the oldest of Joe's correspondence that I came across. There were business letters and several letters from women with whom Joe had had meaningful relationships.

There was one surprise but it didn't actually feel like one; it was more like finding the missing piece of a jigsaw puzzle.

I found a single thin blue aerogramme, those old all-in-one letters where the written page folds into itself to become the envelope, with the fold over sides that you lick to seal.

I read it. There was mention of a son but clearly not Michael. The letter was from 'E' and predated Michael's birth by some years. As I mulled over the words, fragments of conversations with Joe came back to me.

As a lawyer, he'd gone on a court case to a town in the Free State. Staying in the hotel he met E, a legal secretary. I now remember Joe's words, 'she was not of our ilk,' meaning not politically involved. They'd shared a mutual attraction and a couple of nights together. Later she contacted Joe and told him that she was pregnant, that she thought she couldn't—wouldn't get pregnant—and that she intended to keep the child. Her choice, her responsibility.

I'd asked Joe if he hadn't wanted to keep in touch to know that the child grew up okay. His answer was that he had contact with the woman when he was in London, and that the boy was a fine young teenager with plans to join the air force. The aerogramme was written to Lyme Street, Joe's Camden Town address in London and E referred to their meeting up on a visit she made to England.

Joe and I had one more brief exchange, much later, in South Africa when I ventured to ask if he thought maybe his son would be curious to meet him. His reply was that they had agreed that the boy would never be told. The tone of his voice was clear: this topic was not up for further discussion.

The blue aerogramme, Joe's first son; and Michael Sachs, Joe's second son. Two unacknowledged children. One he'd mentioned and the other,

Michael, who everyone in my circle seemed to know about except me.

Some people favor the 'what you don't know can't hurt you' principle. But I have a question, at least for myself: what might my loved ones discover about me when I die that they don't yet know that they might find hurtful?

I think this is a conversation worth having with oneself, worth thinking through and weighing up.

My choice? I want to lessen the chances of my being the cause, post-mortem, of hurting loved ones. I don't want The Mills Brother's song line about hurting most the ones you love to be part of my legacy.

Three years after Joe's death, Michael and I had supper together. In the interim, Michael's half-sister Gillian Slovo had written her family memoir *Every Secret Thing* and revealed several family secrets. Michael's story was splashed across the front pages of South Africa's Sunday newspapers; his biological parentage was now public. He and I talked the length of an unhurried meal. I answered any question that Michael asked as best as I could. He left carrying Joe's black leather ministerial briefcase. It seemed an appropriate gift to the one offspring who has chosen to live in South Africa and work in the government that his parents, Albie and Stephanie Sachs and Joe, spent their whole lives towards bringing into being.

Ten years after Joe's death, I found myself with Michael again—now an economist working for the South African Treasury—on the same delegation to China. We spent almost two weeks on the road. We were a small group, so there was a lot of opportunity for conversation. But Michael and I never ventured towards the personal. One day, as I was sitting alongside him in a boardroom, I glanced down at his notebook. A shiver went through my body. I was looking at the handwriting of my dead husband. Michael's handwriting was identical to Joe's, yet he would never have seen his father's script while growing up. Is motor co-ordination, influencing handwriting, genetically inherited?

Fifteen years later there was a memorial occasion in Parliament to commemorate the passing of politicians who died in office post-democracy. The families would be presented with a bound copy of a selection of the significant speeches made by the deceased. I received an invitation for two people, me and one other family member. None of Joe's three daughters from his marriage to Ruth could fly in from London, so I phoned Michael to ask if he would accompany me. He said he would have liked to but couldn't—he was about to leave on a flight, I think to attend his MBA graduation at Harvard. It felt as settled as it could be.

It was 21 years later that I read the poet Mary Oliver's memoir, *Our World*, a celebration of more than 40 years of living with her partner, photographer Molly Malone. She asks just how well you can know someone, no matter how long you live with them. After 30 years she heard Molly whistling. She'd never ever heard her whistle before. She captured her reflections in her poem, 'The Whistler', which offered me insight and calm.

Twenty-one years, and the peace I yearned for on learning of Joe's secrets after his death feels complete. I thought I'd arrived at a place of acceptance earlier, but when I read Oliver's poem, I surprised myself, realizing that there was yet another layer of understanding that I was adding to my life.

As Caroline Paul writes in her book *Lost Cat*: 'You can never know anyone as completely as you want. But that's okay, love is better.'

To Reveal or Not to Reveal—that is the Question

A friend, a woman whose husband had affairs discreetly, discovered them when reading his journals during her bereavement period after he died. She was also surprised by some of the observations he'd written about their relationship. I asked her if she would have felt less hurt at the time if he'd talked with her about some of those things

> He was a very careful and calculating man. Some of those things he wouldn't have told me because I wouldn't have looked after him so well. I don't think I would have been so nice to him in bed. I wish I hadn't read it in a way. On the other hand, I'm glad I did because it was the truth, but it was the truth in a context and I don't think he could talk about those things. I don't know. I don't know. Look, a couple of those things I wish I hadn't read, but they are real. So, I must own them.
>
> Many men have affairs. And I've always thought that when you are unable to carry your guilt, you feel the urge to tell your wife, to

get the guilt off you and to cause her immeasurable pain. So, I think if you've had an affair, shut up and carry your guilt. I don't think it's necessary to tell your partner. In the same way there were times when I simply turned the other way and did not ever raise things and say things that could not ever be unsaid. And they passed. And I was patient. And I played a long game, rather than a short one. He wasn't perfect. And, in reflecting on the relationship, which was so very happy overall, I'm okay to have lived with the flaws.

Postscript Three

Secrets. Most of us have some. Presumably we keep something secret because we're not comfortable with others knowing the truth. I studied with the US coach and author Martha Beck. I remember her asking a question that made me reflect: 'If there's information that you're not disclosing, is it about privacy or discretion, or is it because of harboring some shame?'

Do we keep a secret when we're ashamed or when we feel that we'd put another relationship at risk if we were to reveal the facts, and that the price of a possible poor outcome in response to disclosure seems too costly to contemplate? Other people adamantly disagree with disclosure. They think secrets should be taken to the grave, and that if post-death revelations do take place then those concerned, those who feel hurt, must get over their hurt, or not, as best they can.

A clinical psychologist advised me that she was always very circumspect about secrets, and was wary that I was including it as one of the themes in the book. She says she regularly advises clients not to share their secret.

What's surprising to me is how many people have spoken to me about the secrets their families live with and the extensive collusion of denial that sometimes comes with it.

Others, like me, learned about a secret posthumously. Samuel told me when we spoke about his family secrets: 'Truth has a way of finding its way out. People, families, differ in how they handle them.'

I found peoples' reflections so thought-provoking. I'd tended towards the 'tell all and weather the consequences' approach, but now I understand the points being made by those who take a different view.

Several people suggested that people should consider how to lessen the hurt of a secret likely to come to light posthumously. The writing of a letter that is left to the person(s) most likely to feel hurt was a favored suggestion, an explanation of the context of the events with the hope of softening the blow.

A secret: to reveal or not to reveal? That is the question. It's a personal decision. There can be no prescription—we are all so very different. I'd simply advocate thoughtfulness, that whatever action or inaction is taken is intentional and is the outcome of careful consideration, rather than no thought ever being given as to how the living might experience discovery.

PART FOUR

Respecting Choices

Love, allowing the other to be a legitimate other, is the only emotion that expands intelligence.

—Humberto Maturana, *The Origin of Humanness in the Biology of Love*

Out beyond ideas of wrongdoing and rightdoing,
there's a field,
I'll meet you there

—Rumi

Gina: I'll Try Everything

My mum, Gina, is a 'give me anything, I'm up for everything' kind of person when it comes to staying alive. It has served her well. Without this attitude, she'd have probably died decades earlier.

Regina Maria Mathilde Klohs was born in 1927 on a farm in an area of Czechoslovakia called Sudetenland in the days before antibiotics and penicillin. She told me that when she was a girl, every year there were kids at school who died, taken out by an infection. Her father's first wife had three children before she herself died; two of the three children died within their first year of life.

Family lineage, on my grandmother's side, traces itself back to Benedictine monk Gregor Mendel, recognized as the founder of modern-day genetics. My great-great-aunt was the village herbalist. Perhaps it was her healing potions that helped my mother overcome the *diphtheria* she contracted when she was seven, and again when she got *scarlet fever* at 16. This aunt also treated my mum with poultices when she *broke her leg* skiing to school one winter.

Mum would show me plants in the Lancashire wilds of my childhood and tell me about them. 'This is the knitbone plant, comfrey,' she'd say. 'It's Latin name is *symphytum officinale*. My great-aunt used this.'

Mum turned 11 on March 4, 1938. Six months later, on September 30, Hitler, Chamberlain, Daladier, and Ciano signed the Munich Agreement which 'gave' Sudetenland to Germany. Soldiers took up residence on my grandparents' farm. My mother watched as a pile of books was taken from their family library, piled up and set alight. 'Too liberal,' said the German soldiers.

The family was told that if they wanted to live out this wartime without trouble, they should 'mind their p's and q's.' My grandparents were once called to the school and told that their daughter had made inappropriate comments and they needed to reform her attitudes. All schoolchildren were forced to join the Hitler Youth brigade. My mother bristled whenever she talked of this brainwashing experience and her forced compliance.

The tide turned and Russian forces pushed back the Nazis. My grandparents piled themselves and victuals into a cart and joined the trek of families trying to keep ahead of the frontline that was coming closer. My mum told me how my grandfather constructed a false bottom to the horse-drawn cart to hide his wife and daughters. People accepted rape and pillage as the consequence of war's brutalization. The one illness my mum had never been treated for is *post-traumatic stress disorder*. As a teenager, I received a gift of a typewriter and sat in my bedroom typing. One day my mother burst in, screamed, and said she could stand it no more. My tapping of the typewriter keys reminded her of the sound of machine guns.

My mother's family were bilingual speakers of German and Czech but in the classification processes undertaken during the war, they were defined as ethnically German. The new political regime that came to power at the end of the war expelled ethnic Germans.

In 1946 my grandparents and five of their children, with their ages ranging between two and 19, made their way to the train station, each carrying the one permitted suitcase, and boarded a cattle wagon. They were just seven people among the estimated 1.6 million who were deported to the American free zone that became West Germany, whilst another 800,000 went to the Russian free zone that became East Germany. As 'displaced persons' they were temporarily accommodated in school halls where families strung up bedsheets to create privacy.

Three years later, when the British were on a recruitment drive for labor, 11 years after the Munich Agreement upturned her childhood life, my mother, now aged 22, accepted one of the free boat passages offered to the United Kingdom in exchange for an agreement to work in a designated job. She worked as a weaver in a cotton mill. She met my Polish father at evening language classes; they found sanctuary in their love for each other. England felt welcoming—a haven in which they could shape a future together.

After my younger brother Martin was born, Mum started having continuous *abnormal uterine bleeding*. I remember watching her when

I was four years old. My brother's nappies would be bubbling in a free-standing boiler and she'd scoop them out with wooden tongs and place them between the rubberized rolls of her hand-turned wringer to squeeze out as much water as possible before rinsing and hanging them out to dry. She looked pale, skinny, and tired. She was *anemic.*

She would make herself a cup of tea and swallow large dark-red pills—iron tablets to help increase the hemoglobin in her blood. Her chronic condition worsened with *pyelonephritis,* an inflammation of the kidney and upper urinary tract. Six months later, aged 32, she went to hospital and had a *hysterectomy.* We children, Roman, Helena and Martin, aged eight, five and two went into foster care for six weeks.

When I was eight and my younger brother had started school, my mum saw an advert in the local newspaper for exams for those whose education had been interrupted by war and who were interested in becoming nurses. Mum sat those exams. She struggled with English as her second language but passed.

Nursing also impacted my mum's health. She contracted *hepatitis*; her case was severe and she was hospitalized again. I remember visiting my yellow-skinned mother—we were older now and didn't go to foster care this time around.

After that her *allergy sensitivities* seemed to get worse—pollen bothered her breathing and certain foods, like strawberries and fish, would cause a skin reaction.

Next, she got a *slipped disc.* It was considered a standard professional nursing injury due to lifting heavy patients in the days before hydraulic beds. My image of my mother in my teenage years is of a plump woman wearing a sort of fat dog collar to support her neck.

As a nurse, you're standing most of the day. Mum often complained of aching feet and would sit with her feet in a bowl filled with hot water and vinegar. Later her legs started to swell—she had *edema.* She took medication to deal with the water retention and started wearing support tights.

In her 50s, she had an *appendectomy. Osteoarthritis* settled in as well as *hypertension*, and she showed up as *pre-diabetic.* She took early retirement when she was 59 years old.

I visited my parents around this time and at breakfast my mother lined up her row of pills on a plate. My father chuckled and said to me, 'Just listen to your mother. All these pills. She rattles when she walks.

But watch it. I swear she'll outlive me.'

And she did. Six years later my father had a heart attack so severe he died within a few minutes—a young-at-heart 68-year-old who'd just begun to enjoy retirement.

Mum decided that longevity would be her life mission. She joked that my dad hadn't enjoyed the British government pension he'd worked so hard to have a right to—so she needed to outlast him for as long as possible to enjoy his pension share as well as her own.

It seemed to me that once Dad was gone, Mum adopted illness as her companion. Coupled together, ill health secured the continued looking in on her by family and neighbors long after the first attentions to her as a grieving widow might have otherwise subsided.

I spent years phoning weekly from South Africa to the United Kingdom listening to my mum's Sunday recital of ailments. Unlike my stoic late husband who never spoke of the cancer-induced pain of his multiple myeloma or his bodily discomforts—the side effects of medication—my mum was fulsome in providing a description, including the color and consistency of her stools. She spared me no detail.

In the first eight years of widowhood my mom had a *hip replacement* and *idiopathic thrombocytopenic purpura*, a blood condition to do with platelets, which was treated with transfusions, steroid treatments and a *splenectomy*, the removal of her spleen. Your spleen helps the body's defense against bacterial infections, and once my mother no longer had one, the doctor prescribed one penicillin tablet per day as a prophylactic.

In her 11th year of widowhood, now aged 76 and sponsored by me, my mother packed up her home and became an immigrant for the third time. Her move from Europe to Africa would be her last.

She bought an apartment five miles from mine. She missed her garden but orchids got the benefit of her green fingers. She did well enough health-wise for the first five years and found that Johannesburg had good doctors. Once, when she was short of breath, she thought she might be starting with *angina*. The cardiologist did an angiogram to get pictures of the blood flow in her arteries. When he came to the ward later he told me, 'Well I hope your arteries are as clear as your mother's.' The shortness of breath, *dyspnea,* was a side effect of the drug, Brufen Retard, which had been prescribed for her in the United

Kingdom for her *arthritic* pain.

Mum spent much of those days in her sewing room, or knitting and doing crochet whilst surfing the many TV channels that her satellite subscription provided. She seemed to me to be the most well-informed person on the planet. I'd drop by her flat to see her and she would begin with, 'Do you know.' Suddenly she complained about not seeing so well. A successful *cataract* operation restored her sight.

Such lifelong health challenges, serious but not life threatening, create opportunities for all of us to start talking about the choices we might want to make about the level of medical interventions in our lives when illness becomes more serious.

Then, in May 2008 when she was 81, Mum showed me a lump under the skin of her breast bone. I took her for tests. She said she wasn't surprised when she got the news that it was *non-Hodgkin's Lymphoma*. She'd read somewhere that people who'd had her blood condition often got cancer subsequently. She was diagnosed as already being in stage four—the scan showed cancerous masses in seven places.

At the time she was diagnosed I'd been a widow for 14 years, but was now engaged to be married later that year. The invitations were out and the venue booked. My mother signed up for *chemotherapy* saying that there was no way she was missing this wedding.

The oncologist suggested six treatments. Mum didn't react too badly to the first one. With the second she vomited a lot. With the third treatment her bodily response was so bad that she was admitted to the hospital's high-care unit to stabilize her. The chemo was killing the cancer but also killing her at the same time. After she was released the oncologist suggested she do at least one more treatment. I couldn't fathom it, but my mum accepted it and I respected her choice and sat with her again in the oncologist's chemo treatment room. As the bag of liquid chemicals dripped into her veins, she told me that she would like to die in her own home and wanted me to promise that I would fulfill her wish.

Mum attended our wedding in October 2008 looking pale but splendid in a silk dress and jacket made from the length of red brocade that I'd bought for her in China. A stylish red hat completed her outfit, covering her bald head.

The next blood tests showed she was in remission but with consequences. Her digestive system was compromised. She had *diverticulitis*—inflammation of the bowel. She ate baby food. Over two years we progressed from Nestum baby cereal number one, to number two to number three. In the third year, she started eating soft, bland invalid food. I tried to become the best rice pudding-maker in the world, but my efforts were regularly rejected, often ungraciously.

Occasionally I'd venture a 'Mum, when you … it makes me feel…' conversation to try to get her to be more appreciative, especially with her two caregivers who I had hired to help her. But I carefully kept a tight leash on my fantasies of throwing the rejected food at her.

Anger begets anger, and I was acutely aware of my mother's vulnerability. She was still the matriarch exercising power from the confines of her bed, but this power was now precarious and shifting. Once I was her dependent and now she had become mine.

Victor Frankl wrote in *Man's Search for Meaning*, 'Everything can be taken away from a man but one thing: the last of the human freedoms – to choose one's attitude in any given set of circumstances, to choose one's own way.'

I have my own mantra when I'm facing a challenge, 'The success of an intervention depends on the interior condition of the intervenor.' This sentence uttered by Bill O'Brien, CEO of Hanover Insurance and a pioneer in creating a learning organization, became one that I've murmured frequently, both at work when on a difficult assignment, and at home when my mother was unpleasant. I could not change my mother and her irascibility. I could only manage myself and how I was with her, and hope that my composure would elicit a different response. She was old and becoming fragile. It behooved me to help her retain her dignity and hope that love would prevail between us.

I wanted to get better at maintaining my composure. I sought out Wendy Palmer, a US expert in Leadership Embodiment, an approach that combines meditation with movement and includes centering practices. She offers a four-day retreat once a year in South Africa, and I was asked to complete a questionnaire to prepare myself.

One question was, 'What is a quality that you have some of, that you would like more of in your life? And if you were to have more of this quality what difference would it make?'

I chose the quality of compassion. And after her workshop, I went to a Sunday market and searched for a piece of chrysoberyl, a green stone which, according to *The Book of Stones*, has the following qualities:

Green chrysoberyl stimulates the heart and helps one move out of judgment and into a state of enlightened discernment. It allows one to have empathy for the life choices and experiences of others, without the weight of judging them. It enables one to be compassionate, yet objective when viewing emotional circumstances. It can help one to honestly assess one's own role in situations and to perceive the highest path toward resolution.

When I got home, I placed the stone on my mother's bedside table, within my sight, as a constant reminder.

My mother survived the cancer, but as a diminished version of her former self. She no longer did anything alone. If she shopped for herself, it was because I took her shopping. If she visited a garden center, it was because I drove her there. She no longer handled her banking or paying of bills. She passed them over to me. She didn't invite people to dinner or respond to invitations, only to mine.

In 2011, I bought an apartment in the same building where John and I lived and moved her against her will—the constant driving backwards and forwards across town was wearing me down. She complained constantly about pain and in 2012 decided to undergo a *second hip replacement* hoping to reduce the pain from her advanced *osteoarthritis*. Post-op she inadvertently took too much warfarin which caused *internal bleeding* and she was rushed to ICU.

After this episode my mother took herself to bed. It was the place she felt most comfortable, and she was totally at peace with her choice. She gave up on TV, saying the flickering light bothered her eyes. She read the history books, biographies, and newspapers I supplied and usually had a crochet project on the go. She took joy from her Skype and phone calls with my brother and her grandchildren, and she relished having caregivers at hand to attend to her every request.

In 2014, two years into her bedridden status, Mum had *double basal pneumonia*. Her doctor asked if she wanted to be hospitalized. She said no, hospitals were noisy unrestful places, where you are constantly being disturbed. She'd preferred to take her chances at home with antibiotics and physiotherapy.

We continued with oncology check-ups every six months. These recorded a steady weight loss, increasing physical weakness as her muscle tone diminished, but the remission from cancer prevailed.

Just after the 2016 New Year holidays, Mum said she felt a new lump under the skin of the breast bone. Her next appointment with the oncologist was for the following week and it was time to get the blood tests done.

I asked, 'Mum, what if the cancer has come back. Surely you wouldn't want to go through chemotherapy again—it made you so very ill last time and you were a younger, stronger self? Would you really want to try chemo again?'

My mum looked at me with a steady gaze. She took her time to respond. 'Well I just might.'

This was a bombshell for me. I wanted to respect my mother's choices. It was the right thing to do to honor her preference and my own integrity and self-respect. But I sat there for a while, astounded, my mind jumping ahead, envisaging the implications of what she'd just said. A little later I parted offering a subdued, 'Goodnight.'

I went downstairs to our flat and told John of the conversation I'd just had. I broke down and wept. Through my tears, I said I wasn't sure that I could go through being responsible for my mum at home again if she chose to go through with chemo. My mind replayed the images of her crisis after the hip operation when I found her in bed amidst blood and feces. Yet I'd made a promise that I would do everything I could for her to end her days in her own home.

The next day the florist rang to advise of a delivery. It was an order made from Brooklyn. I assumed it was from my daughter to cheer her granny up during this time of anxiety. But no, the flowers were for me from my younger daughter and her husband. The note which came with the bouquet said, 'Much love to the caregiver who takes the strain. Thinking of you. Kyla and Andrew.'

My mother approached 90 as the least healthy person I've ever known. But her 'give me everything, I'll try anything' attitude served her well. By this time she outlived my father by 25 years. I've respected her choices. But it hasn't been easy.

A friend asked me, 'Do we do this for our parents out of duty or out of love?' He added that with his mother it was duty and with his father it was love.

I don't do well with duty. It's corrosive. It would steer me into a mood of resentment. In January 2016 I had reason to anticipate a marathon of caregiving ahead of me. I know myself. I would only be able to travel the distance fueled by love.

Pa: It's Enough Now

It was a cold winter Cape Town night when I settled into an armchair in front of a log fire with my friend of more than 30 years. Gonda and I had watched our children grow from babyhood to adulthood, celebrated milestone birthdays together and had been there for one another in times of crisis. We spoke late into the night as the embers glowed and infused our clothing with the smell of burning wood.

That night, Gonda told me about her father's dying and his gift to her—his explicit wishes around his death.

He was in his 80s when he became frail. It was at a time in his life when he carried the burden of attending many funerals of his contemporaries, and he was thoughtful about his own inevitable death. And he himself was in decline.

Getting old can be pretty miserable, not being able to do the things that you want and are used to being able to do. When we walked around the shops together Pa was always very fast. He liked shopping with me because we did things quickly and got out of the shops. But more and more when we went to the shops he couldn't keep up.

Ayanda, my then-18-year-old reproached me. 'You're walking too fast; Pa can't keep up. You must hook his hand in yours. Then you must look at his feet and walk at the same pace as he walks.' I, of course, couldn't do that. I'm impatient. So, there were more times of us finding a bench, him sitting down and me going into the shops alone. Whereas what he really liked was picking out what he wanted for himself, sweets and his favorite, Marie Biscuits.

Gonda and her father had lived together for the last 17 years of his life. She'd moved from Johannesburg to Cape Town, found a job and bought a house big enough for herself and her parents, after her mother became ill with dementia. Things had not always been easy between

85

Gonda and her father but in the months before he died they'd had a good time together.

Two years earlier, Gonda and I had gone for a four-day hike in the nearby Winelands. On one farm Gonda bought *bucchu* herbs and made two bottles of *bucchu* brandy for her father; she put them into the boot of the car. On the drive back, the bottles banged against one another and one of them broke. Gonda and her father laughed about the brandy smell that lingered in the car, especially since Gonda is a teetotaler.

In that moment of shared ease and laughter he told her, 'You know I'm so proud of you.'

He was proud not just because she became a dentist and a deputy dean in the medical faculty at the University of Cape Town, but because 'you do all the things I loved doing in my youth. When I was younger I loved hiking and going up the mountain, and you are the one of all my six children who likes those activities.'

There were 18 months to go between the time of the hike and her father's 85th birthday. But Gonda noticed her father's waning energy and wrote to her two brothers and three sisters. 'Daddy's becoming very frail and I don't think we should wait for his 85th birthday to have a big celebration,' she wrote. 'We should do something this year for his 84th birthday and it would be really great if as many of you as possible can come.'

Everybody made it except the Australian group. Pa's eldest son Anthony had emigrated as a young man and settled there with his family. But he spoke to them on Skype.

This thing was so amazing to him, me walking around with my iPad in my hand and his grandchildren saying, 'Hello Pa' and whatever. It was worth it. He was so happy. That was the birthday that he said here in front of everybody, 'Gonda and I fight a lot. We are always having disagreements. But I love you, Gongie.'

He always called me Gongie. And he had his hands with his fingers together, which he always did when he was making a special point. He was sitting at the head of the table. Aunty Iris, Aunty Margaret, Aunty Thora were here, and so was Olive. We put three tables together so all the grandchildren could sit around with him. It was such a lovely celebration.

And a month and a half later, Gonda's father was dead.

It was the Friday night of Ayanda's matric ball when he said he was feeling a bit under the weather. We took some great photos of her and her best friend and Pa told them how proud he was of them, the fine young women they were turning out to be.

On Saturday morning, we were supposed to go to a funeral; my cousin's wife had died. When I came to his room I found him out of breath. He couldn't even make his bed, something he had always done. I suggested that we not go to the funeral.

'Let's go to the doctor and get you treated,' I said.

'No, no. I must be there for Patrick—his wife has died.'

Walking into the church, he hooked his arm into mine in the way that he never really liked and leaned in on me.

'Daddy, maybe you shouldn't be doing this.'

He insisted, 'No, no. I want to be here.'

When it came to walking up to the altar to receive communion, because he was so tired, I asked him, 'Must I go up with you?'

'No, no. I will do it on my own.'

He walked up and didn't come back down the center aisle straight to our pew. He greeted people—coming back the long way around, down the side. By the time we left the church, even though he was so very tired, he still wanted to go to the hall for tea. I said firmly, 'Daddy, you look too tired. We must go home now.'

On getting home we both fell asleep. It was late afternoon when I woke up and made him a cup of tea and took it to his bedroom. He was lying under the blankets.

'I'm not feeling well,' he told me.

'Should I phone the doctor?'

'Yes, please. Do phone the doctor.'

I had second thoughts. 'If *you* are telling me to call the doctor, you probably need the hospital.'

Pa didn't protest. When we arrived at the hospital, I wanted to stop at the entrance so that he could walk straight in.

'No, no, just park and I'll be fine.'

So he walked his stubborn and dignified self all the way from the parking lot with my sister Maria. Then the three of us sat waiting for the doctor to admit him.

'I don't think I'll be going home,' he said to us.

'Ag Daddy, don't be silly. They are going to do tests and then you'll be fine.'

On Sunday, when Gonda returned to the hospital, all her father was asking for was to go to church.

'I need to go to church,' he said. 'It's Sunday. I've never missed mass. I want to go to church.'

Gonda reassured him, 'Don't worry somebody is coming to bring you communion.'

That afternoon the Catholic Archbishop himself, Steven Breslin, came to visit and gave him communion. The following day, Gonda arrived at the hospital very early in the morning.

'Gonda, I want to go home,' her father said to her. 'It's better if I die at home.'

'You're not going to die. You're going to be fine.'

Then the nurse called Gonda aside. 'Your dad didn't have a good night. I see that the Archbishop came to visit him yesterday. You seem to be good Catholics. I suggest you call a priest.'

It was only then that Gonda looked at his chart; it looked like he had a heart attack during the night and they had to resuscitate him. She called her siblings in Cape Town to tell them, and then phoned her father's priest. His children arrived, all of them surrounding his bed. When Father David started the prayers, he placed his hands on his mouth, part of the ritual of the last rites. After the last rites, all her father wanted was to get out of the ICU. His children tried to persuade him otherwise. But he insisted. After a family discussion, they all agreed to support his request to move to a general ward, where it was more comfortable, with less noise.

The doctor protested, 'Your father needs to be in ICU.'

When the family, united, insisted, the doctor repeated, 'You realize that he is very ill.'

'Yes. But our father requests to be moved to a ward and doesn't want to be resuscitated again.'

After Pa was moved to a general ward that Monday, he became so much brighter, happier, and calmer with all his children around him. Suddenly, he asked Maria and Gonda for help to use the toilet—he didn't want the bedpan, he insisted on the toilet. Everyone else left to give him privacy. The nurses came to help and, as they brought him back out of the bathroom, he slumped and lost consciousness.

'Maria!' Gonda said. 'Look at Daddy, he's going.'

Maria quickly scooped him up in her arms and carried him to his bed. The nurses put the oxygen mask on and resuscitated him. Maria acted like the nurse she was trained to be; it was too difficult for her to act otherwise, but she also started crying and praying out loud, and the whole family poured in when they heard the commotion. The children also started crying while Jackie, Maria, and John prayed loudly. Pa started breathing again.

That night, Gonda and Aunty Margaret stayed with him; Pa talked and dozed, speaking throughout the night to Gonda.

'You've been very good to me. I thank you for all you've done.'

'Ag, Daddy, why do you keep saying these things?'

'I have to say it.'

At another point in the night he spoke but she couldn't make out the words. 'Daddy what are you saying?' she asked.

'I'm not saying anything, I'm praying.'

'What are you praying for?'

'I'm praying for the courage to die with dignity.'

'But why are you talking like that? Just take the medicines and you'll be alright.'

He just laughed. He didn't answer her. Later in the night he called out his deceased wife's name, 'Lillian, Lillian.'

'Daddy, it's not Lillian, it's Gonda.'

'I'm not talking to you, Gonda. I'm talking to your mother—that's Lillian.'

At about three in the morning Gonda's phoned pinged. It was a text message from her brother Anthony in Australia asking when would be a good time to call.

'Tell him to phone now,' Pa said.

He then spoke with his eldest son and his daughter-in-law, thanking them, saying all the same things he had said to Gonda. Before he ended the call, he named all his children and all the grandchildren.

At 6am the family changed shifts. Maria stopped by on her way to work, and their brother John came with his wife. Later they called Gonda to say that Pa wanted some Marie Biscuits. She brought them but he couldn't swallow the pieces; Gonda fed him that morning, gave him tea with a teaspoon, trying to get some biscuits into him. Then sometime in the early afternoon he sat up and drank tea by himself. He joked and laughed with his old friend Mrs. Henry. 'Ooohh I like your *rooi lippe'*—her red lips, because she was wearing red lipstick.

As Gonda watched him laughing, she thought, 'He's turned the corner, he's going to be fine.'

Afternoon visiting hours were from three to four. Pa asked Gonda to arrange to bring all the children when she came back at three. She agreed—she thought the children would cheer him up, so it would be right to bring them along. He greeted them with joy when they arrived.

He asked to go to the toilet again but Maria insisted, 'Daddy, this time you are going to use the bedpan.'

He agreed. While he was sitting on the bedpan, with Maria and Gonda on either side of him, he said to Maria, 'This time if I go, you don't pick me up, you don't do anything. It's enough now.'

'Okay, Daddy,' and she winked at Gonda.

Once settled back into bed, he asked for the children to return and he gave each of them a special message. When visiting time ended, everyone left except for Gonda and her sister Jackie. Gonda lowered his bed and arranged his blankets, and kissed him on his forehead.

He smiled and said, 'Bye bye.'

'I'm going to be right here,' Gonda said.

He didn't reply, he just smiled. Not even 10 minutes passed before Gonda said, 'He's not breathing anymore.'

Jackie said, 'Call the nurse! Call the nurse!'

Gonda asked, 'Just wait a minute.'

Jackie ran out to call the nurse anyway who came back with her, put her ear to Pa's mouth, listened closely and said, 'There is still a flutter of breath.'

'Just leave him, this is what he wanted. Just leave him,' Gonda said as calmly and firmly as possible.

'And then, Pa was gone. Saturday, Sunday, Monday and on Tuesday he died.'

He'd told her he didn't think he was coming back. She just didn't believe him. That's the way he chose to die.

You know, part of why I found it easy to make a decision around my dad and his resuscitation was because of my mother. She'd looked after two old aunts. One of them, Edie, who was blind and incontinent, got very ill with pneumonia. My mother told the doctor, 'Please don't give her antibiotics. Her quality of life is not good anymore. Please allow her to go quietly.'

When it came to my mother, in her ninth year of Alzheimer's, my father did something similar. He'd told us, 'Look, there is a point when you stop.' When she went into renal failure, he said, 'We are not going to treat renal failure. It's enough now. You have to allow her to go.'

He was happy, you know, happy right up to the end. It was like he was being lifted and carried somewhere. He had a kind of joyfulness in him that I had not seen in a long time. Pa was very happy to die. He went peacefully. He wasn't fighting it. He told me, 'I'm ready to meet my maker.'

Lucille: The Conundrum

Matthew* was one of the fittest men in his late 50s that you could ever meet. But then one day he confided in Lucille*, 'Something's not quite right. I can't seem to catch my breath the way I used to on the uphill.' He could still manage the flatness of Rondebosch common nearby their house, but imbibing the scenic beauty whilst running the trails in Cape Town's Newlands forest was becoming increasingly difficult.

It took many tests over the next 18 months, all leading to dead ends, before they got a diagnosis. One day Matthew crashed his car—he just drove through a red traffic light. Lucille took him to the doctor and insisted on a CAT scan, which revealed the ominous shadow of a tumor on the brain.

Matthew and I had, over many years, observed friends of ours getting sick and dying. We'd agreed that if either of us were to be diagnosed with a terminal illness it would be unlikely that we would choose treatment of any sort. We reached these conclusions without any experience of the reality. When Matthew's brain tumor was diagnosed, our first question was, 'What's the prognosis?' We were told we had less than a year but only a few weeks without surgery and treatment.

That pre-illness discussion became irrelevant. We wanted more time. I'm struck, in retrospect, by how we gave intellectual assent to something in the abstract, but when it became real we acted with more emotion.

Here, like in the United States, if you have private health insurance you get the best treatment. Everything was available, all of which was about buying time. We were fortunate middle-class people, well-educated, with the best private healthcare and doctors who told us the truth. There was no, 'Well maybe you will go into remission.' The nature of the aggressive brain cancer, glioblastoma, and the stage of it, made it clear what would happen and that the time would be short.

We went the route of surgery, chemo and radiation. We whole hogged it. We did absolutely everything prescribed. There was a lot for us to read, internet blogs, stories of people nursing their parents and siblings and spouses through this specific cancer, which were mostly hair-raising. I was much aware of my being a white, middle-class South African with two domestic workers, a huge amount of support at home—at least during the week.

The *Harvard Medical Review* had the best scientific paper on the typical end stages. It proved to be 100 percent accurate, precisely as they described, a slow decline of the patient's condition, probable blindness, less and less mobility before taking to bed with anything from a week or two of increasingly frequent seizures before death.

I can't escape from my awareness of class analysis. Poor people with this condition die quickly. Matthew was well-insured. He had good medical aid which paid out nearly R1 million in that last year. In most years, Matthew had claimed only about R10,000, generally for dental care. He'd been a healthy man.

But there's the thing—in the last two years of life you can spend more on healthcare than you've spent in the whole of the rest of your life. With Matthew, it was even more than that. There was limited expense from our side. Medical insurance paid bills of R987,000 and we spent an additional R30,000. Matthew would fall and hurt himself and there were sores that wouldn't heal. There were brilliant wound dressings. Medical insurance wouldn't cover their cost, thousands of rands, but they worked and we paid for them gladly.

Matthew was a professional who contributed to a provident and sick pay fund for professionals. That turned out to be a financial blessing as he continued to receive 80 percent of his salary. While we suffered psychologically we did not suffer financially, unlike many dying people who are plagued with financial difficulties.

We had a happy relationship but in that last year there was an intensification of it, in a way, we were even happier. I have seen it before, in fact, when one person gets sick there can be a closeness that wasn't there before. But I must say I was very conscious of being positive and jolly. There was a sense of the days running out and our need to consciously make the most of every day.

Good information about the nature of Matthew's impending death was helpful. With both of us being very realistic people, not in denial, we got the facts and faced them. We made plans, not all of which came to fruition. We were very alive in that period of Matthew's dying. In that year we traveled, saw friends and family, visited places and attended two weddings.

If I have any regret, it's that I reduced my work to a half-day and I think I should have stopped altogether. We didn't need the money. Matthew would cry, 'Don't go,' sometimes as I left to go to work in the mornings. But every day I scheduled somebody to come mid-morning to take him out for coffee. Matthew loved people's company. But he tired easily, so he'd be out for an hour and a half and by the time I came home he'd had a rest and was ready to have lunch and then another rest. There was something good in his getting out, his being with other people, his feeling connected.

On another level, I'm not sorry at all because I got away into a different world and was distracted by the immediacy of my work. It was a respite for me from the unremitting nursing. *Ja*, I think I don't regret it after all.

We discussed as a couple how Matthew wanted his ending. We talked at length. He had a set of clear criteria of what he deemed to represent the quality of his life worth his living. He defined he would be ready to go when his condition deteriorated to the extent that he was confined to bed, couldn't sit up, couldn't eat and when he could no longer see—the growing brain tumor would eventually obstruct the optical nerve causing blindness.

We followed up our discussions with our families and some close friends. That proved more difficult.

My side of the family was more able to process it and to participate in the discussions. My stepmother, having nursed my father through a long illness, thought assisted dying was the best way of going: be clear about it, think it out and then be explicit. Matthew's family was in denial until the very last days. It was particularly difficult with one sister who would try and stop him whenever he started this conversation. In fact, a few months before his death, she and her husband were visiting and Matthew admonished her, 'I absolutely insist you be quiet and listen to my wishes because it's going to be a problem later if you try to do anything to stop it.'

Towards the end, it was gruesome. Our roles changed so radically because one person is passing on and the other will continue to live, at least for the time being. I wondered how Matthew felt. He didn't say anything, but I was conscious of it, especially in the final days. I would go into the kitchen and see our beautiful old dog, also dying, and then go back to the bedroom to Matthew dying. I found myself talking with our little younger dog, 'You and I are going into the future.' Funnily enough I found it very comforting that I wasn't about to pop off right then.

When Matthew first got into bed he had a tremendous amount of pain and the doctor prescribed morphine. But that made his breathing difficult and he was very far away. I told the doctor I wanted to stop the morphine. He said, 'Do what you think is right. Don't let him be in pain, but if you want to withdraw it, withdraw it.' And I did.

When I stopped it, he came more to the surface. His cognition improved and he could enjoy people again. Obviously if he'd indicated pain I would have immediately given him the morphine, in spite of his being constipated, which the morphine made even worse.

The doctor came twice that week to give him an enema because he was uncomfortable. He didn't eat anything so there wasn't anything in his stomach, but the body still produces waste and getting it out was a nightmare. It was interesting how Matthew's body changed and eventually there was no pain.

Now here's the conundrum. Matthew's criteria for his readiness to die were very clear. He didn't want to be bedridden, unable to sit up, unable to eat or unable to see. You know that man loved food and eating. Three of those criteria were checked within two or three days of his getting into bed, and he was going blind.

But he was still loving being with people. He slept 50 minutes in the hour, but when he was conscious he was fully conscious and enjoyed short visits from friends. Before people entered the bedroom I advised, 'Matthew can no longer see, so announce yourself.'

He was cogent up to the last day. A friend whose mother had recently died came that afternoon and sat beside him and announced her name. He responded, 'Oh, I'm so sorry I couldn't come to your mother's memorial, I wasn't well that day.' He was perfectly with it. They chatted about her children, her husband, her brother and he said how fond he was of them.

The conundrum is that while you set down your criteria, you need to reevaluate them as it's happening. If Matthew had followed through on his criteria, we would have missed what was our last extraordinary week together.

The end happened quickly. I went to bed leaving Matthew with the lovely night nurse, who woke me when he started to have the convulsions that we knew signaled the end. The valium shot did not stop them. The nurse and I sat the whole night with Matthew having these terrible convulsions exactly as we'd read about. We accepted them. By dawn Matthew had no cognition whatsoever and he couldn't see. His breathing was shallow and slow.

It was a perfect time for him to die.

Robin: I Want to Die, but I Want My Day in Court More

Robin Stransham-Ford, lawyer and former soldier, used his own death as the last cause for which he would fight—the right to assisted dying. He wanted his determination and skills to benefit other South Africans who might come to face the same predicament as him.

Robin and his close friend, politician Mario Ambrosini, were both diagnosed with cancer around the same time. Both took Chinese medications and medicinal cannabis to ease their pain, and together they drafted a private members bill asking Parliament to legalize the use of cannabis for healing purposes. Mario responded less well to the treatments than Robin. Within a few months of his diagnosis, Mario was in a wheelchair. He could no longer swallow. He was losing his sight. He could no longer breathe on his own; he needed an oxygen machine. He struggled to speak through the avalanche of tremendous pain that painkillers failed to kill.

Ambrosini rejected the practice of terminal sedation—that's medication used in end-of-life care at such levels to lessen the pain but with the possible effect of unconsciousness, and the moment of death brought forward in time as a side effect. Many opponents of assisted dying are comfortable with the terminal sedation; accelerated death as the secondary side effect is deemed acceptable whereas death as the primary intention of a prescribed dose of a barbiturate is not. A curious logic.

Ambrosini said he wanted the personal dignity of being able to die in a state of full consciousness. He decided to take the time of his dying into his own hands. He wanted agency. As South African law doesn't yet permit access to a lethal dose of barbiturates for the terminally ill, he opted to shoot himself. The head wound that ended Ambrosini's life, the gunshot that his family heard, the bullet that exploded in his brain, created a terrible physical end and intensified the family's heartbreak.

Robin's 11-year-old daughter Epiphany knew Ambrosini's son and did not want her dad to choose the same ending. I'm told she said to Robin, 'Papa, if you are going to do something like what Mario did, I would like to know. I don't want to find out afterwards.'

She had heard her father's war stories and knew of his expertise with firearms. Conversations about dying and death were not taboo between father and daughter. Robin knew from a lifetime of living with death that there's more hurt when such conversations don't happen. These conversations were part of the legacy of love and care that he offered his youngest daughter.

Epiphany's mother Penelope and her father Robin had lived apart for several years. As Robin's health began to decline, they discussed the idea of a dying room in which he would spend his last weeks. Epiphany wanted her father close by. She asked her mom not only to invite Robin to stay with them but also to give up her bedroom. There was enough love, reconciliation, and goodwill for this to happen.

Robin and I first met in November 2014 in Cape Town, in my then-capacity as the chairperson of DignitySA. Robin had offered to be an applicant in a case that the group planned to take to court on the right to assisted dying to request a new law which would be aligned with the new constitution's right to dignity both in life and death. We were looking for a diverse group of citizens, terminally ill, of different creeds, color, and gender; citizens who together would represent all South Africans. The executive committee wanted to be sure that those that represented them be grounded, resilient, and able to handle media attention, and I needed to understand Robin's background to see if he was a good fit for our strategy.

We met in the foyer of the African Pride hotel, one of those double-volume ultra-modern compositions with seating for show rather than comfort. The hotel wasn't far from the houses of Parliament where Robin needed to be because of his involvement in ongoing consultations on the legalization of medicinal cannabis.

The meeting stretched over two hours, with Robin doing most of the talking. It was just 10 weeks after Mario had died and he was deeply disturbed by the manner of his dying. He told me then about his offer to shoot Mario—an offer which his friend refused.

'I know so much about guns,' he told me. 'I'm a professional. I would have chosen the gun and selected the right bullet. I know the best weapon to choose for the least trauma. There would have been no mess.'

Deeply committed to people being able to die with dignity, he wanted terminally ill people to have the legal right to get a lethal dose of barbiturates, if their suffering was such that they no longer wished to live.

Robin filled me in on his background. He was born in Johannesburg but grew up in what was then Rhodesia, now Zimbabwe. His parents owned huge tracts of land, one of the largest agricultural enterprises in southern Africa. They farmed tobacco and exported fertilizer and saw themselves as pioneers, creating employment and earning valuable foreign exchange.

My doctoral thesis, completed in 1993, was on land markets in South Africa and their relevance to future land reform policy; Zimbabwe was a case study. Robin's ancestors had amassed land once belonging to black Africans. In liberation-struggle terms, he would have been considered 'the son of colonial land barons.'

Robin told me about being drafted into the Rhodesian army straight out of high school. His parents wanted him to do military service. His Jesuit education, they felt, had left him too bookish and too academically inclined. Active service would make a man of him. He spent 10 active years in the military, some of this time in Mozambique. Robin had metal pins in both shoulders due to injuries sustained when the helicopter gunship under his command was shot down; later he would show me photos of himself in the bush, standing next to the bloodied bodies of a couple of dead 'chaps,' as he called them. He was the youngest ever officer commissioned into the army and became the youngest major in the elite Rhodesian Special Air Service.

As I listened to Robin, I realized that if we had been in the same locale in Mozambique when he was on a raid, he'd have killed me with a clear conscience.

His history scared me. On the alert for any elements of biography that might impact DignitySA's court application, I feared anything that a journalist could use that might distract our advocacy message. I mentally catastrophized. I visualized billboard headlines, 'Son of Land Grabbers, Killer of Freedom Fighters, Seeks Right to Die with Dignity.'

I composed myself and then asked in my calmest voice, 'Robin, might you consider that you are an unsuitable man to be an applicant for this court case?' He was taken aback but then sincerely engaged with the question. We parted amicably. I did not expect to see him again.

But circumstances dictated otherwise, and our dialogue continued. An understanding evolved. We began to enjoy a warmth in our engagements, not only an affinity for a common purpose.

In late March 2015, when his health took a dramatic turn for the worse, lawyers who'd volunteered their services to DignitySA worked with Robin and his research and administration assistant Rosanne Trollope to prepare the affidavit for his court application to be granted the right to accelerate his dying. They were busy finalizing this when I visited Robin.

I waited in Penelope's lounge for quite some time. Robin was not having a good day. Eventually Rosanne, who'd become his closest friend and companion, emerged, 'It's okay, Robin's ready for you.' I entered his dying room, the intimate, caring space that his daughter wanted for her father.

Robin's welcoming handshake was no longer firm. He was pale and gaunt, that end-of-life skeletal gauntness, the shrinking inwards, the unmistakable signs of life-force diminishing. His shrunken face was already beginning to look like a skull. His once beautiful eyes sat deep in their sockets, larger than ever. He lay on his back propped up by many pillows, knees drawn up under a sheet. His arms were thinner, his skin wrinkled and the veins stood out on his hands. He was exhausted.

In a thready voice, Robin recited to me what he'd been dictating to Rosanne for his affidavit: 'I have severe pain all over my body. I am unable to care for my own hygiene. I am being dulled with opioid medication, at times confused and dissociative. Sometimes I am unaware of my surroundings and loved ones.'

He told me his affidavit would include that he wanted to die at home, not in a hospital or hospice, no matter how good the care might be. He wanted the familiarity of personal space, people and objects and not an institutional setting. And, most importantly, he wanted to die at the time of his own choosing in a conscious state, consciously saying goodbye and not in some random moment when he might be dissociative and unaware.

His perfect death, he told me, would be to have in his possession a legally obtained dose of deadly barbiturates. He would drive to Cape Point, the southernmost tip where the last bit of Cape Town meets the Indian Ocean, and those he loved most dearly would be with him for a final goodbye. He said he was ready to do this now; his disease had progressed to the level of intractable suffering.

Robin, however, felt he needed to keep on living so that his case could be heard in court. Waiting for the date to be set was causing him huge anxiety. How long could he hang in? Even though it was considered an urgent application, it could take another few weeks. He was asking the judge to rule on making an exception to the current South African law, which prohibits assisted dying. He wanted a doctor to be able to assist him to die without the doctor being struck off the medical register for undertaking this humane act. He wanted the court to grant him this wish and thereby create a precedent for all South Africans.

Robin spoke at length about his application, about legacy, of the importance of the shamanistic teachings of Carlos Castaneda and his choice to live his own life, a soldier at heart, in what Castaneda calls the Way of the Warrior. 'One must have something to die for in order to have something to live for,' was one of Robin's favorite Castaneda quotes.

Then he called for Rosanne, asking for a photo of himself. It was an image of his younger, handsome self in army battle fatigues looking at a document, possibly a map. He's deep in the bush in Mozambique in 1976. I reminded him that I was also there at that time. Robin and I served different political masters, he with the Rhodesians and I for the new government in Mozambique. Twenty-eight years later, Robin and I have put our histories aside. Our shared quest for the right to die with dignity created common ground.

He'd been talking non-stop and he was spent. He asked me to pass the plastic bowl that was on top of the lid of the toilet chair. I offered it to him and he retched up a brown, mostly clear, but gooey liquid.

It had a familiar smell. This was Joe in the last days of his life. This nausea—was it his kidneys packing up? I waited for Robin to finish this round of retching, I had to control myself from letting the smell get to me and prompt my own urge to retch. I acted as though what happened was normal, taking the bowl to the bathroom to empty and rinse as though it were just another coffee cup.

When I came back with the clean bowl Robin told me he was done with talking, he had shared what he wanted and now he'd like to sleep. He said he was mostly tired these days, and restless. Sleep did not come easily. I asked to stay and sit with him for a while. Robin said he was okay with that and, almost before the words were out of his mouth, he slipped into sleep.

My eyes wandered around this creation of a dying space, his daughter's initiative. The trees filtered the sun and a soft light entered the room. Pots of acrylic paint sat by the wall on which some visitors had placed and signed their hand prints: Berkeley, Epiphany, Felicity, Georgina, Michael, Papa ... 16 hands so far. The hands of family and close loving friends.

His older daughter Felicity had painted a sun sinking into the sea. 'We are freer together than apart,' was Robin's favorite saying, and it appeared in very large ornate script in red, green, and blue on the cream-colored wall. A couple of white-on-white patterned balloons floated near the bedhead, probably from Epiphany's recent 12th birthday.

On the shelves was a vase with red and yellow roses and along the window sill a rough block of rose quartz, a pendant-healing crystal threaded onto a cord, candles, and an aromatherapy oil burner. A rosary hung on the burglar bars. Someone had glued shells onto the wall next to the window, mementos of walking the Cape Town shore lines.

When Robin started to deteriorate, he'd asked for gifts for this room, artifacts with meaning and strong energy. One gift was a red sash that once belonged to Mario. It was embroidered with the square cross of the Knights Templar. Robin wanted to be buried in Franschhoek, alongside his friend Mario, and requested the red sash be buried with him.

Crystals, crucifix, stones, bones, beads, shells—a hybrid mix—that was Robin. His dying room had become a 'death lodge' of old, bringing into the present some comforting spiritual traditions.

The beautiful artifacts sat side-by-side with the paraphernalia of an illness closing in on life. Brown glass medicine bottles, half-squeezed tubes of ointment, mercury thermometers. The tubular steel and white plastic chair commode was now the most convenient bedside table. It was exactly the right height for the oft-needed plastic bowl, a drinking bottle and my coffee cup.

I closed my eyes to be with Robin on this cusp of his dying. I sat quietly, breathing deeply and then deeper still. My intuitive confidence in this moment was that the calm of my being would find its way into his being. It was a simple offering. It was the only thing I could offer.

Robin slept. I breathed for both of us. It felt as though we were breathing into a bubble and inside that bubble there was a state of grace. I lost track of time. Robin woke to find me still sitting at his bedside, sitting in stillness where I was when he went to sleep.

He smiled and said, 'I can't remember when I last slept so peacefully. It's you. You have a lovely presence. It's like there's an angel in the room.'

I was happy in the core of myself. I felt deeply privileged that Robin honored me with his trust to have me there sitting with him.

I had a lot to think about. The ease with which Robin and I spent time together that day was so different from our first meeting. Robin, without his knowing, had given me a gift. He left me humbled with fresh learning about what's possible when there's no judgment and doors are left open.

Despite Robin's wish to succeed in court, it seemed that his body was ready to shut down. I doubted he would live long enough for the court hearing to take place.

Three weeks later he was still alive and I emailed Rosanne the Mary Oliver poem 'Blackwater Woods' to read to Robin if he had inclination and energy to listen. The words about love, as well as knowing when to let go, are exquisite.

The date for the court hearing was set for ten days later on April 30. Would he make or not?

April 30, 2015 arrived. I was sitting on a train between Baltimore and Washington DC.

PING. An incoming text message from my husband John: 'Robin's application. Judge Fabricius has ruled in his favor.'

How fabulous. Brilliant. This is what Robin had been waiting for. He has been granted the right to medical assistance to die. I am in such awe of Robin's fight to stay alive to get this day in court.

PING. 'Sorry to tell you Robin died the very morning of the hearing without knowing of the verdict.'

I sat in my train seat. Tears rolled down my face. Robin's determination to endure such suffering and live on to secure this act of service to human kind was profound. I knew there would be an appeal to the Supreme Court, but whatever the outcome this was a big step forward in shifting the public debate.

I had once asked Robin what was keeping him going when his body was so obviously ready to die.

He'd answered, 'Don't think that I don't have bad dreams about what I've been part of as a military man. I wake up from nightmares in a cold sweat. What's driving me to stay alive, to have this hearing in court?' The Jesuit within him answered. 'Atonement.'

My eulogy for Robin would include that besides making peace with himself, his dying offered other possibilities of reconciliation, legacy, compassion, and non-judgment.

Legacy. By taking his daughter's request seriously he empowered himself and hopefully helped further build a remarkable young girl.

Reconciliation. In the vigor of life, he and Penelope shared differences and lived apart. In the vulnerability of death Penelope opened her home to him, his extended family, Rosanne, and his friends.

In the vigor of life, Robin and I shared polarized differences. In the vulnerability of death, when compassion and non-judgment were allowed their place, there was common cause.

We all want to die with dignity. We want it for ourselves. We want it for everyone.

Paradoxically, he who wished for the dignity of an accelerated death drew on his every ounce of will power to stay alive longer. He wanted his day in court for himself and others. And he made it. South Africa took one step closer to adopting dignity in dying laws that respect and support personal choice.

Robin Stransham-Ford. I bow my head in gratitude.

Lumimbe: The Artist Who Did Not See

Lumimbe* is a Zambian graphic artist. I've fallen in love with her and her work. For her two-month artist-in-residency scholarship at the Bellagio Center, she was working on a graphic novel in which her heroine is an African female.

'Have you ever thought about it? Batman, Superman, Spiderman— what do they have in common? They are male, white, and straight with supernatural superpowers.'

Lumimbe's heroine Ananiya lives in a futuristic time. She can't fly or time travel or see through walls. Her superpower is a facility that's super-scarce worldwide: the ability to think independently. And that creates lots of challenges for her.

One afternoon, days after I'd done the presentation to my fellow residents of my project, Lumimbe and I were seated next to one another as we waited for people to gather for a lecture. When I took out my notebook and pen, the page fell open to a sketch of a hummingbird I'd drawn. Lumimbe asked me about it and I shared the story of how the hummingbird had first appeared as my totem in California. She told me she wanted to share with me her story about her mother's passing. That evening after dinner, we sat in one of the reception rooms, sipping Amaretto and talking for hours.

Lumimbe was always exceptionally close to her mom. As a child and a young adult, she had bronchial problems. She recalled one hospital visit when she was nine.

It was so difficult for me to breathe, like sucking air through a straw. I remember listening to the sounds of other children playing, and saying to my mom that if I could breathe and play it would be the happiest day of my life.

My mom was always calmly there for me. There'd be an emergency, I'd be rushed to hospital. I used to think about death a lot. I was so tired of being ill all the time and taking antibiotics again and again. The hospital never failed to fill me with dread. But Mom was always there, reassuring, smiling down at me, a constant presence.

Then, at 21, things changed and I became healthy.

It took Lumimbe by surprise when her mother died the previous year.

She got malaria and then collapsed. I was home and took her to the hospital. The malaria caused problems with her diabetes and she was often slurring her words. We were forcing her to take medicines, saying 'Mom, if you don't take the medicines you'll have another diabetes episode.'

Although she was slurring her words, she said clearly that she is going to die. She didn't want to take the medicines. She was ready to die.

In the afternoon before she passed, she said over and over again, 'I'm sorry, I'm sorry,'—about 20 times. I was patting her hands and saying, 'No Mom, you're no trouble at all.'

It was hard being at the hospital; we are a huge extended family.

My mother's siblings were there and so was her mother. Where does a child fit in? It's hard to find moments of privacy.

She said again, so clearly. 'I'm sorry,' and she lay back looking at the ceiling, disconnecting, looking very composed.

Lumimbe, the artist whose eyes are essential to her work, reflected on her lack of seeing.

In hindsight, I can see that my mom tried to prepare us. She knew herself, she knew something was changing. And she was ready to leave us. I think for some time she had carried on living because she was worried about her children. But I think she knew something was changing within her and she was ready to go now that her children were in a good place.

She'd been worried about my younger brother and he'd recently settled down. She'd worried about me and my choice to be an artist, and here I was making a living and winning scholarships.

Lumimbe considered the last six months of her mother's life, and her own blindness.

I knew something was changing, but I also chose not to know, not to see. Like there was the time I needed a portrait photo for the Bellagio application. I didn't have one, so I took my camera to my mom and asked her to take my photo. She wasn't getting it. The photos she took weren't what I wanted. I took a photo of her, and I showed her how I needed it to be, the face in the frame, the light and shadows on the face. Then I put tape on the floor where I wanted her to stand and she took my photo.

Later, I looked at my camera and there was the portrait I had taken of my mom. I looked at it, and looked again, and there was something about the photo that caught my attention. But what? I didn't dwell on it further, I was blind to the signs, but what my subconscious noticed was a lessening presence of her life force.

In those six months before she died, I also had bad dreams. I'd wake up in the morning feeling anxious but I couldn't place my anxiety. I'd go to my mom's bedroom, on the alert, wondering how I'd find her. She would be calmly busy and she'd greet me cheerfully.

My anxiety was subconscious—and I didn't want to hear what my subconscious was telling me.

She was wise and tried to pass on her wisdom to me. I remember coming home from an art exhibition opening and telling her of my frustrations with the artist. I told her, 'He's such a good artist. He's internationally successful. He's made it. He's got people wanting to back him and organize shows. But his opening was so disappointing. He's so inarticulate. He doesn't know how to talk about his art.'

I felt so frustrated, thinking, come on, man, surely you can do better than this! Why didn't he make an effort to learn to speak better, to be more articulate about the thinking behind his paintings?

My mom said, 'He doesn't need to be able to talk.'

'What?' I asked, surprised by her comment.

'He doesn't need to be able to talk. People are different.'

'Huh?'

'You tell me people are buying his paintings all over the world. His paintings do his talking. He doesn't need to talk.'

My mom stopped me in my tracks, stopped my little rant about artists needing to be able to speak conceptually about their work. She made me see it from another point of view. She had so much wisdom.

In retrospect, there were many signs that she knew she was going, and that she was preparing me for her passing. She'd say casually, 'This is where the utility bills are.' And then another day, 'My chain and cross for the church, they're kept in this drawer.'

But I wasn't listening. If I'd seen the signs, her dying would have been different, I would have been different. I wouldn't have been trying to get her to swallow medicine. I'd have been partnering her, supporting her on her journey.

When she died, the church women came. They have a strict set of rituals that they complete for which they needed my mom's things.

'Where's the prayer book?" I scratched my head, then remembered my mom had shown me where it was.

'We need to dress her with her chain and cross.' And I could pass them over.

'And the book with the record of tithes paid?' At first I couldn't remember where to find this, but then I did.

'We need her uniform.' The blue shirt, white blouse and a *kitenge*, a wrap-around cloth for head covering. I went to her wardrobe and found my mother had prepared a clean, washed and ironed uniform, ready to be handed over.

Lumimbe shared with me what she wrote a month after her mother's passing.

Today my mom appeared to me. I'd entered my old bedroom this morning and I was pleasantly greeted by mom's distinctive scent. I thought that I was imagining things at first, but then the scent vanished and then reappeared three times. I gazed in the direction of the scent and asked, 'Mom, is that you?' When I did not get a reply, the skeptic in me took over and decided that her handbag had emitted the comforting scent. It was sitting on top of a see-through box where I'd kept it pending storage of her last possessions.

About 30 minutes later I was taking a shower. Wrought with feelings of regret, I was agonizing about those last few days with mom in the hospital. I should have known that she was about to leave. I should have given her one last big hug. I should have bid her a proper farewell before I left her lying on the hospital bed hooked up to an oxygen tank. I should have, I should have and I should have. Then suddenly I felt her presence next to me as warm water rushed over me from the shower faucet. It was not a vision, just a manifestation.

Mom came to me with that familiar sense of reassurance. She was almost flighty, terribly healthy again! Her energy was like an incessant whispering on the inside of my ear. It felt exactly like those times I'd have long-distant calls with her when I was staying in Norway.

She said that she was fine now, that she was here with us still, and always would be. And that I must carry on in the direction I was going. I cried, but this time no tears fell. I thanked her for letting me know that she was alright and still with us.

Lumimbe reflected.

My mom was always there for me. I wished I'd accepted she was dying. I would have offered her what she always offered to me as a child, that calm presence. I would have said, 'Mom, it's okay for you to go. It's okay. Your work is done, we'll be okay.'

In retrospect, I realize that my mom repeatedly saying 'I'm sorry' in the hospital really meant, 'Goodbye, I'm sorry I'm leaving you.' And her repeating it was her way of trying to communicate to me that I needed to let her go. I just didn't see it. I wished I'd have understood.

The nurses didn't help us to understand. I do feel angry and cheated. They were taking blood, they were checking her pulse and blood pressure, they were doing various tests.

I was asking, 'Is my mom going be okay?' And they kept up this cheerfulness, 'Everything is going be okay. Your mom's going to be absolutely fine.'

If they had told me that she was dying, imminently, that would have made a huge difference.

If the nurses had been honest I would never have gone home that night, I would have stayed. Mom died at two in the morning. I came to the hospital as quickly as I could and found her with the sheet over her head. I uncovered the sheet; she looked so peaceful, her skin so smooth, she looked almost young again. And I felt her and she was still warm.

'Helena,' she told me, 'that part of your presentation the other evening really struck me, about how doctors don't get the training to have the conversations and neither do the nurses.'

I said that was part of my hope, that the more we shared these experiences, the better the chance that the training of doctors and nurses would change the world over. We need them to be again as they once were in the days of old, before technical prowess moved in with such prominence. We need doctors and nurses who are not only healers of life but also easers of death. And, importantly, that they become more comfortable to talk with family members about what is really happening.

Kate: H.O.S.P.I.C.E.

Kate Callahan's mom had smoked two packs of cigarettes a day ever since Kate could remember. As her physical life was diminishing, she was finding it harder and harder to move around, even walking across the room to put trash in the bin became a challenge.

Kate, the fourth-born, but eldest girl of eight children, originally trained as a nurse, was now a respected specialist on end-of-life care. She and her husband consult to many of the dozens of hospices that are mushrooming across the United States. She's known to the public for her part in writing the *Five Wishes* document, a guide to some of the things people might consider having conversations about and making clear decisions about well in advance of the time of dying. The document is legally recognized in 32 US states, and available in 27 languages and in braille as well as online. It includes:

Wish 1: The person I want to make care decisions for me when I can't.

Wish 2: The kind of medical treatment that I want or don't want.

Wish 3: How comfortable I want to be, including pain management, bathing instructions, etc.

Wish 4: How I want people to treat me, including my preferences about where I'd prefer to be, my religious practice and the people I most want to keep in touch with.

Wish 5: What I want my loved ones to know.

Kate and her mom were close. They talked their way through the five wishes; they had the end-of-life conversations that matter. Kate's mom was explicit that she didn't want full code, which is doing everything possible to keep your body functioning no matter what condition your brain is in. Kate's mom specified she didn't want kidney dialysis. She didn't want to be put on a ventilator. She didn't want intubation. Her mother was comfortable talking with her—Kate's seven siblings had shied away from the discussions and decision-making. Kate was lucky. As the eldest girl, and with her professional background, she'd easily assumed that position of responsibility in the family.

When Kate's mom began to feel really unwell, she was admitted to hospital. Kate happened to be sitting in the visitor's chair when the doctor came to tell her mom the results of her tests and diagnosis. The doctor was in her mid-40s, a very experienced nephrologist.

'Mrs. Callahan. You have renal failure. You need kidney dialysis.'

'Doctor. I hear you. But I don't want kidney dialysis. I want to leave the hospital and enjoy whatever days are left to me.'

'Mrs. Callahan. You have renal failure. You *have* to have kidney dialysis.'

'Doctor. You're not listening to me. I'm telling you I don't want further treatment.'

The doctor, exasperated, turned to Kate and asked, 'What's to be done with this old lady who's being impossible?'

'Doctor, do you always insist that your patients have kidney dialysis?'

'Yes. I do,' she said.

'So you want to bully my mom into having kidney dialysis when she's telling you clearly she doesn't want it. How many other patients have you bullied? I think you should respect my mom's wishes and book her into hospice.'

The doctor responded with her own question, 'What's hospice?'

Kate gasped. 'Do you mean that in your 20 years of working as a doctor you have never ever referred anyone to hospice?'

The doctor's answer was a simple monosyllable. 'No.'

'Doctor, please fill in the requisition for my mom's transfer. And I guess you don't even know how to spell hospice, well it's aitch, oh, ess, pee, eye, cee, eeh, H-O-S-P-I-C-E.'

As she related her story to me 11 years later, she had no regrets about the harshness of her tone, the edge of sarcasm in her voice. For Kate, the specialist had lost the plot of what was essential for someone to be a good doctor.

Later, I would hear two other stories of women in their mid-80s who were hospitalized with renal failure. Neither of the women wanted kidney dialysis and they both expressed this wish verbally, they had nothing written down. One hospital respected the 87-year-old's wishes, the other hospital didn't.

Kate's story had a good ending. Her mom got to go home, and hospice offered her supportive and effective palliative care. There were some slow days of siblings visiting and the kinds of conversations that help closure. Kate's mom died in her own bed with Kate beside her and her arms around her.

That's the heart of the matter, the legitimacy of having the personal choice. When you arrive at the point where doctors can't heal you, how is it that you would prefer to die?

Vasu: Permission and Privacy

Pilar Palacia and I discovered we had a common interest. During my time at the Bellagio Center, the head of the Rockefeller residency program and I talked about what we'd both learned in the different end-of-life care courses we'd completed as well as what we'd learned from experience.

Enabling the choice of timing by giving permission to go and offering the opportunity for privacy were the two lessons Pilar took most seriously. She said what a good thing it would be for all people to be more aware of the 'give permission to go' concept, as being most helpful to the dying person to help them let go of their attachment to living.

Pilar told me about her mother's neighbor in Mexico whose 18-year-old son was dying of cancer. He was very sick. But he was holding on because the mother would cry and through her tears would say, 'Don't go. Don't leave me. Don't go, don't leave me.' People gathered by the bed of the boy, surrounding him with a constant chant of prayer.

And at some point, the older sister found her courage and compassion and said in her kindest voice, 'Mom, you have to let him go.' The whole room stopped praying when they heard the sister's clear firm voice. 'He's suffering but he can't go because of you.'

It was hard for the mother to hear these words spoken. But she did hear them. Her acceptance broke a palpable tension.

The mother moved toward the head of the bed and addressed her son directly. 'It's okay son, you can go.' The words were no sooner out of her mouth than he died. Pilar's mother said she had never seen anything like it. He was keeping himself alive, apparently waiting for her acceptance.

The years went by and the boy's mother reflected, 'Had I understood it before, I would have let him go, because all he had was suffering. We all had so much more suffering just because I couldn't accept his dying. I wished I'd understood that I was prolonging his suffering. I would have spoken earlier, "It's okay, my son—you can go.""

Pilar's second observation was about understanding that the dying person might just want some physical privacy.

One of our teachers had worked as a counselor for some years when his own father became sick. He told us of being there in the room when death was getting closer. He comforted the father saying, 'Don't worry' and 'Everything will be okay.' But there came a point when the father said, 'It's you. You don't let me go. Please go. Go away.'

He realized what his father was saying was true. His very presence in the room was holding his father back. 'You're right, Dad.'

He said his goodbyes, left the room and the father died shortly afterwards. It was the father's choice. He needed to be by himself. If we talked about it more often, we would know that there are different styles. Some people choose to be surrounded by loved ones, and some people want privacy.

Vasu got this right intuitively, but it was hard to bring others along with him. Vasu is the Dean of Humanities at Pretoria University in South Africa. He used to be a client of mine when he worked at South Africa's Human Science Research Council. During our coaching sessions, we'd had conversations about what makes a job satisfying, the meaning of life and work balance and what makes a life worth living. Months later, after he was no longer a client, we met for breakfast to discuss his experience of his grandmother's dying and his views on mortality and spirituality.

I grew up with my grandmother and my parents in Durban. She and I had a very close relationship. She lived an amazing life, worked hard, was a strong, dominant, very short woman. Mine are the physical features of my grandmother; we're both short in stature with the same bone structure. She was everything to me.

I am not the oldest grandson, but my dad is the eldest son. He has been the provider in many ways for my grandparents. I have a sense of gratitude for the things that my grandparents did. They worked very hard, my grandmother as a domestic worker and my grandfather as a hawker who sold vegetables. They were illiterate—they never went to school. I've always felt a sense of responsibility for them.

My dad and his generation were Indians who lived all their lives with their parents, literally. They were born, they went to school, they worked, they married. My grandparents were always physically with us. There was no separation—it was a cultural thing but also economics. Stuck together—always three generations in one house. After I left home, when the entire family moved to Johannesburg, I visited my grandmother on a weekly basis.

During the three years before she died at 95, Vasu watched his grandmother become more frail, and in 2011, her life force ebbed. He recalled:

From the beginning of her end to her taking her final breath all happened within three months. She became particularly uncommunicative and she would drool physically. She did not want to eat. She became skin and bone. Basically, she withered away, the body sort of saying goodbye and she became silent.

I normally visited my grandmother on a weekly basis, but I traveled for work and was away for two weeks. When I returned, my grandmother's decline was obvious; she had physically transformed. I have a photograph of her at this time. To me it's a grotesque look, the look of death. And I said to my folks, 'She is virtually dead and we are not letting her go.'

The person who experienced the most difficulty was my dad. I watched him go into the room. He would hold her, cradle her, hold her tightly, not wanting her to go. It was as dramatic as that. Or he would go into her room, stand there and just stare. This kind of anxiety just adds to the anxiety of the person who is about to die. I pleaded with him, 'You should give her permission to go.' I felt this was also my responsibility. I wanted to let her know that it was okay to leave. Nobody else was doing that.

I think what is always very difficult is accepting, knowing that those that you leave behind will be fine, that they will be cared for, that you are not leaving things incomplete.

It is not about the physical attachment, it's about the spiritual and emotional attachment. My grandmother has a daughter, my aunt who is unmarried and who lives with my parents. My grandmother was deeply connected to her and worried what would happen to her. I was very much aware of that. In those weeks of her dying I would sit with her, hold her hand, comfort her and let her know that my aunt would be fine, that I would watch over her and take care of her.

The day before she died, I remember chatting with her, looking at her, stroking her head. I think touch with people who are dying is important. I am not afraid of that and I feel it is important to still connect physically. I said to her, 'It's okay, I would like you to go home now.' Those were the words I chose. 'I would like you to go home now, because it's okay. You worked hard, you are tired and we are all going to be just fine.'

I held her hand and I could feel her hand tighten up slightly, and then it loosened. I know she heard me. She heard that I was giving her permission to leave.

I had a deep sense that was the last time I would see her physically alive. I believe people on their death bed are aware that death is looming. The body is dying but the spirit is still so alive. They are fully aware of their mortality. Even if they do not articulate and express that, you see it in their face, a sense of sadness.

My grandmother chose to die that night. It's interesting that my aunt who normally slept in the same room was not going to be there. My grandma's timing showed that she decided, 'I will die as soon as I'm alone and I've been given some permission to go.' She died a couple of hours after my aunt physically left the room. It was as though there was an alignment for separation.

I was called immediately. I held her hand again and spoke to her, 'It's okay, you are now transitioned. I hope you will be fine wherever you are and we will be just fine.'

I now believe that absolute privacy is needed because the people who are dying know very well that they are going to leave physically. It's an act of love, it is not an act of weakness. They do not want their descendants to see them. Because it is painful. Because death is about physical separation, breaking a physical attachment. It is not fundamentally about breaking the emotional, mental attachment because the love simply continues. Love never dies.

Death is just, you know, it's a continuation of life. Death as it were, as a concept is in my opinion, in my view, a sort of an interregnum. It's a pause, that's what it is. It is not a full stop.

I asked Vasu, 'Interregnum? Do you mean between one world and another?'

He answered, 'Yes. Absolutely. It's like a semicolon.'

Postscript Four

Respecting choices is about love which, in Humberto Maturana's words, allows 'the other to be a legitimate other.'

It seems to be challenging to some medical professionals to respect the wishes of the patient. Gonda's father had a right to ask to leave intensive care and go back to the general ward and have no further treatment. Kate's mother had a right to prefer hospice care to the specialist's recommendation that she undertake dialysis.

Closer to home, my own family doctor told me of his father's admission to hospital after suffering a stroke. His father's end-of-life non-interventionist wishes had been written down, duly signed and placed in his file. But when he arrived at the hospital, he found the staff on duty had explicitly ignored his father's wishes and hooked him up to life support. He struggled to get his father's wishes respected. He is tall and white, with a physical bearing that carries the self-confidence of his own professional standing as a seasoned primary care physician. And yet even he found he needed tenacity to get the hospital medical staff to comply with his father's clearly recorded preferences.

If it was so hard for him, my doctor, how much harder would it be for you or me, mere laypersons, to ask for our wishes—or those of our loved ones—to be respected?

Sadly, it's too easy to be dismissed and feel disempowered in a hospital setting. Institutions establish reputations about their attitudes to respecting patient wishes and/or their disposition to intervene. It's good to know this—that is, if you can choose which hospital you go to.

It is so important to write things down. Current experience shows that it's difficult in certain hospitals to have your wishes respected. It is even more difficult to insist on them in the absence of something documented and when you or the loved one who is the patient is desperately unwell, medicated and not very articulate. The document is most effective when it has legal standing, which in some countries or US states would require policy and legislative changes. The worst imaginable situation is if you've written nothing, discussed nothing and your family is not of one voice.

We need to have conversations to ensure that there are no surprises for our family, for our doctors, that our preferences are clearly shared and discussed in advance. People have told me of their experiences of family members quarreling over deathbed interventions; ugly quarrels damaging loving relationships and intensifying the pain of imminent loss. It's difficult for family constellations to recover from such conflict and find their love for each other again.

Dying is hard on everyone concerned and alignment and agreement may not be possible. I submit that the dying person's wishes are paramount whether it's preference to give a chance to a new drug or treatment or the exact opposite—the arrival at the place of, 'No, it's enough now.'

Conversations about what happens next are invaluable. Respecting end-of-life choices made by the dying person, particularly when their choice differs from yours, is about true love.

PART FIVE
Ritual

The word ritual, in fact, comes from the Indo-European root which means 'to fit together'… All societies have rituals to acknowledge the major life transitions of birth, initiation, marriage and death. Ritual is the conscious act of recognizing a life change, and doing something to honor and support the change through the presence of such elements as witnesses, gift giving, ceremony and sacred intention. In this way human beings support the changes they are experiencing and create a way 'to fit things together again.'

—Angeles Arrien, *The Four-Fold Way*

A ritual is the enactment of a myth. And, by participating in the ritual, you are participating in the myth. And since myth is a projection of the depth of wisdom of the psyche, by participating in a ritual, participating in the myth, you are being, as it were, put in accord with that wisdom, which is the wisdom that is inherent in you anyhow. Your consciousness is being reminded of the wisdom of your own life.

—Joseph Campbell, *The Power of Myth*

Consequences

Rituals underpin all our rites of passage, not only death. I had to learn through experience just how important they are. This story is about a wedding, my very own. It's about how, when Joe and I married, life taught me a lesson when we failed to give to ritual its due importance.

I moved from Maputo, Mozambique, to join Joe in Lusaka, Zambia, in December 1986. We agreed we'd marry during the next year in London, at the registry office in Camden Town. Each of us wanted a specific friend as a witness, both of whom lived close by.

We happened to be in England together for work not long after we made this decision, and we visited my parents in the north. There was a Saturday evening meal of roast lamb, Eastern European-style, cooked with red cabbage and sautéed potatoes as well as mash. Before dinner Joe sampled my father's homebrewed beer, fine-tuned over many years, just the right quantity of hops, just the right spoonful of malt to get the flavor to his taste. With dinner, we'd drunk our fill of full-bodied homemade wine. My parents were exceptionally skilled in these arts of preserving and brewing—their shared legacy of having grown up on farms before the days of refrigeration. Theirs was a childhood in which fruit was dried, fermented or turned into jam; meat was hung and cured into hams or minced and spiced and turned into salami. Vegetables and fish were pickled in jars, cabbage became sauerkraut, and earth pits were used to store surplus root vegetables that would see the family through the long winters. In their retirement, Regina and Toni had ample, unrushed hours to enjoy their skills.

My father and Joe, besides their love for me, shared one other characteristic—they were consummate tellers of jokes. That Saturday evening the jokes followed one after the other, the two men in flow. It's rare to laugh so much in one evening—at times my sides hurt—and I'd beg them to take a pause. I needed respite from laughing too much!

121

Our visit had a mission. We were there to tell them that we were getting married—and that they wouldn't be invited to the wedding. We explained it was complicated; a second marriage for both of us, and children from our first marriages were not easily accepting of our relationship. Our plan was to marry on a Saturday in autumn, with our two witnesses present, and then we'd be joined by their spouses for lunch. No one else was to be in attendance.

My parents took it well. Perhaps, as I'd understand later, this was because it was the very same format they followed for the formalization of their own marital commitment. My father was very clear. He had never seen his daughter so happy in a relationship. He didn't care about political differences, religious differences, age differences—his daughter's blossoming filled his heart and he gave us a blessing we hadn't asked for. Later my mother sent me a gift of jewelry and asked me to wear it on my wedding day. She explained it was her way of being with us.

Come September, Joe arrived in London ahead of me. Harold, his best, oldest and closest friend, his to-be witness at the registry office, invited him to come for supper. Harold's own children, young adults in their 20s, as well as Joe's daughters Shawn, Gillian and Robyn, all in their early 30s, were also invited.

Visiting London was always hard for Joe. While it can be wonderful that your adult children want to spend time with you, Joe's visits were always short and time-pressured and yet he said he found it worked better to see each daughter separately. On this specific evening, however, whoever could make it from the two families gathered. The evening progressed, conversations took off.

'How do you feel about your father getting married next Saturday?' Harold's son asked in passing.

His question sparked expletives. The conviviality of the evening evaporated. It turned out that Joe's daughters were not yet in the know. I had assumed he told them after we'd spoken with my parents. I hardly saw Joe that week. When he wasn't working, he was engaged in long filial conversations.

Saturday was a bubble of a day, completely wonderful. There was a special breakfast with our hosts before we left for the registry office. Joe wore his red socks with exaggerated display for the photographs. The ceremony was simple, the script of words, rings placed on fingers and four signatures. The delicious lunch at a seafood restaurant was enjoyed with merriment. We walked along the Thames Embankment under trees bathed in autumn sunshine. It was an oasis of joyous emotion in a week that had been a maelstrom. Joe told me he didn't expect to feel any different, that he'd felt totally committed to our relationship. But there was something about going through a ritual. Something, he said, 'shifted' inside the very core of his being.

Now what about my children? Also not invited, also not in the know. We decided we would tell them when the Zimbabwean school term ended, when they would be with us in Lusaka for several weeks over Christmas and the new year.

The holidays began well. Tessa and Kyla flew from Bulawayo to Lusaka as unaccompanied minors. They treated it as an adventure and felt quite spoiled by the air hostesses. Kyla, who was almost four, told me they were 'really naughty' on the flight.

'What does "really naughty" mean?' I asked with curiosity.

'When the air hostesses weren't watching,' she whispered, 'we opened the packets of sugar and added them to our Coca-Cola and it fizzed.'

We swam, we read, we baked, we cooked. We arranged playdates. We went to Carols by Candlelight. The children seemed grounded and settled, so, sitting at the dining room table just after dinner one night, Joe and I decided it was a good time to tell them.

'Joe and I have some news,' I began. 'We got married…'

I didn't get a chance to continue. Tessa choked on the juice she was drinking, burst into tears and left the table, ran upstairs and locked herself in the bathroom where she wailed and sobbed.

I had not anticipated such a dramatic response. It had been four years since her father and I separated, and Joe and I had now been living together for a whole year.

Tessa, who was about to turn eight, was inconsolable. I spent what felt like hours trying to talk to her through the locked bathroom door. It was traumatic for both of us.

At some stage I went downstairs and sat again at the table, dejected, my head in my hands. I felt defeated. I felt out of my depth in navigating parenthood. I seemed to be doing it so badly, getting too much too wrong, at least for my elder daughter.

Kyla, who'd remained sitting at the table composed, watching and listening, looked at me wide-eyed and concerned. 'Mama, why is Tessa crying?' she asked. 'Isn't getting married supposed to be nice?'

I still feel that catch in my throat, that choking up with emotion, when I replay that evening in my mind. My younger self, so naïve, with such a lack of understanding of the enabling power of ritual. I'd wanted privacy for self-protection. I did not want to expose myself to any further hurt by one, two, or all three of Joe's daughters possibly turning down an invitation to our wedding.

My older self feels differently. Joe's daughters, my parents, and our friends should all have been invited. We'd have survived the varying responses. Tessa and Kyla should have been our flower girls. Sure, Tessa may still have been unhappy—it's normal for children to hold onto a hope that their estranged parents will reconcile and Tessa's hopes were dashed with our announcement. But imagine if there'd been an inclusive wedding, with all the paraphernalia of ceremony, the choosing, making and fitting of bridesmaids' dresses, their having a role in this occasion. Would it not have made it easier for everyone to find their place of acceptance? That, in part, is what ritual is about. For better or for worse, the ritual happens. And then the family constellation, with acceptance possibly more enabled by the enactment, rearranges itself like the pieces in a kaleidoscope and the relationships find their way to fit or misfit together again.

I learned respect for ritual the hard way, learning from my mistakes. Not that I learned everything all at once, but at least I enrolled as a student.

Totsie: The Wedding Before the Funeral

A text message popped up on my phone: 'Watch the news. Listen to the radio. Phone Totsie.'

Totsie and I had worked together at different times over 20 years and enjoyed a deepening friendship. I learned there had been a death in her family, in fact two, and they happened just before a wedding ceremony was to take place.

The *lobola* bride price had been paid, but for the traditional marriage to be completed, the welcome ceremony at the house of the groom's mother still needed to be done. The rituals would begin at the front gate of her future mother-in-law's house.

There would be gifts for the groom's parents, aunts and uncles. Patterned blankets of the best quality the family can afford are the favored gift. An animal would be slaughtered, a goat, a sheep, or a cow, and the gall bladder extracted. Totsie once mentioned that the goat is the animal most often chosen for this ceremony; it has a way of crying as it is killed, a bleating sound, that is gentler to the ear. Wamu, Totsie's nephew, was the groom-to-be. Someone from his family would anoint the bride with the green paste from the gall bladder on each of her toes and her forehead. This part of the ritual was the act that finalized the marriage union and completed the welcome of the bride, known as the *umakoti*, into her husband's family.

Wamu and Wendy had set the date of the welcome ceremony for mid-January. But on the weekend before the ceremony was to take place, they were the victims of a double murder. They were found in their Johannesburg bedroom, bound and strangled to death. The assailants drove away in Wendy's car, taking their bank cards.

On the following Thursday, I attended the most moving memorial service. The grace of singing together was balm to the hearts of family, friends, and colleagues. The burial was to take place two days later. When I hugged Totsie, she told me they were about to sit down to have a family meeting.

Wamu's family wanted the couple to be buried together. At the meeting, Wendy's family insisted that a joint burial could not happen unless the wedding rituals were completed.

'If you wish our daughter to be buried with your son,' they said, 'we need to fulfill all parts of the ceremony.'

After much discussion, they all agreed this would happen the next day, the Friday evening before the Saturday burial.

Wendy's parents went to the funeral parlor on Friday and returned to their Soweto home in a hearse that contained Wendy's coffin. They dressed their daughter in a traditional cream-colored dress of woven cotton, decorated with beads along the borders. Then they had to drive to the home of the groom's family for the official start of a ceremony that has many scripted parts.

Sandile, Wamu's father, went with his sister Totsie to the funeral parlor to collect his son. Sandile entered and went privately to talk with Wamu for the last time. Totsie, who long ago decided that she preferred not to look at people when they are dead, stayed at the entrance. She was adamant that she wanted the memory of her last sighting to be one of when they were alive. Whilst she waited, she inhaled the scent of eucalyptus. This was the funeral parlor to where she'd brought her mother when she died, and she appreciated how they did things so beautifully here—no lingering smell of either death or cleaning fluids.

Totsie and Sandile got into the hearse that now contained Wamu's coffin. The plan was that both hearses would meet at the halfway point on the highway. It was a stressful car ride. It was Friday late afternoon with traffic at its busiest, and it was essential that the bride and groom arrived at the same time at Wamu's mother's home as the next part of the ceremony would officially begin outside the entrance to the house. Wendy's parents stood on the shoulder of the highway next to their hearse, frantically waving their arms, anxious that Totsie and Sandile might miss them.

The ceremony duly began at the wrought-iron gates. There were wedding songs to be sung, and these were sung, however much the hearts of those singing felt like breaking. The 'welcome-to-the-family-gifts' were offered. Totsie, as aunt of the nephew, received two blankets, one for herself and one for her deceased mother. Her twin sister, Ntsiki, received two blankets, one for herself and one for their deceased father.

The final ritual was the anointing ceremony. That was when Totsie heard her name being called to step forward.

'What!' she exclaimed. 'Not me?' She'd thought that the mother-in-law did this part of the ceremony—but no—tradition specified that this was the role of the groom's eldest aunt. It fell to her, the very one who always avoided looking at a face in an open casket; she was the one who would have to anoint each of the ten toes and the forehead of her nephew's dead bride. She could not refuse. Totsie had to step up and make this contribution that mattered so much to the grieving families. She moved forward, breathed deeply, steadied her trembling hand and did what was expected of her.

With the wedding ceremony now complete, the joint funeral could take place. Wamu and Wendy would be buried together.

This should have been an occasion of joy, not one of weeping. But there was gratitude for the presence of ritual.

On the week of the second anniversary of Wendy and Wamu's murder, I phoned Totsie just to say... this must be a hard week for memories and that I was thinking of her, noticing on Facebook that Sandile was about to publish a book of poems which he'd written on his journey of grief.

Totsie told me it was still hard, and family members differed hugely in their grieving, and in what they had chosen to share publicly and what they had kept private. They were having to try to be respectful and non-judgmental and allow that each person has their own way of moving forward.

She had conversations with the other family members about having shared this story for this book. She added, 'You know, at the time, I thought Wendy's parents were crazy in their insistence that the wedding rituals be completed prior to the funeral rituals beginning. But now in hindsight, I can see how good it was for us as a family to have had those conversations and completed the rituals. I'm so grateful they insisted.'

In a modernizing urban world people often let go of rituals, judging them as archaic. But grief can make us feel that we're about to disintegrate into a million little pieces, and in these moments the observance of ritual holds, cradles and soothes, at least a little, the sharp deep pain that death inflicts on us.

Maggie: Her Final Fling

My brother Roman and his friend Maggie* talked as they walked along the seashore at Sefton in Lancashire, where *Another Place*, Anthony Gormley's installation of one hundred naked, full-size, cast-iron men is fixed into the sand. The Iron Men of Crosby Beach look out to sea and disappear and reappear as the tide comes in and goes out. No one knows what they're going to see of them until they're there. After 10 years, barnacles have begun to grow on the sculptures, making them even more interesting.

Maggie and Roman walked as colleagues and confidantes who shared a love of gardening and swapped plants, going to flower shows and, most importantly, were there for one another in difficult times.

Maggie was chronically ill by then; she'd contracted hepatitis from a blood transfusion which compromised her liver function. It didn't seem life threatening, but it certainly influenced how Maggie lived her life with zest, more mindful than others of its fragility. After she died, my brother Roman described how he admired her and the influence she'd had on him.

Maggie had organized a small community garden where she lived. She was part of a very tight-knit group of families on a social housing estate of about a hundred dwellings called the Village Close. It's just about a mile down the road from here, not far from the beach where she used to walk. She'd bring driftwood home. I remember one year she created an amazing Christmas tree out of her collection of driftwood and shells.

Many of the people still living on the estate were residents who originally moved in when the houses were first built. It was a bit like the street we grew up on, where you could leave doors open or leave keys with neighbors. And if you were working a full day, your neighbor would go in and take the dog out for a walk or borrow a cup of sugar and then give it back. There was a car park and yard area in the middle and Maggie's house was close by. When Maggie married Ted, they had their wedding do right outside her house. They put up a marquee in the parking lot.

Maggie was very much a free spirit, which included being anti formal religion. She hated it. She hated it for what it had caused —the wars the world over, for centuries right up until this day. She hated how religion could be used to manipulate people. But she also respected other people's need for religious belief.

As caregivers, we had weekend rotations and there was one guy who wanted to go to church Sunday mornings, whenever possible. Whenever she could, she'd swap out with him. While she kept a distance from religious establishments, spirituality, her own and how other people found it in their lives, was important to her.

Her son from her first marriage was in the army for a few of the years that I knew her. He did a couple of tours in Afghanistan and, because we worked with her, we all lived through that with Maggie. We lived with her anxiety. Every time something happened, she'd be distressed when she didn't then hear anything from him to say he was okay. And then there'd be an email and we'd see her relax.

Her son's girlfriend had a baby boy. She had good reason to consider it wasn't his child. But her son accepted his responsibility as father and so she, Maggie, also accepted her part as grandmother. That relationship ended, but nothing changed for Maggie. He was her grandchild. She had him for sleepovers, took him on holiday, the things that grandparents do.

You know it'll be like that for me when my stepdaughters have children, their little ones will be my grandchildren. Bloodline can't stand in the way of love. At least not in my book of life.

Roman told me that Maggie was a great soul fan, she especially liked Motown. She still went to a northern soul music club. She couldn't always dance when she'd not been feeling that well physically. But she'd still go listen to performances and rave about the music.

Maggie died, quite quickly, unexpectedly soon, one summer. Her liver deteriorated and she started with internal bleeding. The doctors tried blood transfusions and treatments to see if they could restore the liver function. Some days she was in absolute pain and agony. In the end, she died of heart failure.

My brother said Maggie inspired him—her values and the rituals she chose.

'The funeral was superb,' he said. 'She'd taken time to think it through. She'd discussed with her husband Ted about what should happen once she died. She was very clear about what she wanted.'

'A cardboard coffin for me,' she said, 'that's what I want when I die.'

Maggie's funeral gathering would be the last party she could plan, and she'd be present in spirit if not in person. The invitation requested those attending to:

- wear brightly colored clothing;
- bring a plant for the community garden;
- bring Post-It notes, on which you've written down your memories or messages;
- be ready to stick the Post-It notes onto the cardboard coffin.

The funeral was beautifully organized. Roman described it in detail, as though it were yesterday—such was the deep impression it left on him.

There was a printed program. They had a master of ceremonies. Her husband and her son delivered brilliant eulogies. Ted said, it was 'his privilege to be part of Maggie's years of adventure of living in this world.' Maggie's first husband was there to support his son, which was good.

Maggie had 53 years. All of us present were a part of some of those years because we'd worked with her or been neighbors or whatever. Each one of us had a plant to be planted. I took an arum lily, my big church lily, I call it. I chose an arum lily because once before I'd given her one, and I liked the memory of that occasion that it brought back to me.

She'd made a playlist of her favorite songs. We ended up having this great big party for her, right outside her house, with the marquee up. People had cooked food. And at the very end of the night there were fireworks going off high into the sky. My wife Pauline and I had already left by then, but we could see them from our house, a mile away. It was a real celebration. We exchanged stories. We laughed and we cried, but it wasn't a sad occasion at all.

I would like people to celebrate my life like that. I've talked to Pauline about it. It might just be that I pass before her. And yes, I want the cardboard coffin, or at most a basket-weave coffin. I want a woodland burial. I don't want a stone. I don't want a grave that people must visit and maintain, instead I would like a tree to be planted. I ask that people choose to remember me kindly, fondly.

As for a party, I said to Pauline, maybe we should lay by a few bottles of my favorite red wine, Spice Route Chakalaka from outside Cape Town, and then everybody can have a drink of something 'proper.'

She said, 'Bugger that, we need to be enjoying that together while we're both alive.'

Ashes

When you follow the rituals of religious practice, making decisions becomes simpler. If you don't have a stipulated ritual, things can become problematic.

I've heard at least a dozen stories of family debates and even fallouts about what should happen to ashes, exactly where should they be placed. Should they be in one unit? Or separated? Or perhaps added to the ashes of a predeceased spouse?

Stefanie, Dave and I sat together contemplatively at the end of their telling the story of Nicholas's dying. Without being formal, it was almost as though we had a minute of silence to honor the joy and healing he'd brought to our family relationships.

Afterwards, we found ourselves sharing stories about rituals whilst we sipped our bedtime cocoa and the theme of disposing of ashes came up again and again.

Stefanie told me that long before Nicholas died, it had been important for her to think about exactly what she was going to do after Nicholas stopped breathing. She worked out a soothing ritual: she would give him a wash and put his favorite pajamas on—well, the ones she liked most on him—and then read him a story, his favorite story, *Little Bob*. It's about a little lamb that goes missing and then cried for his mommy.

She wanted a service that would be celebratory in mood, where no one was to wear black. With the help of her family, she decorated the church with colored balloons and asked that people come with more balloons, which they later let go in the park. They requested that people wear bright colors. Stefanie chose a bright pink top, a white skirt, and posh white shoes which she later wore to her wedding when she and Dave married. As rain was expected, they asked people to use bright umbrellas. Indeed it rained. I'd seen Stefanie's funeral umbrella earlier that day when we'd walked her daughter Cerys to school in the rain— it's transparent with big circles of yellow, turquoise, and red.

Nicholas's ashes were scattered in the Garden of Remembrance outside the church without any memorial tablet. Stefanie explained that she's never liked seeing neglected grave sites, and that's why she didn't want a grave for Nicholas. 'This way when I put flowers down, I feel as if I put them down for everyone who's in the Garden of Remembrance. And that feels right for me.'

The ashes story I shared was about my late mother-in-law Rachel, from my first marriage, and how her family's decision had influenced mine.

Rachel was born in India and arrived in South Africa as a young adult. She married and raised her children in Johannesburg and then retired to Victoria Island in British Columbia. She wanted to be near her daughter who'd emigrated to Canada. When she died, her children easily agreed that her ashes should be divided and taken to the places that had been important in her personal geography. I liked this idea and I took part in the scattering of her ashes in Johannesburg.

I've written up my request that I would like my ashes to be split into three. One third must go to the Pleasington Cemetery near Blackburn—my first roots were in the north of England. They don't need to be added to my dad's grave, they can just be scattered in the woodlands. The second portion is to be scattered in Mozambique. It's where I had my children, it's where I had my first job, where I became politically literate, and where I divorced and fell in love again. Living in Mozambique was fun—that decade, more than any other, was a big part of shaping my life, my friendships, the person I became. The third portion can be scattered in South Africa where I've lived for the longest part of my life. I have a plot available in Avalon Cemetery next to Joe's grave, but I'd be happy if my ashes were simply scattered in the aloes of the botanical garden in The Wilds, close to where John and I now live.

Some friends have exclaimed, 'Oh no! You can't split up your ashes like that!' You'd think that I was requesting the dividing up and transporting of sawn-up body parts. We are so very different in our choices.

Dave followed me with a story that was exactly about that—people being upset about the idea of splitting up the ashes. Of the stories I've heard about family differences on what to do with ashes, the one that Dave told us that night was the one filled with the sharpest conflict.

A colleague told me of a mother, a widow with three sons, who had died. She'd been quite specific in her request for cremation, not burial. The oldest of the three who'd made all the arrangements went to pick up the container of her ashes. He didn't feel especially bothered about what would happen to them, but when he asked his younger brothers for their thoughts, he discovered they had very fixed and very different ideas.

One of them wanted their mother's ashes to be scattered in the River Mersey because that was near where she grew up and she'd always told them stories about the river. The other sibling wanted the ashes in a particular cemetery. They were at loggerheads, shouting at one another. In the end, they parted in a huff and stopped talking.

Apparently the eldest spent a lot of time thinking how to break this logjam. Eventually he phoned each brother and delivered an ultimatum.

'Right,' he said. 'I don't mind. Either of those scenarios is fine with me. You decide between yourselves, and let me know your decision by this date. If I don't get an agreed single outcome from you, I'll be splitting the ashes in two, and putting each half in the post to you. You'll both get your package delivered by the British Royal Mail. You can take your own half to do with it what you want.'

Hoo-hah. There was a hue and cry over this. But it got them talking again and they sorted out a compromise. They were in such fear that their mother's ashes would be divided and put in the post.

I added two more stories to our late-night conversation over cocoa. While some people get the shivers thinking about dividing up ashes, how about the ashes of a couple being mixed together?

One of my acquaintances went through a bitter divorce. I don't think it's an understatement to say she'd come to hate the father of her children by the time they separated. Decades passed and her ex-husband died; their daughter collected his ashes. Another decade passed and my friend died. Her daughter collected her ashes. Now in death the daughter could reunite the two people who'd once loved one another! That's exactly what she did, she mixed their ashes together, hired a boat and scattered them ceremoniously at sea. I felt that my friend would be turning in her grave if she'd had one!

In her book, *Can't We Talk About Something More Pleasant?*, *New Yorker* cartoonist Roz Chast described how a discussion about the mixing of her parents' ashes came about and how she ended it. Her father died and had been cremated, and his ashes were in a box inside a blue, velvet, drawstring bag. Her mother died two years later.

'The funeral director asked me if I wanted their ashes to be mixed together,' wrote Chast. 'I told him that my mother had been so dominant when they were alive I thought it better if he had a little space of his own.'

Her mother's ashes were placed in a box inside a maroon velvet drawstring bag.

She drew a cartoon that showed the packages in her closet, one on top of the other, and captioned it: 'Still close, but independent.'

The three of us concluded that, firstly, we should all spell out exactly what we want to happen once dead, in detail, and that way such family dramas could be avoided. And secondly, it's also best to have inclusive conversations so that different points of view can be heard and discussed.

That necessity, of course, falls away when you are adhering to religious rites and the decisions are made for you. Then the prescribed rituals after someone's death simply demand that you fit into the flow of roles ascribed and follow the requirements.

That simplicity of following religious rights and roles was true for Vasu. After he'd finished telling me about his grandmother's dying—how permission to go and privacy had proved to be so important—he then spoke about the after-death rituals so essential to his Hindu spiritual practice. And being the sociologist he is, he commented on how men and women are assigned different roles.

'Death in my cultural context is a very cathartic process,' Vasu reflected. 'People are given permission to cry and wail, to be emotional and express their feelings.'

Whilst his father didn't cry at the actual time of his mother's death, when he saw her body enter the furnace at the crematorium, he wailed for about 20 minutes. Vasu thought it must have been prompted by the stark reality of seeing it so close.

When I grew up people would cry out loud, wail at times, or be quiet and calm in their way of expressing grief and mourning. But wailing is allowed, even expected. And central to the culture I grew up with is to look at the face of the deceased, and the body, and to acknowledge: 'This is a dead body.' When neighbors returned from a funeral they would be asked, 'Did you look at the face? How was the face?'

Vasu noted that although after-death rituals are considered important, in Hindu tradition women are excluded. 'Women,' he said, 'are not allowed to visit the gravesite, in fact from the moment the body is taken away from the home, they are not part of the ritual. They are not allowed to be in the actual furnace room.'

This is a 4,000-year-old ritual. The Hindu Vedas believe that cremation releases the trapped soul from the dead body. The ritual requires starting fires on the body itself. Nowadays gas and electric furnaces are used so the last rites take place in the furnace room. Vasu's first experience of this was when he was 11 years old.

The body is already in the coffin and the mourners spend time together in the furnace room starting the fire on different parts of the body. You use sandalwood by preference, ghee, and rosewater —all things that have spiritual connotations—and you create fire on all parts of the body. The ritual gives thanks to the elements. Water is also thrown in: it's fire, water, air, and earth. With a Hindu ceremony, you must also place cooked rice inside the coffin for the afterlife. And to complete the ceremony there are verses intoned by the person leading the ritual. The coffin lid is then lowered and the coffin is put into the furnace. The furnace door closes and the button is pressed. This is the most difficult part, the part where you find men who don't normally wail begin to wail because it is so final.

And then you leave and wait. An hour to an hour and a half later you go back to collect the ashes, and sometimes you might arrive while the person who is working in the furnace room is still processing the ash.

It is also part of the Hindu ritual that mourners participate. They don't leave and come back to pick up a package on another day. What often happens is that the bigger bones don't completely cremate. It all comes out on a big tray and then they put the remains, bit by bit, into a grinder. Picture like a coffee grinder, okay? You add about a liter of milk—which is also what makes the ashes whiter —and you press a button. It's incredible to watch and listen. You would be surprised how much comes out.

Then the ashes are put into a small urn, a clay pot, and the excess of it is wrapped up in a white cloth. And then we go to the river. The ritual stipulates that the ashes are to be dispersed in moving water.

We took my grandmother's ashes to one of the Hindu temples in Pretoria. At the river, it's a short ceremony, not more than about 10 to 15 minutes. You light a campfire, give thanks to the body, and say

135

we now commit this body to the water. And that's it. It's so amazing, the beautiful rushing of the ash. It's literally taken away by a little wave and it goes.

Remember, the water must be moving: a river or the ocean. There are interesting superstitions: if you drop off the ash at the edge of the ocean, as soon as you've done it, you must never look back at it. You must just walk away. Otherwise, it's said that the spirits will follow you.

To tell you the truth, as much as it is painful, the process of disposing the ash brings home the finality. There's the process of cremation, getting that done, but the last act of taking the physical remains and returning them to blend with the elements is the moment of completion.

'Is this what will happen to you when you die?' I asked Vasu.

'Yes, the very same. What I have done for my grandmother will happen to me.'

No confusion. No decision-making. Roles assigned in an accepted dance of ritual. Simplicity.

Mapi: I Have It in Writing

Ngiphiwe Mhlangu, or rather Mapi, as she's called by everyone in our book club and all her friends, grew up in the township of KwaMashu, 20 miles from the Durban city center. Her mother was a life-long teacher who taught many people in the community, often offering a second home to youngsters for whom things were not going well. Widowed young, she used her earnings carefully and built a three-bedroomed brick house with an inside bathroom as well as another in the yard next to the room used by so many in KwaMashu when they were facing difficulties.

Mapi was her youngest, the love-child of a liaison during widowhood. Exit man—leaving Mrs. Mhlangu pregnant with a daughter she treasured and imbued with the deepest sense of self-worth. As a young professional, Mapi started making her own way in the world and she and Ma Mhlangu would settle on the bed, eat cheese curls, and talk through the travails that Mapi found herself confronting in her early days as a sound technician at a regional TV station.

Mapi worked her way up the ranks, moving from Durban to Johannesburg to join the public broadcasting company. That's when we first got to know one another. She was working alongside John, who was a radio talk show host at the station, and the man I married a few years later.

By her late 30s Mapi's career had seriously accelerated. She became the head of eNCA TV news, the most watched 24/7 news channel in South Africa. As *the* professional success in her biological family of three sisters and one brother, it's Mapi who pays what's called the 'black tax,' money dispensed among relatives for covering school fees, help with rent or for bulk packs of chicken pieces for the meal that accompanies the 'washing of hands' ceremony after a funeral. It's called the black tax because it's the price paid by many successful black professionals making their way forward without the benefits of inheritance. With official unemployment at almost 30 percent, but more likely to be 40 percent if those who've stopped looking for work were to be included, then those fortunate enough to get jobs spread their salaries around the extended family's several households. It's not a uniquely South African story; my American friends of slave descent now living in Baltimore and Washington DC respectively share the same social and economic legacy.

Mapi told me the story of her mother's illness, the challenge to integrate her Zulu traditional rituals and Christianity, and her claim at the age of 25 to the family leadership position in a culture which has patriarchy as its default setting.

The first time I knew my mom was ill was around local government elections in April 2004. My mom already found out that she had cancer, but hadn't told me—she was waiting for me to finish with that year's election coverage. My mom's friend Mathilda, a matron at King Edward VIII Hospital in Durban, phoned me. 'You know your mother has not been well. You need to come home soonest so we can tell you more.'

I left the election center at the earliest opportunity and I took a bus for the 400 miles to Durban. Mathilda was waiting there, all teary. She said, 'Your mother has colon cancer. It is too advanced; she can't do chemo. They are giving her six months to live.'

As we talked I saw the fear in my mom's eyes that maybe I would just fold up. I quickly realized how important it was for my mother to see me strong rather than falling apart. She had this bigger thing to deal with. I started joking and said lightly, 'I mean, if this is the case, you know what I want? I don't want the house; I want only the china.' My sisters were there. My mom made it clear she had thought about how to divide everything and indeed the china was to be mine.

During the rest of April, May, and June I caught the bus home every other weekend. I watched her deteriorating. At first, she could still walk and insisted that we go out. We didn't have a car then so we would use public transport. She was losing weight; I was giving her clothes because suddenly she was thinner than me. I have this memory of walking with her to the boutique shops on Musgrave Road. But things quickly turned for the worse; she wasn't even going to have the six months. I exhausted my savings on alternative treatments, hoping they would work or at least make her more comfortable. And I took leave in the last week of July and went home expecting her to die.

A lot of things were not going well. She was living with my nephews and my brother but it was Aunty Msomi, our housekeeper, who really looked after my mom. She was very caring and prepared special meals. My mom was on morphine and in pain but she didn't want to go to the hospital. She began to need help to go to the toilet. She was so self-conscious; she didn't want to mess the bed. But we couldn't do everything ourselves, so the neighbors would come and we would put Mom in the bath and wash her, put baby oil on her, change her bedding and help her back into bed.

When I arrived one weekend, she said she felt like cake. A friend of hers said, 'What's the point? You can hardly swallow.' But I wanted her to have whatever she still might enjoy.

'I will go to the shops and buy you a piece of cake. Mom, if you want cake, you will have a cake today.'

After that I started a conversation with her. 'You know you are not getting any better, you know now you are dying and you know we have tried everything possible and there is nothing more to be done. How do you want your funeral to go? What songs do you want sung? Who is your MC? Who must speak for you?' We got into all those details.

Initially my sisters were completely uncomfortable when I told them I wanted this discussion. So, the first talk took place just between me and Mom.

I asked what policies she had and we looked at the files together. About the funeral, she said, 'I want to be buried on Thursday because it's Mother's Union Day.' That was one thing in her retirement she'd always looked forward to. She would put on her blue church uniform and go around with other mothers who were dressed the same. She said she'd like a blue coffin, the same color as the uniform. There was a youth leader in her church, and she wanted him to be her MC. She named the reverend to officiate. She named the friends to speak, she named the songs. She was very clear which funeral parlor she wanted to go to.

Later, I called my sisters to sit with us and my mom repeated her wishes. I made sure they became part of the conversation. It was difficult for them but it happened in such a way that when we were finalizing the funeral program—my sisters are great singers—they started to sing the songs our mother chose. They warmed up to that idea of having a plan. My mother dictated her wishes and I wrote everything down in an exercise book as she spoke, witnessed by my sisters.

My mom also stipulated, 'Do not slaughter the cow in the house because I don't want the blood in here. Buy it and get it slaughtered outside and once the cow is slaughtered you can take it to this butchery and then it will be cut up there.' The husband of one of her teaching colleagues owned a butchery and we learned she had already made this arrangement.

By the fourth day of my visit she was in more pain, even though she had morphine smuggled to her by a friend. I took her to the clinic because she had boils coming out of her body. They were not helpful and the service was so bad. She messed herself. I was so angry that I lost it. I think I complained to everybody, even the head of the health department in KwaZulu-Natal.

I didn't want my nephews and nieces to continue to see her in this state, and I also didn't want them to find her dead or crying in pain. I decided to take her to the hospital knowing that at the end of the week I had to return to work in Johannesburg.

She didn't want to go; it was against her will, really. But eventually she was admitted to Mahatma Gandhi Memorial Hospital, which I chose because we had a family friend who was a nurse there. The boils were coming out of everywhere, and the public hospitals sometimes don't dress wounds properly. I went with Mathilda to bathe her and clean out the boils.

She was just getting worse and worse. All her organs were failing; her whole system was collapsing. She was losing her mind. My mom would give me this look and I just knew she was going. There was no doubt whatsoever. The only thing I could do was to talk and reassure her, 'You know I have a great job, I am your last born, you are with your star.'

By Thursday she didn't recognize me. She was hallucinating, talking to people, talking to the dead. She was crying from the pain. On Saturday I had to return to Johannesburg on the overnight bus, and I stopped at the hospital on the way to the station. It wasn't visiting hours but they allowed me in. She was in such pain as I said my goodbyes.

I left her and told my sisters who'd been waiting outside, 'I think this is time.' I didn't think she'd last a week. They said, 'Don't talk like this.'

After I left, I called the hospital every day asking to find out what was happening. When I phoned on the Wednesday morning, they told me she had just passed.

My older sister was writing exams so I couldn't call her. I called my brother, not my biological brother, but Emmanuel, who had become my mother's son, the one who always remembered Mother's Day. He was a school principal and had a car. 'It has happened. Just go there and make sure that you finalize the process to get her death certificate and move her to Doves funeral parlor.'

When someone dies in our family, the first thing people do is cry. But I couldn't because I was in that organizing mood of, okay things must be done right. I called the neighbor who had helped me wash Mom and asked her to clear the dining room for the mourners to sit in. My mom did not want people to sit in her bedroom, even though that is tradition. I insisted that it must be the dining room as was my mother's wish.

When I landed in Durban from Johannesburg, those meeting

me at the airport were crying and falling apart. I was the only one thinking and organizing: 'Let's just stop by the Checkers. We need to get juice, chicken, and other foodstuff to feed people who will come to pay their respects.'

With all the immediate practical arrangements made—food for visitors, spaces created for mourning, and the funeral home organized—Mapi found herself facing a much more complicated challenge.

On occasions like funerals or the traditional ceremony that takes place a year after someone dies, the elders in the family always take charge. But I just couldn't let them. People tried to advise me: 'You have relatives in Ladysmith and Johannesburg. She died on a Wednesday. The relatives proposed that the funeral should take place a week on Saturday.'

There was tension because culturally men are used to being in charge. My biological brother had never assumed any family responsibility whatsoever—he never even came to the hospital once. But now he expected that when the relatives came, they would make sure that we women recognize his role as the oldest male.

For me it was just one of those things. I could not accept my brother taking over. I needed to step up. I had my own selfish reasons. I wanted to make sure that what my mother requested would be done. I knew once I gave power away they would bury her on the Saturday and do all sorts of traditional things that my mother did not want.

I took out my exercise book and told them. 'I have it in writing. These were her wishes. It's going to be done this way. Our mother will be buried on a Thursday. The coffin will be blue.' I became this young woman who was stubborn—no one could overrule me. I needed things to be done just the way that my mother had wanted.

Mapi straddles tradition and modernity. Slaughtering the cow away from the home was the one wish she was unable to fulfill because of the outcry from older family members who brought the cow and slaughtered it at home, in the yard outside the house. Only after the slaughtering ceremony could Mapi organize for it to be taken to the butchery where her mother had arranged for it to be cut up.

The elder aunties from the Mhlangu family moved in to assume their mourning tradition of sitting on the mattress and praying in the days leading up to the funeral. Mapi assumed her role of dutiful daughter tending to their every need.

They wanted pap—soft corn porridge—so I would make it. I would also make eggs with a salsa. Then daily I started cooking a huge pot of curry and Aunty Msomi did whatever else was needed.

Afterwards I would leave with Emmanuel, driving around to finalize arrangements. There was laughter between us; we had so many good memories. We laughed until the day we went to the mortuary to bring the blue church uniform. We saw her body and we could see she died in pain. She had the same expression I'd seen her making in hospital.

Various family members volunteered to wash my mother. But she'd been explicit about not wanting anyone near her who might apply traditional oils and other substances. The funeral parlor washed her. They put on make-up and lipstick, and when they brought her body home on Friday, she looked beautiful.

When Thursday came we buried my mother following all her requests. There were pictures of her and a printed program. We sang the Zulu songs she asked for, like *Dwala Lami Laphakade* which translates as Rock of Ages. They were the songs she used to sing with her friends in the choir. I still remember her funeral so vividly—several busloads of people. My mom the teacher, known by everyone. So many people came. It worked out just as she wanted.

It's true that Mapi paid the money to supplement her mom's funeral policies, which helped when her older brother tried to claim his patriarchal space. But at 25 Mapi had imbibed her mother's wisdom. With foresight, she'd secured her mother's voice, in writing, to support her determination to bury her mother according to the wishes she had so carefully and clearly set out.

Getti: A Couple of Dropped Stitches

Getti, the gift of friendship I received through my marriage to his friend John. Getti, the mensch who visited my bedridden mother daily for 43 days when I got my writing scholarship in Italy.

Over the 12 years I've known him, he's the one who has lived on a roller coaster. In part, he had the time available to choose to visit my mother because Alan, his life partner, had died of cancer. A couple of years after Alan's passing, Getti and I talked at length.

My gratitude is that we had all the time we needed to engage deeply. It was an extraordinary gift to talk through what Alan wanted at the end and exactly how he wanted it. He was a staunch atheist, and I'm a Christian, but our differing convictions proved not to present difficulties. I'm what's called a Cafeteria Catholic. I go through, I pick up what I like and ignore what I don't.

While Alan was an atheist, he also liked tradition. He came from a small town outside of Johannesburg where there's a church where his sisters got married, where his father's funeral was held and his grandmother's funeral as well.

Alan set me a task: he also wanted his funeral held there but only if the minister would acknowledge that he was both gay and atheist. This was a challenge for the exceptionally nice minister whom Alan had known for 35 years who, when I inquired, asked, 'If Alan was an atheist, how come he made a substantial donation every year?' I answered that the church was well-known for its stunning welfare work in the surrounding townships. Alan always specified that his money was specifically for this program. Surely his donation did not disprove his atheism?

Alan realized he was popular and people would want a proper funeral. He was a *Harold and Maude* figure—you know that famous movie about a young man and an old lady who meet because they go to peoples' funerals? He never missed one. He said they had an important social place and function: comfort of the bereaved and people reconnecting. He always came home from a funeral in a cheerful mood, upbeat, having seen people and distant family members that he wouldn't have seen otherwise.

Alan had already dealt with the issue of choosing a coffin when his father died. His father was a modest man who, despite being quite wealthy, couldn't bear show. A Jewish coffin resolved that choice: a plain pine box, with rope handles. Perfect. Alan wanted that for himself. He wanted cremation and for his ashes to be scattered near the sea at the same place as his father's. Importantly, he didn't want his ashes separated. His mother had divided his father's ashes; half into the church's Garden of Remembrance and half at the sea. He once told me, 'Oh darling, whatever you do, please don't separate me, it gives me the creeps.'

A few months before Alan's death, I said that when it happened I would pull up the drawbridge and be quietly home alone with him. But as it was happening I realized that isolating him from his friends and family was not what he most wanted. Once Alan took to his bed, I phoned ten friends and said to them, 'Please phone X, Y, and Z, and if you want to see him, please come this week.'

Seventy or eighty people came that last week. They came in droves. That was interesting! The WASPs arrived expecting to be served a drink and a snack. The Jews and Muslims were the only people who brought food. I became so conscious of cultural differences. I was going to the bloody home industry shop every 10 minutes to get another cake. In my southern Italian culture, when you go to visit a sick person, you go with a meal. Not generally a cake but a meal for the family to eat when you're gone.

'African culture too,' I interjected. 'At birth as well as ill health. I remember enjoying delicious food after giving birth in Mozambique. People would come to see the baby and they brought food, a ready-made meal. That's what you most need. Sometimes they didn't come in, especially in the first week, they just rang the bell and handed over their dishes.' Getti added:

I must tell you, a very funny thing happened. A Jewish friend came to the door and said, 'I'm not coming in but I've brought you this.' It was beautiful looking lasagna. I said, 'Thank you very much,' and went inside. I hadn't thought about supper. I said to my son, 'Turn the oven on and put the lasagna in. I'll make a salad.' When we sat down to eat and cut into the lasagna—it was a cheesecake!

Salad and cheesecake! But that was how it was: only our Jewish and Muslim friends brought food.

Getti was quiet for a while. Then, he took a deep breath and continued.

Nothing prepares you for the reality of death. It's such a strange thing. After I had washed Alan's body, our little dog got on top of his body as it grew cold. He just lay there trying to give heat to his owner. The undertakers came some hours later, as per my request. After his sister left, I had four to five hours to sit with him in our bedroom. It was peaceful.

'What made you able to wash Alan?' I asked Getti. 'It's one thing that many people tell me that they recoil from?'

We are all influenced by how we grow up. In my family, most people die at home, and my mother always washes them. There is no rushing. You die and then a doctor comes to complete a form that states the cause of death to give to the undertaker. It's a very, very nice space. Of course, you know the funeral parlor is going to do whatever they do, and that is out of your control. But I find the washing nice and gentle.

Of course, there's all the busyness of logistics that starts to happen, but we had planned and Alan's nephew helped. I didn't feel overwhelmed or worried or unsure. What had to be done and how Alan wanted it was all pre-prepared, like the death notice for the newspaper. It's useful to do these things in advance because when the time comes you can't think clearly, at least I couldn't. If you plan beforehand you don't need to think. I had my list of all our friends who needed to be informed set up on my computer, there was no need to gather contact details.

Everything proceeded as Alan had wished, his choice of coffin, the church, the minister's acknowledgment, the cremation. Months later, you were with me when we scattered Alan's ashes at the sea all in one place. The rituals were comforting, helping me and his family and friends towards acceptance and closure.

We sat quietly together basking in Getti's sense of accomplishment and gratitude.

'Anything you'd consider doing differently?' I probed, in a gentle voice.

Getti reached for his cigarettes and lit up. The irony of it all. Alan the super-fit athlete—gone. Getti the chain-smoker, the one who expected to die first, here conversing with me about his beloved Alan's death.

> Just a couple of dropped stitches. One thing we never considered was getting married and our not going through the formal ritual had consequences. One of my close friends, a judge who pioneered the recognition of gay marriage in South Africa, urged us to get married. Neither of us felt it was important. Our legal affairs were entwined with everything equally shared. Between us it was never an issue. But from the minute he was diagnosed until his cremation, it became a problem when dealing with medical insurance—and even the pharmacist.

'But you were his partner of 20 years—his common-law spouse!'

> Well, that proved not to carry enough weight. At one point the matron at the hospital told me, 'You can't sign. You've got to get one of his sisters to sign.' We had not thought about such things arising in a country where gay marriage is legal and constitutionally protected.
>
> Then there was the day of the funeral. The family was together outside the church greeting people as they arrived. Then my mother and I got ready to walk down the center aisle. The oddest thing happened as we were lining up. Alan's sisters, nieces, and nephews took precedence in the order of walking in. And when we got to the front of the church there were no seats for us. They had taken them all. Every single seat taken. Nobody vacated for us. I found that absolutely startling even in my semi-conscious state. As I stood there, I had that thought, well you know, you didn't get married.

I shared with Getti that I saw him looking along the row, telling him that what made it even more noticeable was when the minister said things to acknowledge him; everyone watched as the minister looked over the heads of the front row to make eye contact with Getti who'd found seats on the far end of the second row.

> But there was one more dropped stitch. Alan and I never discussed peoples' need for an after-funeral gathering. But at the church a lot of people asked me, 'So what time shall we come around to the house?'
>
> I realized to my horror that people were intent on coming. I found that very difficult. It was a very trying, very long evening of wonderful people who drank too much mostly and who just wouldn't go home. As you know a lot of Alan's friends are heavy drinkers and party goers. I'd bought a case of whiskey and there were only two bottles left. Eventually, after midnight, I asked a friend who's capable of throwing his weight around if he could just clear everybody out. It was mid-winter and I was freezing cold and exhausted. The place looked like a tip. I suppose it was important for others, and afterwards I was glad to have done it.

Getti's story got me thinking. I needed to revisit my wishes and specify that I want a gathering the evening before. I went to one such pre-funeral event—Christians call it a wake—although it was a Hindu colleague who'd died. The coffin had been placed in a small hall. People came and went informally throughout the evening. They sat quietly, thoughtfully, and every so often someone got up to speak—unplanned and unscripted.

The talking happened, the connectivity happened. People had a chance to share and say something without being on a speaker's list. The next day there was the service, a combination of African and Hindu rituals, the 'washing of hands' and then a meal, after which people dispersed. We had a 'washing of hands' ceremony for Joe. African tradition includes placing bowls of water containing aloes and when mourners arrive they literally wash their hands and then sit and eat and drink together. I grew up in a community of Irish Catholics and a gathering after the funeral is part of having a good send off.

We sat in quietness. I could sense a movie playing in Getti's head. He'd rewound the reel and was reviewing his story. When he eventually spoke, he said:

I do feel enormous gratitude for the experience that I had. There was anxiety during the period of illness before the diagnosis, then we had 323 days post-diagnosis that were quite different. We lived in that period in a way that was very alive and happy. We talked, we did things well, and the rituals helped. We dropped just a couple of stitches.

Respecting Ritual

On a Sunday in February 1995, four weeks after Joe's burial, Tessa, Kyla, and I visited his grave in Avalon Cemetery which lies on the southern edge of Soweto, some 45 minutes' drive from home.

It's a huge cemetery where up to that point only black people had been buried, with the exception of anti-apartheid activist Helen Joseph who, in 1992, two years after the release of Nelson Mandela, requested to be buried alongside her close friend, trade unionist Lilian Ngoyi.

I was not familiar with the roads through Soweto so Joe's former driver Sipho Sibeko* offered to help. I followed him carefully, memorizing the route for future visits.

We had gone to buy flowers the day before. Tessa chose white and yellow daises that would be resilient in the fierce February sunshine. Kyla's choice was classically shaped roses of a delicate porcelain hue. My offering was a mix of tuber roses, lilies, and eucalyptus leaves. We'd respectfully dressed in what we considered appropriate Sunday graveside attire, knee-length dresses and low-heeled shoes.

A metal surround, almost like a child's cot with slatted sides, had been placed over the spot where Joe's coffin had been lowered into the ground. I'd been told that Joe's African comrades who prepared the cavity had placed within it all the necessities for his afterlife: a reed sleeping mat, a digging stick and various seeds, although I can't remember Joe ever growing a single plant in the 19 years I knew him.

The grave was a mess. We realized straight away that we should have worn boots and brought gardening gloves. There were several thousand people at Joe's funeral. The metal surround was overflowing with the dozens of wreaths brought by mourners. Twenty-eight days after the burial, the flowers on the top were dry but underneath they were decomposing. The smells of rotting leaves broke through as soon as we disturbed the surface.

There were so many cards, so much red in the ribbon trimmings, even baubles. We took them off the dead wreaths and put them aside to add to our collection of Christmas decorations. Some artificial arrangements had weathered well; a large clear plastic dome covered with artificial flowers sent by factory workers. There was a red circle of cloth flowers inset with the emblematic yellow hammer and sickle from the South African Communist Party. A Jewish six-sided star arrangement made of green moss still looked lovely. I wondered who sent it. The ink had run and the writing was illegible.

Tessa, now 15, and Kyla, almost 11, helped me clear and sort. We filled several large black garbage bags with dead wreaths and bouquets of once beautiful flowers. We fastened the artificial arrangements on the sides of the metal surround. We hadn't brought a spade so I kicked the earth flat with my heeled shoes. Tessa and Kyla tied ribbons from the discarded wreaths and bouquets to the sides of the metal structure as their finishing touch.

We stood back and surveyed our work with satisfaction. It was good for us to have done this together. Joe's grave no longer looked like a bad compost heap. It looked gay, almost carnival like. With solemnity, we placed our three fresh flower arrangements in the middle space we'd left clear for them, and we stood together silently, each within our own thoughts.

We noticed a small dust twister on the other side of the cemetery. Time to go, the weather was about to change. We hurriedly piled everything into the trunk of the car. We were already seated and I was about to turn the key in the ignition when we noticed the dust twister had switched direction and was coming across the cemetery towards us. The twister danced, swirling and turning. We watched it pass over Joe's grave, roughly rearranging our very neatly positioned flowers.

Kyla cried out, 'It's Joe. It's Joe. He's on his way to heaven.'

The twister danced a little more and then fizzled out.

I envied Kyla and her uncomplicated delight. I'd lost those beliefs without any replacements. I let go of my Catholicism after my discomfort with the proselytizing I'd experienced at the mission school where I worked when I first went to Zambia. In university, it never seemed right to me that one religion claimed superiority over another. In *God is Not a Christian,* I appreciated Archbishop Tutu's writing so lucidly that religion, for most of us, is not a choice but an accident of birth.

It seemed appropriate for a Rabbi to say Kaddish at Joe's funeral. He was an atheist, but Jewish in culture through and through. He respected liberation theologians, the role played by many church leaders in South Africa's liberation struggle. On attending a gathering of political and religious thought leaders, he had once said:

> It is my contention that there is major convergence between the ethical content of Marxism and all that is best in the world's religions. But it must also be conceded that in the name of both Marxism and religion great damage has been done to the human condition. Both ideologies have produced martyrs in the cause of liberation and tyrants in the cause of oppression. Let us, socialists and believers, stop the debate about whether there is or not a paradise in heaven. Let us work together to build a paradise on earth. As for myself, if I eventually find a paradise in heaven, I will regard it as a bonus.

But I found myself grappling with the lessons I'd learned the hard way, my acknowledgment that ritual enables, ritual soothes, ritual supports. Joe had described his childhood experience of his mother's dying and the rituals that followed, the covering of mirrors, the sitting Shiva for seven days. I wondered what could I access that would assist me in my mourning.

A friend gave me the *Tibetan Book of Living and Dying.* I accepted this as synchronicity. I'd discovered that many cultures believe in a transition period between the drawing of the last breath and entering the afterlife, and that this interim time is taken very seriously. I gratefully followed the rituals prescribed for the 49 days following Joe's death. They offered me a framework. I found them comforting.

According to the book, the end of the fourth week is important for the spirit, especially at the precise time that death happened. I decided that at midnight on that 28th day I would do a vigil. I replenished the aromatherapy burner with lavender oil and re-read parts of the book. I meditated. It was peaceful. I felt good and strong and very close to Joe.

On day 50, however, I woke up feeling blue. I'd forgotten! I'd lost track of the days. I'd let Joe and myself down by not observing a vigil on the 49th day. I went to bed that night feeling desolate. I lit the oil burner and again chose lavender as the fragrance that soothes. I read until I could no longer keep my eyes open.

When I woke in the morning I recalled a fragment of the previous night's dream. It was Joe, in a car, ready to drive. I got in the car. I couldn't believe my luck. This was a real gift, a bonus.

'I never expected to meet you again.' I laughed joyously, and so did he.

'Are you real?' I asked. 'I mean, are you solid?' And I pressed against his shoulder. He was solid!

'We are all real in our dreams,' said Joe.

I told him how sorry I was that I'd missed doing the vigil on night 49. My Joe-in-spirit said generously, 'It's fine. Anyway, you saw me go. I went up with the dust twister.'

Meeting Joe in my dream took me time traveling back to 1989, shortly before the fall of the Berlin Wall. We'd been in Vilnius, Lithuania, visiting his birthplace in the nearby village of Obelai.

All around us Lithuanians were demonstrating against the USSR. We watched a candlelit vigil surrounding the Vilnius Cathedral, demanding it be re-opened to use again as a place of religious worship—something the communists did not tolerate.

During this trip, Joe was writing on the question: has socialism failed? He asked me what I thought of what he'd written. I ventured that his focus was on the material, on comparing the longevity of poverty under capitalism with the improvements achieved under socialism. While Joe had chronicled some errors of socialism, it also seemed to me that the denial of spirituality had been deeply alienating. My comments were a conversation stopper; there was no ensuing dialogue. I respected Joe's consistent focus on political rights and material well-being. But this focus was too narrow for me; I wanted spirituality and the support of ritual as part of my life and the society I live in.

Years later, I read a quote from Arnold Van Gennep's *The Rites of Passage*: 'One dimension of mental illness may arise because an increasing number of individuals are forced to accomplish their traditions alone with private symbols.'

Spirituality is important to many people who are not comfortable in a religious church setting. Many individuals cut ties with the religion they grew up with in their family of origin. Yet this respect for independent thinking can leave us more vulnerable; we no longer have the container once provided by a simple reliance on formal religion.

We may find ourselves consciously thinking about creating our own new supportive rituals, developing what the German philosopher Martin Heidegger called a 'mindfulness of being,' paying attention to ourselves as humans connecting with other humans, sharing this planet. But it's not easy. We're composite, complicated beings—physical, emotional, intellectual, and spiritual. And the latter is non-denominational, and even includes atheism.

Ritual is said to be a form of expression that enables focus, that marks and enables transition. My advocacy of ritual is not without reservations. Many people experience ritual as harmful; the removal of the clitoris of young girl children is a ritual that continues in some countries.

But ritual, at its best, can offer support, comfort, connectivity, inclusiveness, acceptance, and create beauty. My younger self and extended family once paid a high price for the lack of it. My older self is mindful, respectful, and still learning.

Postscript Five

Maryse is my colleague and friend with whom I teach Time To Think™ courses at Henley Business School in Johannesburg. Our clients are from the corporate world and the coursework is about creating the conditions we need to do our own best thinking as well as apply this to how to run business meetings efficiently and effectively.

I knew Maryse had officiated several ceremonies. I asked her what she considered as the essential components of designing a ritual. She answered fulsomely.

Clarity of purpose. This is the first and most essential component. What makes you want to mark this specific occasion with a ritual?

Element of visibility. Ritual, secondly, often includes the element of visibility of being seen. I knew from my work on bereavement that, for so many people, the public acknowledgement of their loss was important and public ritual provided this.

Making a declaration. The ritual may include the making of a declaration as its centerpiece. This is certainly true for marriage rituals. The speaking out loud of vows is a declaration of commitment and to do so in the presence of witnesses is what makes a huge difference emotionally and psychologically.

Participation. Fourthly, participation is often an important part of the design. It may be participation in an activity such as the lighting of candles, the sprinkling of soil at the burial or an object being passed around. Our rings being blessed by everyone in attendance at our wedding was the participation ritual that John and I chose for the occasion.

But Maryse noted active participation is not essential—the act of witness can be enough. She reminded me of the words of the cross-cultural spiritual teacher, anthropologist Angeles Arrien. Her most well-known book is *The Four-Fold Way: Walking the Paths of the Warrior,*

Teacher, Healer and Visionary. She teaches that when we witness, there is an impact; that we are changed by what we witness; watching the action unfold in front of our eyes leaves its impression.

Special clothing. Special clothing is often an important part of ritual, whether for the officiant or the participants. People choose to mark the day by choosing a dress code that symbolizes the special occasion. Clothing also denotes status which is psychologically enabling, hence the judge, the pastor, the bride all step into 'costume' that holds meaning in society.

Embodiment. Ritual often includes the physical. Stepping through a decorated archway may be used as symbolic of crossing a threshold to a new life. Singing, chanting, dancing, swaying, lifting someone in the air!

A love bath? Oh, yes, I had one of those on the eve of my marriage to John, when 30 of my women family and friends wrapped themselves around me in a tight spiral. I felt truly bathed in their warmth, love, and blessings.

Simplicity. Finally, 'Keep the design of ritual simple,' Maryse said. 'As I get older, I understand more about what works best and that's simplicity. Keep it simple.'

After reading all the ritual stories again, I decided to add two more components.

Specificity. Be as specific as you can about you wishes, especially if you are diverging from the conventions of your family religion.

Conversations. Have inclusive conversations thus pre-empting surprises, especially when your choices deviate from the cultural norms in your family.

PART SIX

Bereavement

What emotion do we most associate with bereavement? Grief ... it is the easiest for society to deal with. The feelings that are much more difficult to deal with are the more private ones – like guilt, feelings of going mad, vivid nightmares, shock and the socially unacceptable ones – like hatred, anger, joy, hallucinating. The multitude of weird and peculiar feelings is not only oppressive for those who experience them first-hand, but also frightening for those who witness their friends experiencing them. It's quite natural to find that most people are far less uncomfortable with the idea that their friends are feeling suicidal after the death of someone close – a ghastly but understandable reaction – than they are in the grips of wild dreams ... that they spy their loved ones around every corner, that they smell strange smells or feel they are emotional zombies.

—Virginia Ironsides, *You'll Get Over It: The Rage of Bereavement*

Only people who are capable of loving strongly can also suffer great sorrow; but this same necessity of loving serves to counteract their grief and heal them.

—Leo Tolstoy, *Childhood, Boyhood, Youth*

No Stages

At Joe's funeral, in a soccer stadium surrounded by 80,000 people, I tried to appear calm and dignified. Jackie Kennedy was my role model. As a child I'd watched on TV the funeral of her assassinated husband, President John F Kennedy. She presented the image of grief contained.

The psychoanalyst Darrian Leader, writing on how the disappearance of public ritual and mourning is making bereavement a more difficult experience in our modernizing world, wrote, 'Jackie's calmness became emblematic of a grief that was internalized and not displayed. Although some saw this as a model of courage and fortitude, others shared the view of one commentator that it "set mourning back a hundred years."'

But once I was out of the limelight of that public day there were no constraints. There was nothing remarkable, nothing magical, in my experience of bereavement after Joe died. My diary, written in the months that followed his death, reads like a repetitive, monotonous recital of misery. The entries had a pattern. Statement of emotion: 'I am so miserable' followed by a description of the triggering incident, followed by the description of tears. I was so miserable, more miserable than I thought humanly possible to bear.

I don't think of it as having been a personal growth experience. One of my least favorite adages is, 'What doesn't kill you makes you stronger.' But it's true that I also took time to reflect and acknowledge my deep gratitude for the love we'd shared. Later in that first year, my earlier 'I am so miserable' diary entries were complemented with others which were in complete contrast.

I decided to write up cherished memories: the first concert, walking Scotland's Crieff nature trail, buying wedding rings in Moscow's Arbat in the old USSR, a sunlit balcony in Maputo. This impulse was in part driven by the fear of forgetting. But it proved to be a double-edged activity. You are recording your times of happiness in the past whilst living in the now with the knowledge that you are *never* going to experience this joy, this intimacy, with this person again—and possibly never in life again, at least not in the same way that's unique to this relationship.

The poet Elizabeth Alexander describes this experience tenderly and poignantly in her 2015 memoir, *The Light of the World*. Life was flourishing for Elizabeth, her artist husband, and their teenage boys; Elizabeth's career as a poet, essayist, and playwright had blossomed. At the presidential inauguration of Barack Obama in 2009, she recited the poem she composed for the occasion, 'Praise Song for the Day.'

Three years later, four days after his 50th birthday party in April 2012, Elizabeth returned home after attending a poetry reading of the Kabbalah and called out to greet her husband. Her son found him in the basement, slumped alongside the treadmill which was still running, a gash on his head. He was dead.

Of the many personal grief memoirs in my library, it was reading Elizabeth's chronicle of the pain of her loss and a joyous meditation on the love she shared, that most took me back to my first year of widowhood 20 years ago. It was a bittersweet immersion into personal history. She wrote:

> My bed, the bedroom, the house, was suffused with sorrow. Sorrow like vapor, sorrow like smoke, sorrow like quicksand, sorrow like an ocean, sorrow louder and fuller than the church songs, sorrow everywhere with nowhere to go.

One of the last films Joe and I watched together was *Three Colors: Blue* by the Polish director Krzysztof Kieślowski. The film starts with a family laughing, and in the next second their car crashes. When the woman, played by Juliette Binoche, comes out of her coma the TV is on in the hospital ward and she looks up at the screen and finds herself watching the funeral of her only child and her husband, a nationally acclaimed composer. The film storied her grief and journey of forgiveness and conciliation (she discovered her husband had a mistress, pregnant with his child) as she stumbled to find a way forward to live a new and different life.

Later that evening, at home over a whiskey, Joe said, 'You will be alright. Eventually.' I guess he knew that viscerally; he had found his way to joyous living after Ruth's terrible and unexpected assassination. Earlier that year, we'd celebrated my 40th birthday. He sat pensively, and after another sip of whiskey, added, 'I'm glad I'm dying while you are still young enough; you'll have a chance to build another life.'

Two weeks after Joe's funeral I went to Cape Town to pack up our things in the ministerial house at Groote Schuur, the parliamentary estate. According to government rules I had one calendar month to vacate the house. Tessa and Kyla were already back at school in Johannesburg but joined me for the weekend. On the Friday afternoon, I drove to the airport to pick them up. I cried myself to sleep again that night. The airport arrivals hall triggered another visit to the space of 'never again' which offers no comfort. The space of never again, a tear-jerking, unbearable place of heart-wrenching thoughts. Joe will never ever meet me off the plane again. I will never again be enveloped in his warm embrace. I'll never again listen to a warm loving message on the answering machine. 'Hello my darling, I just called to say I love you.'

On the 23rd day after Joe's death, we arrived back home again in Johannesburg. Now we needed to try to find our way to the new normal. It would be our very first supper, home alone, since Joe's death. All the days up to that point had been an interlude. The tougher part was about to begin; living an everyday life without him. I laid the table. I started to cry. I was disarmed as I laid only three placemats instead of four. Joe was not working late. He was never coming home to join us for supper, ever again.

This was our own house, not the rental accommodation and constant moving of the last 15 years in Maputo and Lusaka. This beautiful house, graciously set on a slope surrounded by jacaranda trees. Our home of joy became the place of my sorrow.

I cleared the bathroom cupboard and top drawer of Joe's medication. It was startling to line up what had been prescribed in the last year: anti-gout, anti-nausea, an incredible array of pills. The cancer caused pain, the anti-inflammatory pain killers caused constipation, the constipation needed suppositories. I noticed the phial of Arsenicum Album, the homeopathic remedy prescribed for Joe's restlessness in his last days. The homeopath's response to my asking what she'd thought about his restlessness: 'Too much focus on living, not enough preparation for dying.' I sorted and discarded. It felt as though I was discarding him, a part of our lives together for the last four years. But I knew I needed to take care not to live in a trapped-in-time museum of a once shared life, now over.

I kept a diary in those first weeks:

Another devastating heart-sore morning. My heart aches. The alarm clock rings. There's no Joe to go wake the kids; a once established rhythm now broken. The 'used-to-be' replays in my mind: Alarm rings. Joe moves. He wakes Tessa, and is keen to wake Kyla. She's a snuggler and creeps into our bed to be in the middle of a sandwich hug. Time up. Joe off to the kitchen, makes me a cup of tea, brings it to me in bed, runs the bath whilst shaving, and calls me to tell me the bath is ready. Then he'd do the morning school drive whenever he could. 'You were spoiled, Mama,' said Tessa.

The time after supper proved to be the hardest part of the day. Tessa and Kyla were lovely. They gave supportive warm hugs often, but they would go back to whatever they were busy with—homework, TV, whatever. This was the time that Joe and I would most often have an after-dinner whiskey. This was our talking time when Joe was alive. I missed him. I sat alone, I cried again, as quietly as possible.

Saturday nights were the most challenging. They were the confirmation of singleness and the absence of adult conversation. And yet, I turned down invitations. Being lonely seemed easier than being sociable.

I cleared the medicines. I started on the clothes. I wanted to keep too much. I held the clothes to my nose as I handled them, hoping to be able to still smell my beloved. I recalled associated memories which I jotted down before putting the item aside to be disposed of. I got a yearning to see my favorite tie again—the one I'd sent to the undertakers for Joe to be buried in. Now I wished I'd kept it.

People gave me books to read on bereavement, including Elisabeth Kübler-Ross's *On Death and Dying*, and her five stages of grief. I didn't experience those stages she set out: denial, anger, bargaining, depression, and acceptance. I kept waiting for anger but it never arrived. And I couldn't fathom out if or how denialism was expressing itself. Only two out of five: I experienced only depression and acceptance. Already upset, now I found myself even more upset because I thought I wasn't normal, that there was something wrong with me.

I cried quite a lot when Tessa and Kyla were at school. I was not fine. I felt mostly terrible. The dull ache, the backwash of absence persisted, interspersed with flash photographs of memory. I missed companionship. I missed our loving. I missed the political conversations. There seemed to be no easing to the pain. My diary was where I could put aside my public face. Over and over, day after day, the basic gist of my journal entries was: 'I miss you. I miss you, oh how much I miss you. How absolutely awful it is to be living at home knowing you'll never be here again.'

I contemplated suicide. That would cauterize this pain, quickly, once and for all. My contemplation didn't go far. I chose to have children. Surely, I should stay in this world to be a parent for them? But what kind of parent was I at this moment?

Kyla, almost 11, told me, 'Mama, you said that once Joe had died, you'd have more time for us. And it's true, you have more time. But you're not here with us—you're in your head somewhere.'

She was right.

I didn't know this version of myself. I was adrift; I'd lost my centeredness. And I was so tired—exhausted. My doctor gave me a sick note for one month's leave from work, and then a second month and then a third. A few months earlier I'd been appointed associate professor at the University of the Witwatersrand's School of Governance. I was overwhelmed by the thought of preparing lectures and delivering them in lecture halls filled with large numbers of students. I craved quietness. I still couldn't identify any patterns in my grief. There were just waves of misery that came crashing in and regularly took my feet out from under me. I was self-absorbed for many months, spinning in my vortex of grief. Friends enquired with genuine care and concern, 'How are you?' It was a long time before I was engaged enough to reciprocate, 'And how are you?'

I held onto the Sufi aphorism, 'This too shall pass.' My faith in those words was my comfort and my crutch. If I could just get up day after day and get through the logistics of living and try somehow to be a good enough parent, I trusted that the pain would eventually begin to ease and that somehow, slowly, over time, I would indeed build a new life.

I don't know how long I might have stayed spinning in this cycle of immobilizing sorrow if I hadn't been offered a new job. I was asked to become the advisor to Mandela's newly appointed Minister of Land Affairs Derek Hanekom. He wanted me to be his troubleshooter, apply my mind and engage in discussion to resolve particular issues. For instance, decades before, the apartheid state had dispossessed African landowners from good land near Humansdorp in the Eastern Cape, and removed them to Keiskammahoek in what was known as the Ciskei. In the first year of democracy, the white dairy farmers had been bought out so that those once dispossessed could return. But they had not returned. There were unresolved issues, some of which involved burial grounds. My job was to research the issues and, as an emissary of the minister, consult with all parties concerned and come up with a recommendation for a way forward. Meaningful work, gathering and collation of facts, interspersed with meetings that my creativity called for—it was a blessing. It was also a balm, a job that contributed to healing a land, which also healed my heart, creating fissures in my grief, thin openings through which the light of joy filtered, slowly, back into my life.

The year progressed and I marked the passage of time through birthdays, public holidays and religious festivals. It simply became easier to sit with, recall and let myself be with the 'grief bursts,' so I've heard them called, the explosion of memory into sadness which would mostly end in a flood of tears. I began to believe more confidently that 'this too shall pass.' My ability to recompose myself after tears, my recalibrating, happened more quickly. The grief bursts became less intense and fizzled out fast like small fireworks.

The year after Joe's death, Tessa and Kyla were to spend Christmas and New Year with my first husband, Ed. I still felt somewhat fragile, I feared if I stayed home I'd dip too deeply into memories and sink into melancholy. I took up an invitation to join good friends on a trip to India, a place I'd never been to with Joe—a chance for new memory making.

Thinking back on that holiday has always brought a huge smile to my face. My former colleagues from Maputo days, Marc and Maureen, had been teaching at the Centre for Development Studies in Trivandrum, Kerala. Four of us joined them: myself, Marc's wife Anna, their 19-year-old daughter Ilundi and Maureen's partner Mandy.

I loved Trivandrum, its energy, the flow of people, cars and animals in the town center. I found an entire shop full of books on homeopathy, Ayurvedic medicine, and alternative healing, which I'd become interested in during Joe's illness. I felt excited by the different culture, food, and belief system. Ilundi's lovely energy made it easy to share a room with her, and Anna and I discovered our stamina for shopping and bargaining. We trawled the beach jewelry shops together, bought paper lanterns and pashminas. On New Year's Eve, the hotel organized a huge party. Marc and I were asked to sit on the panel of judges to select who were the best dancers. It was hilarious!

I had wanted to be alone on the night of the first anniversary of Joe's passing. I ended up alone while surrounded by hundreds of people. I sat at Madras airport in a crowded terminal. The logistics of my journey home, Kerala–Madras–Kuala Lumpur–Johannesburg meant I had six hours, from 11pm to 5am, to wait between planes.

I began the recall of Joe's last 24 hours, Mandela's visit and our own final conscious touching. I went over the whole last five months of accepting our parting which culminated in our last wordless embrace. In the end wordlessness seemed best. I didn't want to utter the word goodbye. I didn't want to say again, 'I love you.' I didn't want to create any pull-back into this world.

That last evening, I had precious private moments of lying close to Joe, shaping myself for the last time into that jigsaw puzzle fit of contours as he lay on his side in those final hours. I touched, oh so gently, those body curves which had now changed so drastically, this body, such pleasure, for so many years, so many more years than expected. As I lay I tried with all my spirit to imbue his spirit with my feelings of wishing him well on his way.

My tears began to slide silently down my face in this hot Madras airport where the sound of CNN competed with the whirr of the mounted rotating fans. People positioned themselves to catch the waft of moving air, others wiped their faces with dampened cloths. I felt safe that my quiet tears went unnoticed. I had an amazing sense of privacy and anonymity in this crowd.

I took out my journal and spent the time writing. Totally immersed in pouring out my heart onto paper, I captured my reflections of the years that Joe and I had spent together. I regularly looked at my watch and calculated back to the time in Johannesburg, I was counting down the hours towards the time of Joe's last breaths. At 3am, the hour of his death, I took off my wedding ring as a symbolic gesture. I shivered. My finger felt naked, strangely cold, with a band of skin more pale than the rest. But I felt ready to acknowledge, that what was, was, and what would be, would be. I felt at peace, with deep gratitude for what I'd had, and optimism for my life ahead.

Not that it was easy. I walked, then stumbled, walked again, then fell and got up again, like a toddler learning to walk.

A few months later I tentatively ventured into a new relationship. I still lived in the house that Joe and I bought together. Brendan* sat in Joe's chair. I looked at him and thought, he's sitting in Joe's chair. It wasn't cerebral. It was a gut reaction. Later I reasoned with myself, thinking, I can't get stuck here. I'm 42, I need to move forward. I can't be living in a house and looking at a man and thinking, 'You're sitting in Joe's chair.' I moved house—a radical expense-incurring solution.

So, it's true this too did pass, but not without the occasional reappearance. My life with Joe and his dying shaped who I became. Even now, 21 years later, there are moments of grief bursts. It feels okay to just be with the sadness now and again. It's no longer the prevailing, all-consuming mood. It has a place, and it knows its place. Meanwhile joy, which once pushed its way tentatively through the cracks in my grief, has firmly jostled its way into the forefront of my life.

Agira: A Matter of Acknowledgment

Agira* hailed from Nairobi but worked for a global non-profit in Washington DC. We found ourselves sitting next to each other for dinner on a Wednesday at Bellagio's Villa Serbelloni, on the one evening of the week when residents dined with guests from the nearby conference center. Whoever sat next to you was a matter of chance.

Agira asked what I was writing about during my residency. I briefly described my project and she immediately got into a flow, telling me she was finding some things about living in the United States really challenging—one of them being the apparent national awkwardness when talking about death.

The topic was raw. When her mother had been visiting her just a few months ago, they got a call from Nairobi with the unexpected, unwelcome news that her father had suffered a heart attack and died. Agira took leave and she and her mother flew home to take part in the rituals, the funeral, and the memorial.

Everyone at work knew her father had died. There were so many meetings at which her absence was noted and the reason why was mentioned. When she returned to work a full two weeks later, she would come home from work day after day wondering if she lived in a parallel universe of norms and customs. She found it incredible that nobody spoke to her about the fact that her father had passed. Not a single person said, 'Sorry for your loss.'

'This was *so* unlike being at home in Nairobi, where everyone descends on your home, family, friends, and colleagues—and for months after, when you meet someone face-to-face that you know has had a loss, before you start with your professional discussion or whatever, you say the words that acknowledge the person's loss. It's customary. It's not awkward. It's comfortable. It's respectful,' Agira said.

Her first response was to feel deeply hurt and to second-guess the good standing of her relationships. Who were these colleagues? There was even a couple who she'd begun to think of as friends prior to her father dying. It took some deep breathing and reflection not to blame them, not to feel angry with them, but to accept that she was experiencing a peculiar aspect of American culture—discomfort and denial around death.

A few weeks later a colleague's mother died. Agira had worked side-by-side with Charlotte* for 18 months. Agira asked for the details of the funeral and the venue and the following Saturday she drove two and a half hours to the small town where the service was taking place. Charlotte was astounded. A colleague of hers, giving up a Saturday and doing a round-trip drive of five hours to attend the funeral of someone she'd never met?

'This is what we do at home,' Agira told her. 'We honor you and your loss. It doesn't matter that I never met your mother. It's about being there for you, my colleague, my friend.'

At the end of the evening, Agira and I exchanged contact details.

I asked if I could include her story, which would underscore the importance of acknowledgment. 'Sure, please do,' she said. 'Just don't use my real name or my organization. I don't want to hurt anyone. It's just the way I've found things to be in America.'

I've discovered that in South Africa, in our multi-cultural, multi-racial work places, we are sometimes confused too. It seems we don't talk enough about each other's cultures and because of that we don't always know enough to be respectful of them. It's customary among some black Africans to gather money from friends, colleagues, and relatives towards the funeral proceedings. When my husband Joe died, indeed his African colleagues gave me an envelope with the money they'd collected towards expenses. I worked in an institution where, when a black person's parent died, there was an email sent out advising you and an invitation to donate towards the funeral. I never saw that happening with other races. Like Agira, I noticed that black Africans were the most comfortable in expressing public acknowledgment when there was a death in someone's family.

Darian Leader, the British psychoanalyst, posits in *The New Black* that healthy mourning 'requires other people.' He makes the distinction that 'grief is our reaction to loss, but mourning is how we process this grief.'

It used to be that private grief and public mourning were entwined—a common experience wherever you were in the world, whatever religion you were born into. Every culture had a way of publicly acknowledging the death of a member of the community, whether it was the curtains drawn (the United Kingdom); a sash on the door (Italy); the wearing of a black armband (Mozambique); the wake (Ireland); or the wearing of white in China and India, or light blue in Syria.

Leader refers to anthropologists who hypothesize that the decline of public mourning rituals in the West was linked to the mass slaughter during World War I. 'The surplus of the dead—and bereaved—was far more extreme and concentrated than in earlier warfare and so profound changes were forced on society,' he writes. Leader opines that, the 'erosion of public mourning rituals' continues today. 'Mourning and burial rituals that have been practiced for hundreds of years are now being abandoned or abridged.'

More personal suffering would seem to be the outcome of this loss of ritual in which acknowledgment was a part. 'A loss, after all, always requires some kind of recognition, some sense that it has been witnessed and made real,' Leader writes. That, he argues, is what commemorations are about. For relationships that had no public life, the mourning process proves more challenging for the bereaved.

There was the man who told his family he was getting engaged, but his fiancée was killed tragically before they ever met her. As Leader wrote, 'We need other people to share our feelings, to make sure that we have really lived them.'

I sat with Leader's opinions, mulling over them. Is mourning more difficult today because of this erosion of social mourning rites? Let's take 'yes' as the answer, and know that the reclaiming of the practice of public acknowledgment is one of the steps needed for a healthier engagement with death with the societies we live in. Whatever our race, religion, or culture, this is a question of sharing a common humanity, which begs for a practice of acknowledgment.

How exactly will we unlearn our awkwardness, our hesitancy, and confidently know what exactly is appropriate to say to someone when you know they've suffered a loss? A friend of mine, whose wife had just died, confided, 'If one more person comes up to me and says "she's in a better place" I shall explode!' An afterlife does not fit his belief system. He was so irritated by their choice of words.

I went to visit my friend Amelia* in Miami who is a member of the International Women's Forum, and she introduced me to another member, Joann Lederman, a clinical psychologist who hosts a support group for bereaved women. Joann knows Letty Pogrebin, author of *How to Be a Friend to a Friend Who's Sick*, and Letty's writing prompted her to ask the women in her group what were the sentences they found most annoying, insulting or flat-out useless no matter how well intentioned:

- Everything happens for a reason.
- You need to be strong for your kids.
- We're all in the same boat.
- Maybe it happened for the best.
- You're so brave.
- Chin up.
- God works in mysterious ways.

'What can I do to help you?' wasn't well-received either.

'That's such a well-meaning statement and it's not cruel at all,' said Joann. 'But the bereaved person is often in such a state of confusion. My suggestion would be that instead of asking what to do, just do something. Drive the two hours to help with the paperwork. Bake some cookies. Organize a gathering of friends. Get me dressed!"

Amelia chimed in, 'People don't often mean it when they ask, what can I do?'

She was speaking from experience. When she was 53, having been one of the first women partners at a prestigious New York law firm, Amelia was working her last couple of days before starting her early retirement. She and her husband had lived modestly compared to their peers to be able to afford this. The first part of their retirement plan was to sail around the world. She was closing their apartment in New York when she got the bad news. Her husband was sailing with crew and supplies to the dockyard where she would join them when they hit rough weather. The crew told her they heard a thud. Did he slip and hit his head? Did he have a heart attack? He was washed overboard; they saw his body being tossed about in the waves—but could do nothing.

When people ask, 'What can I do to help?' it's often not meant. And it is understood to be not meant. That is the big difference with saying, 'What can I do?' and actually doing it. The people most likely to say what can I do, are not going to do anything.

The problem, at least for me, was that people didn't know what to say. Maybe this is an American thing. Suddenly there was this wall created between me and everyone I knew. They didn't invite me to the dinner parties I had always been invited to and all kinds of other things. I was philosophical about what happened and wanted to shape a new life. They expected me to be sad and were perplexed when I wasn't. I think in a way that was why I moved to Florida. I walked away from my New York life—it was too difficult. It was much easier for me to restart with people with whom I didn't share that background of life as a couple, our history and the burden of that.

Amelia wondered how much impact people more easily having conversations about death and with bereaved people would make in changing culture. How might her life have been different if people had been more comfortable talking with her, socializing with her, when her husband died? She might never have felt the need to make a new start in an entirely different city. It's possible we wouldn't be sitting, having this conversation, on the banks of the Miami River in Florida.

Elysa: The Dinner Service

Virginia Ironside's book, *You'll Get Over It*, tells of a woman she knows who discovered that her mother's employee had been given a necklace she coveted. Her aunt had made this gift after her mother's death as a thank you to the employee.

The daughter believed her mother meant for her to have it. It was as though her mother and the love lost with her death were embodied in that one necklace. The daughter says of the necklace and her actions, 'It wasn't especially valuable, though the stones were real, but I just couldn't let the thought of it go. This cleaner deserved it as she had been loyal to my mom over the years.' But she found herself, 'tormented with want, eaten up with resentment … feeling that if I didn't have it I'd die.'

The daughter spoke with her aunt who refused to intercede to ask for it back. But her son advised her to make a request directly with the understanding that it might be refused. She followed his advice:

I got a virtually identical necklace, rather more expensive actually, and sent it … explaining the situation. She sent me back the original necklace at once, with a lovely letter saying she completely understood. I can't tell you what it meant to me, getting that necklace back. I could sleep properly at last.

'The truth is that after a death, things are no longer mere trinkets,' wrote Ironside.

Pieces of furniture are not bits of wood; money is not cash; houses are not bricks and mortar. The loved one has gone, so the possessions take on this mysterious meaning, as if they are the last link with the dead people, often becoming imbued with their very lost selves, talismans of their souls. There is a particular saucer, for instance, that 'is' my mother. Whenever I look at it, she's there. If someone else were to take it, I would be furious, and fight for it. To outsiders it would seem as if I were squabbling over a piece of cracked china; I would actually be fighting for a dear part of her.

Ironside's insight was at the back of my mind as I listened to Elysa telling me the story about her mother's dishes. Elysa is the Director of Environmental Stewardship at Clif Bar, the US maker of all-natural energy and nutrition foods. She's also an honorary research associate at the New York Botanical Gardens and holds a master's degree in forest science from Yale University. As a member of the Greenhouse Network, she regularly tweets on global warming. When I met her she was on sabbatical in Bellagio, accompanying her husband Chuck who was finishing a book on sustainable harvesting in forests.

She and I took a day off to go to the World Food Expo in Milan and we had lots of time to talk. Elysa's mom had died a couple of decades ago but there was something that puzzled her. Why did she get so obsessed about needing to have her mother's dishes? Dishes that she didn't even like very much.

She told me that some of her earliest childhood memories were about being concerned because her mother seemed very distant. She has an abiding memory of asking, even before she started kindergarten, 'Mom, is everything okay?' Elysa grew up always feeling a little worried about her mother and her distance which in turn created more distance between them. When she was 14 her mother became ill and stopped teaching. Only later did Elysa learn that the 'illness' was a nervous breakdown. She couldn't understand what was happening—people around her said, 'All women go through change of life, this often happens.'

As an adult Elysa continued to worry about her mother, but she 'always felt there was a barrier I couldn't break through. It was with me my whole life—with me always wishing that I could be closer to my mother.'

She was already married in her mid-30s and had given birth to the first of her two boys when her brother phoned to tell her that they had a half-sister, Debbie, who they didn't know about. Debbie had hired a detective to find out who she was and where she came from. She'd been adopted in Santa Barbara, California, by loving parents, but all her life she'd wanted to know more about her birth story and meet her birth mother.

Elysa's mother had gone to college in Idaho and, while working in a rural town, she got pregnant. They believe the father might have been the gym coach. Her mother felt she could never go back home to her own very strict, religious mother in this situation. So, she went to California with her best friend, also a teacher, had the child and gave it up for adoption.

Two years later she married Elysa's father. It was Elysa's dad that Debbie first called and he confirmed to Elysa that her mom had shared the adoption story with him.

Elysa's father invited Debbie to come and meet her mother, warning her that she'd had something like a stroke, was in a wheelchair and could not speak very clearly. 'I think it was sad for her to meet my mom but not to be able to have this mother–daughter conversation that she always wanted. But in a way, I didn't get to have that conversation either.'

The next time she visited her parents, Elysa asked her mother, 'Did you think about her a lot?'

Because of the stroke, her mother struggled with her speech. But on this occasion she enunciated very clearly.

'Yes, I thought about it all my life.'

Elysa says her mother's response was like a shaft of insight for her.

Wow, this is the why. There's been a terrible secret here. And it's been painful. Now I know she thought about it all her life. I used to see her looking off into the distance and I would wonder—that's probably where she was. I was about 34 at the time when I felt I started to understand my mother a little more. She'd grieved her whole life about this loss; it was something she felt she couldn't tell anybody about.

Years later Elysa's father died and they found a frail care home for her mom. Her brothers cleaned out the family home. Elysa wasn't there; she missed this process of sorting stuff.

Chuck and Elysa spent five years in Indonesia and that's where they were when her mom died.

I remember getting the news so clearly because Chuck had broken his ankle very badly and was on crutches. I got this call that my mother died and I collapsed. I fell into him, but he couldn't help me because of the crutches.

And then, I don't know when it was, I started to think about my mom's dishes. There was this set of china that had a pattern we would use every special holiday. I was always a little disappointed in that pattern because it was a brownish color, drab, not fancy colored flowers that a child would love. It was a pattern of a stalk of wheat, which you'd think I would like. When I think about it, the pattern was very much like my mother.

I remembered just becoming obsessed with this desire to have my mother's china. I'm not a sentimental person, so my feelings about the dishes felt strange and not my normal self. I would wake up in the middle of the night and just think about those dishes with that wheat stalk pattern. My brothers told me everything was gone—there were no dishes. I was so mad at myself that I hadn't spoken up when they were sorting stuff. That obsessing went on for two whole years—I'd wake up thinking about those dishes.

A few months after I was back in the United States after years of being away, my brother and I were talking on the phone, and he told me, 'I've got a box of Mom's stuff. I packed up the crockery.'

'I want that,' I blurted out. 'I so want those dishes.'

Here it was, the holy grail. When he brought me the box, I opened it up and was, like, 'Oh.' It was disappointing, and I felt not just disappointment but also surprised at myself. Why was I so desperate to have *this* china? Now that I see it, I don't need it. And I felt a kind of shame about it. I just shut the box. I didn't take it out and look at the coffee cups or anything. I shut it and I haven't really looked at it ever again. But it did feel like closure. Do I still have it in the attic? To be honest, I don't even remember. It's probably still there in its box.

Until we started having this conversation I hadn't considered that my obsession with the material objects was possibly really about the relationship, the pain that was there for me about not being close to my mother. There's something there in my wanting those dishes so badly. Although maybe even someone who had a close relationship with their parent would also obsess about some material object.

I shared with Elysa the story about the woman with the necklace in Virgina Ironside's book and how when my father died my one brother got his tools and my other brother got his ring and how I kept thinking, okay I'm the girl around here, what do I get?

I wanted something that was his, that was part of his everyday life and could then be part of mine. I like how an object can just stop and make you think appreciatively about somebody. I took a measuring tape, one which has both centimeters and inches. I keep it in my bedside drawer; it's not just any tape measure—it was my dad's. And I have a screwdriver of his, one of those old ones with well-worn natural wood handles. When you use it, and your hands touch the smooth wood, you sense there's another generation in your family that used this. It's a funny kind of heirloom, priceless, but with almost no monetary value.

I think grief often creates a temporary imbalance and we are not kind enough to ourselves and each other about the madness that sometimes happens with it. And sometimes it plays itself out in its attachment to things. Afterwards, the pain of loss ebbs and you kind of think, 'I really wasn't myself at that time!'

Novella, my Italian friend, told that me candidly that she was in a terrible state after her mother died. She said, 'I wanted everything. I wanted all of it. I didn't want my siblings to have anything. I told them I'm the oldest child. It matters more to me than to anybody else.' She said it was two years before they could start to have a reasonable discussion.

Elysa sat back thoughtfully.

Well, I've always told my story of obsessing over the dishes, humorously, against myself, thinking about our attachment to material things. But after this conversation I feel differently. Understanding the link between grief and how it can get connected with something that belonged to that person—it's like, oh, there's nothing to be ashamed of with that story because there is a connection made between objects and grief. I'm thinking, I now have a different and deeper perspective. My understanding of my own story has changed, so how will I tell it the next time?

Getti: Three Losses

Getti's partner Alan died in May, just two months after they'd marked their 20th anniversary of a shared life. They'd intended to have a celebratory Sunday afternoon garden party at a Johannesburg country club. They prepared their guest list but it didn't happen. Alan was already too sick.

They'd expected to retire to a house in a small rural town set within a few acres of olive groves a couple of hours' drive from Cape Town. They'd had their first virgin olive oil pressed from their own trees the year before Alan died. The property included an enormous garage. Three pristine decades-old cars sat with their gleaming paintwork kept under wraps. The cars got an airing on weekends and during their end-of-year holiday. In their dotage Alan and Getti expected to breeze around the country roads and take a spin to the Atlantic Ocean some 20 miles away—an imagined life no longer possible.

'I started going to bereavement counseling before Alan died, and for more than two years after his death,' Getti told me. 'I wanted the support to help me through Alan's dying and my grief.'

I asked about his choice for counseling during Alan's illness; it's unusual to start so early. He told me he knew very soon that he wanted support through Alan's dying. One of the issues he faced almost immediately was a change in their respective roles.

I think typically when somebody gets sick, in a couple, roles have to change. The truth was, if you looked at us in a gendered way, I was more the wife than the husband. I looked after the house, the domestic workers, and the food and shopping. Alan took charge of our finances and paying the bills. When he became ill, he either couldn't or wasn't interested, and just simply didn't do it without telling me he'd stopped.

You know the electricity got cut off one morning. I got the fright of my life. A guy came and disconnected it. Alan just laughed and said, 'Oh well, you'd better go down and pay it, hadn't you?' I didn't go to work that day; I sat for hours trying to get reconnected.

All sorts of things changed. He always drove if we were together but with his brain tumor he couldn't drive anymore. He always made the arrangements if we were traveling and he couldn't do that anymore either. I was conscious of these changes. I was challenged by them, not distressed, but quite startled by how much there was to do, and that I had to do it all and I had to do it right. His state of dying meant he became unaware of my feelings or how tired I was. I think that's part of dying, that you are involved with this process you are going through that's profound. There isn't a lot of space to think about other things and other people.'

I asked Getti if there had been surprises for him in his grieving. 'Look, for the first year I actually had a lot of difficulty accepting the reality he had died. To this day, nearly two and a half years later, I still find myself saying, "God, I just can't believe he's dead."'

The one truth, for all the people I spoke with, is that grief is different for everyone. I told Getti of Professor George Bonnano, who's researched grief over 30 years and who's written a line of argument that our only commonality is that we are hardwired to recover: our ancestors couldn't sit around too long moping—they needed to hunt and be on the alert for danger.

Getti agreed.

Friends of ours, the wife died and within four months the guy was married again, and at the age of 60 he was having a new baby; he married a woman of 32. I'm not there. At present, I have no interest in another person, which is not to say I shan't have any interest forever.

What was useful for me was to accept that it's not all Elisabeth Kübler-Ross—neat, with all those different stages and emotions that she set out. To my great surprise, I haven't had any anger. And I haven't had any denial, although I suppose unconsciously I have it; I still grapple with the fact that Alan is dead.

I shared with Getti what Zimbabwean editor Irene Staunton wrote to me in an email about losing yourself as you were in the eyes of the other: 'It seems to me that when someone you love dies, you have not only lost the person and the relationship, but the self that was reflected back to you through them; and that if the person was much beloved, it was their presence that gave yourself a unique dynamism; so one also loses a self.'

Absolutely. You also lose that intimate language that you have with somebody, where just one word conveys eons. So there is a loss of a certain kind of intimacy. I mean, there is also a loss of touch. I go and have a massage at the Chinese place every month or so. There's loss of sex, but that you lose long before the person is dead because dying people don't have a lot of sex. For me there is a huge reluctance to go into those spaces. I don't feel that I'm ready for it. I don't have the urge for it. And I don't know how that will play out, but for the moment it just doesn't feel like something I want.

It's the happy things that make me miss him most, like when I went to his uncle's 86th birthday. He's a delightful man who came every week when Alan was sick and Alan loved his visits. At the end of the meal, after there had been various speeches by others, the uncle stood up and gave his appreciation. Twenty-four people, and he went around appreciating every single person in a very beautiful, simple way. When it came to me he said he'd known me for so long and that every time he sees me he thinks of Alan. I wept.

I did my spousal duty of going to mass every Sunday for a year for Alan. It's a Catholic thing, and I find ritual helpful. I valued the sense of discharging a spiritual duty even though I've got so many difficulties with the church. I enjoyed every single minute at the services, they were contemplative and lovely.

I also made a couple of good decisions. I decided after his death that I should accept every single invitation I received unless I was otherwise occupied. I kept to this doggedly, even if I ended up going to blooming Coconut Shy in Germiston 20 miles away. I made decisions about being as happy as I can be. And I am. I'm not miserable. Another thing is that I'm training for a new career and I think that's been very good, something new amidst the debris of the past.

I maintain very close relations with his family and I look after Alan's mother and her money and that's nice. She's nearly 90, with dementia, in a nursing home. I'm the family member who visits most regularly. I like that we have tea and cake on a Sunday morning once a month. I bring the nurses a bottle of whiskey for the small nightly tot that Alan's mother is so fond of.

I am on a long and winding road with a sense of the good fortune of class. Here we are sitting, reflecting, and thinking about bereavement. What a privilege it is to be so consciously thinking these things through. So many working-class and poor people just get on with it. Nobody asks them how they feel or what they are thinking. I'm so conscious of that. I'm thinking of my grandparents and their tough lives as immigrants. There wasn't a lot of space for feelings or for this kind of reflecting. It's a class privilege: counseling, medical insurance, sick pay.

I just think about my grandmother and her very harsh, very poor upbringing in which there was very little space for feelings, or for discussion of feelings. You had to pull yourself together and get on with it. She was widowed at 42. Get a job? She'd never worked in her life. The widow's pension from the state—my grandfather was a magistrate—was small. Her children, my mother and my uncle, also had to get on with it. And I don't think anybody ever asked my grandmother what her feelings were.

I don't entirely agree with Getti. I ask him, is this poverty or modernity?

American Derrick Jensen, radical environmentalist and social commentator, writes prolifically. In *A Language Older than Words*, he's written about the losses we have incurred with so-called economic advancement: loss of physical security, loss of ritual, loss of stable employment, family constellations spread across an intercontinental diaspora.

I ask Getti to consider rural societies such as the San people of southern Africa or Native Americans, who have lived with spirituality very present in their rituals, specifically in their way of embracing and accepting death. They built death lodges on edges of a village, creating psychological readiness for separation. They've clung onto their rituals more than most other cultures in the world.

I pointed out that was what he created for Alan in his last days, a sort of 'death lodge' with gentle light and music playing in the room where people visited him. I believe that for people who haven't modernized and lost that, this is what happens; ritual supports acceptance.

We sat quietly, companionably. The winter sun lowered itself in the sky, bright rays filtering through the trees. Dappled light shadows danced on the veranda walls to the accompaniment of birdsong.

After a considerable pause, Getti told me he'd 'been fired' by his bereavement counselor who said his bereavement is over, that he'd gone as far as he could on that journey for now. I asked Getti what, if anything, was different or harder than he'd expected?

> Well, I'd studied Kübler-Ross at university, and had these sociology ideas about what it was going to be like. It's been much more difficult than I would have imagined. At times, I felt such profound loss, not only of him, but of us as a couple. An interesting thing that came up is that I have lost a lot of status. I'm now a single person. I'm the odd man at a dinner party. Singles are not as easily accommodated as couples. I have been very fortunate with my friends, but I feel a profound loss of status around being part of a couple and that is forever lost. I would never have predicted that.

Three losses: losing the person you loved, losing the unique intimate self who you were in the eyes of that person, and finally the loss of social status.

But Getti ends our conversation on an unexpectedly upbeat note.

> Oddly enough, I feel more confident just being who I am, more than ever before. Part of my need for Alan was to prop me up and to calm my anxiety and to find me lovely just as I was. But I wouldn't construct a new relationship like that; I would want something much more equal. I'm different. I'm an older self and I'm a two-and-a-half-year widowed self. I've changed a lot. I've had to.

Cathy: An Elegy for Raphael

Raphael Barnett. Born and died January 3, 1986. Tombstone Ceremony: May 2015.

'You think I'm one of triplets, don't you?' my friend Daniel asked me one day. 'I'm not. I'm one of four. You should talk to my mom. It's quite a story.' A few months later, Daniel's mother Cathy and I met in Cape Town for coffee. I set up my recorder and over cappuccinos she poured out her heart.

Cathy told me that in 1986 she gave birth to Orli, Daniel, Tali, and Raphael. She wanted others to learn from the story of her grief that lay dormant and unresolved until 27 years after Raphael's stillbirth, when it surfaced and finally boiled over.

I was 25 when I was pregnant and carrying four babies. They hospitalized me for four and a half months, on intravenous drips the entire time. I've since discovered the medication they gave me has so many side effects that now they won't use it. I was warned by the gynecologist of the huge risks of carrying four babies, and that the pregnancy wouldn't be expected to go any further than 32 weeks. I was warned but my husband Graham and I had tried for a long time to fall pregnant and I was excited.

My gynecologist was hell-bent on telling me about the dangers, and I was hell-bent on not hearing. The pregnancy progressed and once I was hospitalized I had a sense of security of being in a controlled environment. Never for one moment did I imagine losing a child.

At only 28 weeks it looked as though I would start with contractions at any time. They gave me a bronchial-dilating drug which had a side effect of holding the uterus, to prevent it from contracting. They kept on increasing the dose; another of the drug's side effects was a crazy heart rate. Pre-eclampsia symptoms started. I'd read a lot and knew the symptoms that indicated a life-threatening situation. I started getting all of them; the doctors were grave and anxious. But everything was being monitored. We got to 29 weeks. It was hellish for me. They discussed using steroids which were experimental at the time. The choice of timing mattered. There was a window during which the steroids were most effective in boosting vitality which was after 24 hours but if you delivered only 48 hours later, they'd have lost their effectiveness.

Things started to get bad. My kidneys failed. Each leg was swollen. The edema became unmanageable. I put my legs up, not knowing that fluid was going onto my lungs. My health became critical. They kept up the dose of the bronchial-dilating drug. They decided to inject the steroids and wanted to keep me going to the next day to give the babies a better chance. My gynecologist spoke to me with a calm urgency. 'Listen, we will deliver in the next 24 hours. Know that you will be in ICU afterwards. You've got fluid in your lungs. We need to deal with that. Everything is okay.'

In the morning, when the anesthesiologist checked me, I said to him, 'I can't see. I just can't see you. There's all these dots and stars; my head's exploding.'

He took my blood pressure. It had gone berserk. Over 200. I had full eclampsia. 'Get her into surgery!' He was screaming at the staff. I could not see—it was just black stars. They called my husband Graham, and they called on all the staff that could come to help deliver four premature babies, including healthcare providers from other hospitals.

I felt them lift me onto the table—then I started with a massive fit. In those moments, they reckon everything constricts and the blood to the babies cuts off completely. The gynecologist tried to give me a spinal as there was no time for an epidural. As they put me under he just tore me open and they tore out the babies—literally. It was a traumatic birth. I've never told my children just how traumatic. They know they were in critical state: born at 30 weeks, 10 weeks premature. There were two little boys and two little girls but one of the little boys died.

My husband came and I asked, 'What happened to our baby? I was obsessed. It was the only conversation I wanted to have. 'Where is the baby?'

Graham said, 'They took the baby away.'

'Who took the baby away?'

'The Chevrah Kadisha took it.'

He said he wasn't allowed to see the baby, that the hospital took control. We don't know who called the Chevrah Kadisha, the Jewish burial society. But we knew they buried the baby; we just didn't know where.

I learned that the three surviving babies couldn't be looked after in the hospital we were in. They were not coping and so critical that they had to be transported to the Mowbray Maternity Hospital where a pediatric doctor worked. Within the next 24 hours I had another fit and lost consciousness.

I couldn't deal with it. I didn't want to come through. I remember my mom's voice, 'Cathy, come on, you have to come back, the babies need you. You must come through. Come on. You are needed. Wake up.' My mother pulled me through together with the assistant gynecologist. He spoke to me as I laid there, telling me, 'Yes, one of the babies died. Yes, it's terrible, but you've got these three. They are fighters and they are fighting. Please, they need you.'

I felt I could choose whether I wanted to come here or not to come back. I came around eight days later.

We lost a baby, and I hadn't allowed myself to think of that possibility. But I had three critical babies, all hospitalized, who I had to look after. Orli had quite a severe heart problem and Tali also had problems related to prematurity but not life-threatening. Daniel was so premature that it took three months before he had the minimum weight of 5 pounds for us to do his circumcision. I was told, through my husband, that we were just very lucky to have three babies alive; there was nothing we could do about our fourth baby being lost.

I needed to get well again. My hair had fallen out in clumps. I was losing fluid, felt and looked awful. All I knew was that I had to get to that hospital every day to be with those babies. At the bris, the circumcision ceremony, we name our male babies. Daniel and Raphael were the first two names on our list for boys. Raphael would have been the name of our dead baby.

Cathy felt massive gratitude as each baby was discharged, that all three, despite the drama of their birth, came through. They were born critical and got less critical as the weeks went by. Orli came home first, then Daniel eight days later, and finally Tali after a further eight days. Mentally they were okay; physically they needed help.

'They had low tone, there would be lots of physical therapy and a six-year catch-up period was predicted, but I had to live in a state of gratitude. That's what got me through.'

With time, Cathy buried the reality of losing Raphael deeper and deeper.

It was something that I couldn't deal with. I'd been told this was traditional Jewish law, upheld by the Chevrah Kadisha. My husband and I were both young, completely restricted by our belief that you couldn't question religious authorities. The Chevrah Kadisha had taken over; they believed this was the best way of supporting young parents who'd lost their baby. That was how things were, and how things are. But my soul always said, 'Surely, this cannot be law.'

In the deepest recesses of her mind it simmered and bothered Cathy that she'd had no closure for the fourth baby.

Two years ago, I started studying a course in Judaica. One session dealt with death and mourning taught by a Rabbi's wife who I knew very well. On one of the tea breaks I asked her, 'You know the triplets? Well, actually, I had four. I lost a baby when they were born, and I don't know anything about my fourth baby. I don't know where he is buried. Is it law that the parents are not allowed to know?'

'I don't think it's a law,' she said. 'I think it's custom that's evolved.'

That was the beginning of my journey of resolution. I became dogged. Why did no one call Graham and tell him about our baby, where he was buried and when and in which part of the cemetery?

Eventually we found out that the Chevrah Kadisha had buried him in the Cape Town cemetery in Pinelands. Graham searched the registry and found, 'Baby Barnett, January 3, 1986,' along with the number of the plot where he was buried.

There was a separate section in the cemetery for children who died under a month. That practice has changed; children are now buried in the main cemetery. But then they were buried in the furthest corner, the derelict side of the cemetery. There's a row of mounds without tombstones. Why no tombstones? I learned that babies that are either stillborn or pass in the first 30 days don't get to have a tombstone. Apparently, this comes from medieval times and it's not just a Jewish concept. The thinking is that the soul does not enter the earthly being in the first month, therefore the baby cannot be acknowledged as human. When I found the place, it was so horrendous that I'm still battling with that. The place itself said, 'These were not truly human beings.' Thirty days. So many parents who have given birth to babies that died in the first month haven't been allowed to erect a consecrated gravestone.

I knew I had to confront this. It became my mission to put up a tombstone to acknowledge the life of our baby.

My persistence to learn more about our son's death also took me back to the gynecologist who responded with shock that I was asking. 'Anything you want to know about the babies you need to ask the pediatrician,' he said. He told me that everything that he'd predicted could go wrong, went wrong and more, and that his full attention was on trying to save me. Apparently, my blood platelet level was so low that if one of the placentas had detached, I would have bled to death.

Cathy approached the now elderly pediatrician. She explained her need to talk with him about what happened almost 30 years ago. She needed to know what happened at the time of birth, about the baby that was lost. 'I have to know because I have to start grieving for that baby,' she told him. 'The triplets need to grieve their brother and as a family we have to heal.'

The pediatrician, quite a religious man, became emotional. His face dropped and he started to shake. He described how, when Cathy had the fit on the delivery table, there was a period of time when the babies were not breathing. And as the babies were pulled out, they had to decide whether to resuscitate or not. He told her, 'You've got to believe me that, thank God, I wasn't on my own, because it was like playing God. We had to assess each baby and whether to ventilate. We felt that the second boy had the least oxygen; if we succeeded in resuscitating him, how brain damaged would he be? We felt he was not viable.'

Cathy asked if he would describe her son as stillborn. He became even more emotional at the memory. 'Yes,' he said. 'He was stillborn. Yes, in those minutes of giving birth he wasn't breathing. Neither were the others, but the life signs were more positive with the other three; the color of the babies, the way they were lying.'

As I started pursuing the truth, I felt the consequences of not having grieved this child. I was filled with guilty thoughts. What kind of mother doesn't acknowledge the loss of her child? The grief and loss and guilt was massive.

There was never the space, except just after the birth when I lay there unconscious. I know I grieved then. I was obsessed in my thoughts. I didn't want to come into the real world to deal with it. When I did come back, I buried the grief. I think if it had been our only baby, we would have found a way to grieve. I've since found out that in Israel they are even stricter with this one-month ruling but there are active lobbyists trying to break down this social practice that is treated as law. There is a swelling of people who have lost babies who want to put up a stone as part of acknowledgment and healing. Our experience was devastating; there was no way to acknowledge a baby that lived for seven months in the womb. There was love for this baby. The Chevrah Kadisha denied us the opportunity to acknowledge and grieve. For many years that grief remained buried, ready to surface.

I hadn't spoken to my mother-in-law at all about any of this. I decided to visit and tell her what I'd been doing and about setting a date for a service. She grabbed me and she wouldn't let me go, saying, 'No one has ever allowed me to talk about this baby, my Graham's son. Our son lost his baby. We lost this grandchild. I cried so much. We were away. We couldn't support you, and we couldn't support Graham. When we came back there was no grave to go and visit. There was no conversation. I can't face dying without knowing that that baby has a recognized place to be. Thank you for doing this. I can't thank you enough.'

My mother-in-law! I knew nothing of the pain she had held in for so long.

Cathy persevered with the memorial stone arrangements even though her ex-husband Graham was reluctant. She went against the grain of custom in laying a stone for a baby who was less than a month old. She was supported by her mother-in-law and Daniel, her eldest son, who said, 'If Dad doesn't want to be part of this, Ma, we are doing it. We need it.' Two days before the consecration Cathy went to see the tombstone.

We chose a white-ish granite. I saw it in its wholeness and felt such happiness. This was my time of release. I sobbed and sobbed some more. I went back to my car and sat there for about an hour immersed in total acknowledgment for this child.

We chose a Rabbi to come to put up the stone. Now, for a Rabbi to do this, he had to check that it was not law; it may be customary social practice but it's not actually law. He confirmed this and then fulfilled our request to officiate.

The consecration was a very special day. Graham had Daniel by his side. It was tremendously healing for the triplets, perhaps an edge more so for Daniel who'd lost the brother he would have grown up with. I've noticed a difference between the three of them. There's a bond between multiple births that's closer than between any parent and child. I think our family had a wound and that day was unbelievably healing.

Loss, I don't think it can be denied. My task became personal, to acknowledge that I had to grieve my lost baby, to acknowledge that my ex-husband Graham suffered loss, as well as his parents and our triplets.

We've now come to a place where we feel resolved. I did that, I had those conversations that I never dared to have earlier: with the doctor, the physician and mainly with the Rabbi. And I did it because there are going to be other people that need to do it. I felt and feel very proud and liberated. If a Jewish parent with a baby that's died were to come to me now, I would support them.

Postscript Six

The Greek philosopher Heraclitus said, 'You cannot step into the same river twice.' The water flows, but when you step off a river bank the next time, the earth on the side of the riverbank may be the same but the water you immerse yourself in is not. Bereavement will differ each time we step into the experience. Bereavement somehow seems unpredictable, there's no advance knowing how you're going to respond.

There are many books by healthcare practitioners as well as numerous personal memoirs. Most of us are unlikely to read extensively. I'm going to risk naming the insights that have emerged for me as I've encountered bereavement in my life, and as I have borne witness to the bereavement of others.

The phenomenon of resilience. Apparently, our brains are hard-wired for resilience. Our ancestors at the Cradle of Humankind could hardly sit around immobilized in their sadness. They'd have soon found themselves becoming food for other hunting creatures in the vicinity. I find the resilience concept comforting because then I can anchor myself in the adage 'This too shall pass' and sit with the pain of grief, be patient with it, confident that, in time, it will ease.

Readiness for the unexpected response and timing. I'm not sure that anyone gets more skilled at navigating grief. The deaths of a spouse, a lover, a parent, a child, a colleague, a family pet are all different. Response may be influenced by the age and relative wellness pre-death of the deceased; caregivers may even feel release and gladness alongside sadness. And then there's timing, our readiness to allow ourselves to grieve. People have told me they did not cry at the time of the death of a loved one, but only months later, often when another incident (the death of a pet) prompted the release.

Counseling. I never accessed bereavement counseling. Now I think in those first few months after Joe's death, or even in the months before, it would have been wise for me to have done so. My children might have had an easier time of living with their grieving mother had I benefitted from conversations with a skilled counselor.

Stages are a myth, and emotions have no sequence. I've discovered other people who, like me, were given Kübler-Ross to read on the five stages of grief, and then grappled with the confusion that it made them feel that they were 'not normal.' There is new scientific research on bereavement that invalidates Kübler-Ross's pioneering attempt to conceptualize a theory.

Language matters. The language of 'getting over, letting go' that are common parlance may not be helpful. I am who I've become because of the love and influence of many of the deceased in my life. I don't want to 'get over' their death or 'let go' of my attachment to them. Rather I want to 'let in' and integrate their influence, accept their absence and 'move forward' with that sense of integration.

Curb judgment. However difficult it may be to be in a relationship with someone who is utterly self-absorbed, selfish, lost in the suffering of their grief, it's empathy, compassion, and love that have a better chance of contributing towards their finding a new equilibrium. On the other hand, some people find their equilibrium very quickly.

Acknowledgment matters. I now try to be more careful and attentive about acknowledging loss when meeting a friend, colleague or acquaintance after bereavement. We've lost not only the outward display of loss using black arm bands or drawn curtains or a sash on the door, but also the art of conversation around death and bereavement. Many people are awkwardly unable to acknowledge loss and express empathy. It would be quite something to regain that social practice as a new normal. Perhaps when children have their life skills lessons at school they could be taught about the importance of acknowledgment and do a homework practice of writing a condolence letter. Imagine that!

My husband John shared with me that this is the meditation that he drew comfort from when his sister Harriet chose it as a reading when their father died. After Mandela died John posted it on his Facebook page and it attracted hundreds of Likes. Since then whenever he's acknowledging a death and offering his condolences by mail, he often chooses to attach this meditation.

WHEN I DIE

When I die,
Give what's left of me away
To children
And old men that wait to die.

And if you need to cry,
Cry for your brother walking the street beside you.

And when you need me,
Put your arms around anyone
And give them
What you need to give to me.

I want to leave you something,
Something better than words or sounds.

Look for me
In the people I've known
Or loved,
And if you cannot give me away,
At least let me live on your eyes
And not on your mind

You can love me most
By letting hands touch hands,
By letting bodies touch bodies,
And by letting go of children that need to be free.

Love doesn't die; people do.
So, when all that's left of me is love,
Give me away.

—Mishkan T'Filah, *Meditations before Kaddish—A progressive
Siddur*

PART SEVEN

Money. Planning. Emotions

To be sure, on certain occasions, emotion can be a substitute for reason. The emotional action program we call fear can get most human beings out of danger, in short order, with little or no help from reason. A squirrel or a bird will respond to a threat without any thinking at all and the same can happen to a human. That is the beauty of how emotion has functioned throughout evolution; it allows the possibility of making living beings act smartly without having to think smartly. In humans, however, the story has become more complicated, for better and for worse. Reasoning does what emotions do but achieves it knowingly. Reasoning gives us the option of thinking smartly before we act smart, and a good thing too: we have discovered that the emotions alone can solve many – but not all – the problems posed by our complex environment and that, on occasion, the solutions offered by emotion are actually counterproductive.

—Antonio Damasio, *Descartes' Error: Emotion, Reason and the Human Brain*

Money: Hard Talk

Money and death. It seems to me that in many families it's almost easier to talk about death than it is to talk about money. And yet to avoid talking about money can have such significant consequences.

In late December 2003 I was invited by my friend Gillian* to spend New Year's with her in Durban. It was the ninth year of my widowhood, of being single after living in coupledom for the previous 20 years. Invites for singles don't come so easily; I was grateful. One of Gillian's brothers still lived in Durban and would be hosting a New Year's Eve party. I looked forward to great music and dancing.

Gillian and I shared a room together in her mom's compact two-bedroom townhouse. Her mother had lived alone for several years since the death of her husband. She had three children and was fiercely protective of her privacy and independence, especially when it came to money matters. A few months earlier she began to suffer ischemic strokes, a mini stroke, that leaves little impairment after the episode. Her three children worried on two counts: her living alone with no one at hand to attend to her should a more serious incident occur, and secondly they were concerned about finance. They were all financially stretched—spending on their children, school fees, and mortgages.

Gillian decided to venture the conversation, to ask her mom to consider a joint account so she'd be able to access money in case of emergency. Her mother's immediate response in their first discussion which quickly became tetchy was a, 'There's no need, if anything happens I'll simply write a letter to the bank.' They were sitting together privately in the lounge but the tenor of their voices and their tension was palpable throughout the small house.

Gillian's mom, perhaps a little embarrassed that a visitor had overheard their raised voices, came and spoke with me and said she hoped that I was not upset with her not agreeing with her daughter's suggestions and that, being a widow myself, I surely understood her need to be independent in her decision-making. I responded that I hoped she understood that my friend, her daughter Gillian, was talking to her from a place of good, a place of concern, not avarice, and that I hoped they would find a way that could work for all of them, herself and her children.

Later, after reflection, when the point settled in that indeed the joint account would be for when she was incapacitated and could not write to the bank, Gillian's mother a little grudgingly said, 'Alright, I'll talk to the bank' and she made the arrangements for Gillian to have access to her checking account. Her mother had indeed found a solution she thought would work for both parties. The checking account was not where the real money was kept. Gillian would later discover her mother had moved the bulk of her money into a savings account, for which she did not create access.

Three months after our visit, Gillian's mom took ill on a Thursday and was admitted to hospital and died within a week. If she had had a prolonged incapacitation, there would have been an unnecessary and challenging financial situation for her adult children—the very thing they had tried to engage with her on.

I'm not sure what my mum would have done without me. I had paid her medical insurance for the last 14 years and as she became more frail, my costs increased to include caregivers and night nurses. Many of my friends find themselves in the same situation.

It's no wonder that my own fears revolve around longevity, that I will not die soon enough, that I'll outlive my savings and then face financial difficulties when I am old-old. The women in my lineage have mostly died on the cusp of 90. Whenever someone tries to sell me life insurance I refuse to engage, saying what I need is money for my elderliness.

A friend of mine shares this same fear. She and her husband emigrated to New Zealand. She's retired and her husband, also retired, has had some health issues. She's worried about finances. He tells her not to worry. He reassures her that they have enough, that although when he dies the bulk of his assets will go to his children from his first marriage, that she should have confidence that he's made provision for her. But he won't actually disclose the financial facts and tell her exactly what the provision is. Her natural disposition is anxiety and this uncertainty feeds into exacerbating her worry.

Financial planners tell me this is not unusual for married couples. It's more often the woman in the couple who is not fully aware of the assets that are owned and what monetary situation she would face if she were to be widowed.

And apparently, so say financial planners in countries which don't have generous government pension schemes, it's as few as 2 percent of the elderly that have done their financial planning well enough so that they do not need to draw on the contributions of the younger generations in their family.

Rene August, a pioneering Anglican reverend based in Cape Town, shared with me that while her job as a parish priest was to tend to the spiritual well-being of her parishioners, she found herself drawn into the practicalities of their lives when there was a death in the family. She found families facing crises, and that she was facilitating discussions on wills, downsizing, retirement annuities, so much so that she organized a series of Saturday workshops.

I can't say 'there's no escaping it,' because people do escape it; they avoid thinking ahead and then there are consequences for their families. A TV presenter told me of a friend of his who had a car crash. He was on life support. By the time his wife agreed the machines should be disconnected several weeks later, she was financially impoverished. She had dipped into the mortgage on their family home to pay medical bills depleting all the capital which they had built up in their years of marriage. After his death, the woman had to move out of their home and into rental accommodation. Another friend told me of a member of his book club whose husband had died, leaving her to find that there were unresolved debts for which she was now liable. She had to move to a smaller house and find less expensive schools for her children.

My observation is that people find themselves in financial difficulty mostly in three situations: when they have lived a very long time and don't consider downsizing but find it difficult to cover the running costs; when they have many medical expenses with insufficient health insurance coverage; and when they get into debts over honoring family rituals at any stage of their lives. There's one more time when facing financial decisions seems most challenging and potentially creates difficulty and that is during bereavement. It's difficult to be rational and make sensible decisions when you are in a maelstrom of emotion. And yet fairly soon, after a funeral is over, the practicalities of life kick in.

Nokuzola: Ritual. Money. Emotions

Whatever society we live in, weddings and funerals are the occasions that we often spend the most money on. We're emotionally vulnerable at the time of death and sometimes the expenditure on ritual becomes the final, public manifestation of love.

Nokuzola is a Xhosa domestic worker in Cape Town, who works two days a week for a close friend of mine. She told me the story of how she spent more than R20,000 on her husband Simon's funeral. He was employed in a butchery. He became ill in 2009. The clinic diagnosed TB and he died in hospital in 2015, leaving her with two boys aged 15 and six. She borrowed R17,000—the equivalent to five months' salary for her part-time job. Simon's colleagues and boss had a collection at his workplace, and gave her R2,500, and she also got a pay out from her savings club. She's now working to pay off her loan at R500 a month; it will take her almost three years to clear this debt.

Nokuzola's funeral expenses, whilst huge for her, turn out to be quite modest when compared to what people can spend.

My friend Mapi, the South African TV executive, sat and did her math with me for her own imagined funeral costs, writing out every detail, and arrived at a total that was almost 10 times more than Nokuzola's.

The greater expense was because Mapi envisages a memorial service in Johannesburg and she'd have to make financial provision for family members, who live across the country, to attend this, since she is the main breadwinner of her extended family. The traditional burial in her birthplace in KwaZulu-Natal would be attended by several busloads of people; this would be expected in her family, as Mapi is the daughter of a deceased teacher, well-loved in the community, as well as the fact that Mapi is seen as the local girl made who made it big in Johannesburg.

When Mapi finalized her total she was shocked, and exclaimed, 'But this could buy education policies for my two nephews!' She began to second guess her fidelity to tradition and told me she was going to lobby family members about the acceptability of having a cremation.

But for Nokuzola, it was important to fulfill all the rites of passage irrespective of expense. When she and I talked several weeks after Simon's death I gently asked why she did not consider paying into a funeral policy. She told me that when Simon first became very ill, she fasted.

> Maybe a week, no food, no drink, fasting as a sacrifice for his life. I told myself God is going to heal him. We went to church together. He was better, better, better. And we were happy, it's like the first time we met each other. So the reason I didn't take out an insurance or funeral policy was because I believe in God. If I were to take out a policy, what am I saying, that I want him to die and get the money? So I just told myself it's going to be fine. But God, he knows everything. I'm not blaming him. I still believe in him. I still praise him. Maybe there's something he wants me to learn from this.

She described in detail what it meant to fulfill all the rites of passage. Her husband had to be wrapped and placed in a coffin ready to be transported. She bought Simon a fluffy maroon and blue blanket and a coffin with gold-colored handles which cost R3,900. Funeral businesses are set up to accommodate the needs of workers whose traditions require them to be buried in their ancestral home. Nokuzola's husband was to be buried in his birthplace of Graaff-Reinet, 420 miles from Cape Town. The cost for that was R11,000, including a vehicle with a driver and space for ten passengers, with the coffin packed with ice and placed on a trailer behind.

People would travel overnight on Friday and come back to Cape Town on Sunday. Nokuzola traveled ahead by bus on the Wednesday to prepare things. She hired the Graaff-Reinet undertaker and a hearse for Saturday morning. She rented a large tent to erect outside the house, as well as 50 chairs and a four-plate stove with a gas bottle. She bought three sheep—R700 each—two to be eaten when they came back from the graveyard, and the other to be eaten on Sunday morning at the closing ritual ceremony. The ritual of slaughtering an animal, called *umkhapo,* is performed to help the spirit of the person who has died move more easily into the afterlife.

Simon, in his coffin, arrived on the trailer on Saturday morning at 5:30am. At 7am, women gathered with Nokuzola at the family home for a special Xhosa ceremony in which they encircled the coffin and sang specific songs. The men waited outside until 8am when the pastor arrived and the coffin was loaded into the hearse and driven to the church for the Christian service.

Nokuzola had organized one hundred programs to be printed. Mr. Hlungu, from Nokuzola's church in Cape Town was the program director. He'd traveled on Friday night after conducting a short service at Simon and Nokuzola's home in Khayelitsha in Cape Town. It was a two-hour church service with readings, preaching, and a eulogy interspersed with many songs. Nokuzola said she sat alone next to the coffin, while the wives of Simon's cousins stayed back at the house to do the cooking.

At the graveyard the coffin was lowered into the ground with the items needed for the afterlife. On returning to the house, people washed their hands in large basins of water filled with leaves of aloes, a healing plant.

The funeral feast began. The sheep, now cooked, was served with cabbage, carrots and cornmeal, and homebrewed beer. Several hours later, when everyone except Simon's family-in-residence had gone home, Nokuzola washed *all* his clothes, clean and dirty. In one month, they would be ceremoniously divided and distributed to different members of the family. At that time, the spades used for the digging of the grave would also be ceremoniously washed and put back into use.

Nokuzola traveled back to Cape Town overnight on Sunday to be back at work on Monday. Her employers were moving house and she did not want to let them down. She had a day off on Tuesday and that's when she allowed herself to feel her emotions. 'When I woke up on Tuesday I was feeling so wrong. I started crying, just crying loads. My sister was there, and my cousin and my kids. Everyone just looked at me and left me alone until I stopped.'

People get into debt trying to do what they consider is the right thing. Archbishop Tutu told me in one of our interviews that he wanted his funeral service to role-model modesty when he dies. He's specified a goat, not a cow; cremation rather than burial; modest refreshments, not a fully fledged funeral feast, and that his memorial stone should not be expensive.

He explained:

My concern is not just about affordability; it's my strong preference that money should be spent on the living.' He has applied the same thinking to end-of-life medical expenditure, 'You have to ask questions, why is money being spent in this way? Money should be spent on those who are at the beginning or full flow of life. Of course, these are my personal opinions and not of my church.

Caitlin and Amber: The Double Cost of Outsourcing

There was a time when the rituals undertaken when a person died were mostly simple, inexpensive, and involved everyone in the community either actively or as witness. It was only the wealthy in society who would have more elaborate and expensive rituals.

The range of diverse practice is huge and what is essential in one funerary ritual is considered inappropriate in another. The gathering of witnesses to start a fire to release the soul trapped in the body is essential to Hindu practice whereas cremation is considered to be an ill-fitting spiritual end by orthodox Jews whose interpretation of Jewish law, the *halachah*, is that the dead must be buried in the earth.

I've heard North Americans comment that African burial rituals and the huge community turnout for a funeral and the associated costs are astonishing to them. But looking from the outside in, there's a lot happening in the United States to be astonished about. Handling death is increasingly outsourced and the involvement of family, friends and community has become increasingly minimized; the practices of embalming and building of mausoleums may be considered as extraordinary in other cultures.

It was death away from home, the return of dead bodies to their relatives from the battlegrounds of the Civil War, which first created a high demand for embalming. It gained even more legitimacy as an American funerary practice after Abraham Lincoln was embalmed in readiness for his journey from Washington DC to his hometown of

Springfield, Illinois, 800 miles away.

The embalming process involves cutting the carotid artery at the base of the throat and inserting a tube through which formaldehyde and other preservatives are pumped into the body. The jugular vein is cut simultaneously so that as this carcinogenic liquid diffuses through the body, the displaced blood drains away. The mortician then uses a trocar, a short, sharp, three-sided jabbing instrument with a cannula, a hollow tube, to puncture the deceased's stomach, intestines, bladder, and lungs. The purpose is to suck out waste fluids and release gases. This process has been the life blood of the US funeral industry which, in 2014, accounted for $20 billion worth of economic activity.

Mausoleum space, an above-ground burial space, is the other expenditure which some American families choose to make.

'As someone who has recently been "adult orphaned"... the fact that I can't even find a decent mausoleum space, for less than $30,000, in the fourth largest city in America is depressing,' so wrote Georgia Todd in response to an article in the Los Angeles-based *Refinery 29* on what happens to people once they're dead. I don't know how much Georgia Todd earns per month but $30,000 would certainly be the equivalent of several months' salary for many North Americans, just as Nokuzola had also spent several months' salary in another country and another culture.

I had never considered mausoleum space in the 21st century. Those I'd seen in Mozambique and Italy were built long ago in an era that I thought was over, but it seems to still be a thriving enough business in the United States. I read advertorials online for mausoleums. The sales pitch is worded to pull at our heart strings. 'Building a mausoleum is one way to bury our kindred dead that shows our love and respect for them. Even in death we value them so much to build them a place where there is a mark and they can never be forgotten.'

In the mausoleum, a coffin is placed inside a dry sealed chamber. There are indoor and outdoor mausoleums, and offerings of a single crypt, a side-by-side crypt or companion crypt. A family crypt is designed to accommodate many members by stacking them. What about if the person has chosen cremation? A columbarium is designed to hold cremated remains—the niches are smaller than the crypts in which coffins are placed.

Forever Legacy advertises that it will co-design with you a custom-built private mausoleum for $250,000. 'Forever Legacy creates eternal monuments, private estate mausoleums made by master craftsmen,' reads the company's website. 'Forever Legacy specializes in providing elite services to discerning clientele.'

Their press release describes one 15-foot tall mausoleum constructed of Vermont Blue Gray granite for a 'beloved philanthropist.' The Forever Legacy price includes a video of the construction of the mausoleum showing footage from the quarry, 'where everlasting granite pieces are quarried and split with expansion wedges. The granite loaf is cut with a diamond saw to exact measurements. Diamond sandpaper is use to create a polished surface.'

In comparison, Georgia Todd's $30,000 seems to be a steal. But to be fair, I found other adverts for crypt spaces in communal mausoleums at the comparatively modest price of $4,000 dollars.

In my childhood people spent their dying days at home, were washed and dressed by the family and laid out in the front parlor, and after an inclusive wake, they were buried. Now most people die in the hospital and families pay a funeral home to prepare the deceased's body for burial or cremation.

In the United States you can now make online arrangements with a funeral parlor so that you are totally uninvolved—you don't ever have to speak to another human being. The body of the deceased will be picked up, cremated and the ashes posted to you via the US Postal Service which is strict about the packaging: they require heavy brown tape and explicit labeling, with a stamp reading 'Human Remains.'

Caitlin Doughty, mortician and author of *Smoke Gets in Your Eyes*, described some extraordinary instances of emotional distancing. There was the man in Pennsylvania who wanted his money back, claiming that the package had leaked. 'He gave up on his story when I told him how the urn was packaged.' Doughty writes. 'We came to find out that he'd never even gone to the post office to pick it up.'

The story that upset Doughty the most was that of a nine-year-old girl she calls Ashley*, who had just finished third grade. The child had died in the hospital, 'where her parents left her body, went home, typed their credit card into a website, and waited two weeks for her to appear in a box by mail... The idea that a nine-year-old girl can magically transform into a neat, tidy box of remains is ignorant and shameful for our culture. It is the equivalent of grown adults thinking that babies come from storks.' And yet, comments Doughty, there are many who see this option as 'the future of low-cost death care.'

Doughty has teamed up with Amber Carvaly to open their Los Angeles mortuary business, Undertaking LA. There's a meeting of minds. Doughty wants to challenge the current norm that 'talking about death is deviant,' and has produced a series on YouTube called *Ask a Mortician*. She also runs the website *The Order of the Good Death*.

Carvaly, when interviewed, talked about her theory of mourning and said, 'Because we shroud and protect society from death, you don't understand what level of grief to feel for things, so everything is blanketed at a 10. Because we make it such a taboo subject there's no barometer.'

She regrets she hasn't come across any academic studies so far to prove her views. Doughty supports her, interjecting, 'Anecdotally, everything I've seen is that when you're involved in the death and you're present and you let things unfold as they naturally unfold, and you see the small changes in the person ... you are much more ready to let go of the person and their body at the end of the process.'

Doughty and Carvaly are committed to spending time talking to their clients. It may be emotionally more demanding, but that's what makes them passionate about the work they do. They're also environmentally responsible. You don't find toxic embalming as a service offering on their website. And they now have a facility that accommodates up to 50 people for a memorial service.

They are cost conscious. Undertaking LA's price of a direct cremation (with no service and no viewing) is $995 dollars in February 2017, compared to other funeral homes in the area where the cost has crept up to as much as $3,400.

But environmental commitment does not come cheaply. If you lived in Los Angeles and were to have the idea that you might wish to have a green burial, wrapped in an environmentally friendly (unbleached) shroud ($487) and buried at the Joshua Tree Memorial Park, the starting price is $7,500 dollars. What's euphemistically called an 'alternative container'—that is a cardboard box—costs $20 so you could make a saving of $467 dollars if you got buried naked without the shroud, but the ballpark figure for the burial would still be above $7,000 dollars.

Undertaking LA are one of several pioneers in the funeral industry. One South African funeral company, Tony Wyllie & Co., offers brightly decorated eco-friendly 'cardboard' coffins. The decorations are themed and currently include golf, surfing, and daisies, and they're currently exporting to Australia, Belgium, and Germany. Owner Andrew Wyllie says, 'It sounds cheesy, but it's putting back the fun into funerals.'

I'm not entirely sure about his view on 'fun' at funerals. I like the idea of celebrating a person's life. I admire the Mexican Day of the Dead rituals when the whole community throws a party in the graveyard to remember the deceased. But at the time of the death and during the disposal of the body of the deceased, what seems to matter most to our future well-being is our emotional engagement with the whole process of dying and ritual.

Of the funeral homes I've read about, my favorite is in Bergisch Gladbach, near Cologne in Germany. Fritz Roth ran the Putz-Roth funeral home for more than 30 years, and in 2006 he created the first woodland private cemetery. They provide lounges for families to gather. You can make your own casket from a kit, and paint it if you like. They've had families rent a room for up to three weeks. David Roth, who's run the business since his father died in 2013, says it's important that people spend as much time with the body as they need.

Funerary practices in our modernizing, urbanizing world have generated concerns about their expense, as well as the increasing lack of emotional involvement in some cultures. The first concern includes the extent to which people are willing to take out loans to pay for funerals. This seems to be especially true of southern Africa where people combine both indigenous ritual with Christian practice involving the whole community. At the other extreme, the USA takes the lead in paying for ritual to be outsourced, and minimizing their engagement with death—they pay to distance themselves and their emotions.

Money, ritual, emotion. It is not an easy combination. What is true is that it would serve us to deliberate carefully what it is that we truly want that will ease our family's mourning process and to consider the cost of those wishes.

Anything more than the direct cremation service, the 'we'll do the body pick up and you'll receive the remains by post,' is a significant expenditure. The adage 'cut your coat according to your cloth' has relevance. A financial plan and its implementation to secure the possibility that the rituals important to you can be paid for, and attended by the people that matter most to you, cannot be over emphasized.

Helen and Roger: Planning for Longevity

Carol Abaya, a US-based expert in aging and elder care, uses the image of sandwiches to help people understand where they are in terms of their dependence on other generations and how others depend on them. According to her, I am a club sandwich—four slices of bread not two. I'm one of 'those in their 50s or 60s, sandwiched between aging parents, adult children and grandchildren'—my mother Gina, my adult children Tessa and Kyla and my grandchildren Benjamin and Livia.

Over the last four years my mum's health had declined considerably. She moved into the same apartment building as me. She stopped cooking; she took to her bed. At first I cooked, then stopped. I was equating the cooking of food for her as an expression of love. It was too hard for me not to feel emotionally rejected when she shook her head (ungraciously) and pushed the plate away. I realized I could find other ways to express my love. So, I bought in readymade meals and the food bills went up. When she began to fall, I hired caregivers to be with her every day, and eventually every night. More expenses. Her digestive system played up, and she'd have diarrhea accidents—'Sorry I thought it was just going to be a little fart.' The washing machine was always on the go. I reckoned I was the biggest single purchaser of stain remover, automatic washing powder, and fabric softener in our entire suburb— we went through kilos every month. I bought a wheelchair, a bath chair, an orthopedic bed. Eventually we'd transition to diapers.

My brother told me how fortunate my mum was to have moved to South Africa from England and have me supporting her, that the quality of care and bang for her bucks and mine added together, got her a level of care that would have been unaffordable for her in the United Kingdom.

I have friends, also in the club sandwich generation, with parents and grandparents in care facilities. I've listened in to their discussions in which they've calculated. 'How long before the money left in a trust runs out?' or 'How much money do we siblings need to collect between us to cover the difference between our parents' pension and what we're actually spending every month?'

I'm resolute that I want to do my financial planning so my children don't have this predicament. I read that if I succeed in doing this, I'll be part of a very small minority of elderly, around 2 percent—that's the estimate of how many elderly people are able to live without receiving financial assistance from their children.

I was on the lookout to learn from others ahead of me on this curve and by pure chance, when visiting Maputo, I met Helen and Roger from Old Lyme in Connecticut. They were doing serious homework on packing up their family home and moving to Washington DC into what's known as a Continuing Care Retirement Community (CCRC). The principles of such facilities seem to be similar the world over. I live in Johannesburg, my one daughter lives in Cape Town and the other in New York. Who knows where I'll end up living out my elder years?

I met Helen and Roger in 2010. My friends Zé and Guida planned to travel for three weeks. Would I like to stay and have some quiet writing time in their Maputo apartment? Yes, please. There's a line in Peter Hoeg's *Smilla's Sense of Snow* when Smilla enters her apartment which describes my feelings perfectly: 'I feel the same way about solitude as some people feel about the blessing of the church. It's the light of grace for me. I never close the door behind me without the awareness that I am carrying out an act of mercy toward myself.'

I settled into Zé's office. Joe's good friend, an architect, erstwhile Secretary of State for Urban Planning in the period following Mozambique's independence in 1975. He designed this very apartment building; there's a small window, thoughtfully set into the wall. When you look up from your laptop, you gaze at the blues of the Indian Ocean and the play of clouds in the sky.

But I couldn't get the internet to work. Which of my friends could I bother for internet access? Polly? But Julie's house was a pleasant walk and across the road from a good bakery. She was going away and introduced me to Helen and Roger, her house-sitters. Helen had helped create a master's program for the local health faculty and was updating course materials. Roger worked with a church charity twinned with his church in the United States.

Every day they offered good coffee, and we chatted before I settled into my agreed-upon 60-minute stint on email and Skype. Helen and Roger, 73 and 68 respectively, were debating how they would choose to live out their elder years, assuming the possible onset of frailty, and taking into consideration their family geography. They were contemplating a move to Washington DC where their only son lived with his wife. They were not yet facing health issues, but others in their age cohort had been less fortunate.

They had worked out their criteria. They wanted a place that would support their independent living and not require them to move if and when they could no longer care for themselves. An apartment in a complex offering access to frail care as well as access to nearby shops, movie theaters, and restaurants was their ideal. They also wanted to be close to a metro line so that when they could no longer drive, public transport would be in walking distance; it would also make it easier for family and friends to visit them. They visited several places and gathered information slowly without committing to anything.

The events of just one day changed the speed of their decision-making. They'd gone on a trip to the United Kingdom for a family wedding, and had a great time. The next day, Helen and Roger went to a local country pub. Over lunch, Helen asked Roger about what he planned to say in a lecture that he would deliver on his return home. But she could not understand what he was trying to tell her. Nothing he said made sense. His words had lost their composition, their orderliness, their meaning-making.

A doctor by training, she decided they should return to their accommodation. In the bright light of their room, unlike the low light of the bar, Helen could see Roger's mouth drooping on one side. She called emergency medical services. While sitting in a Durham county pub, between one minute and the next, Roger had had a minor stroke.

Back home in the United States, one of the first things Helen did was contact Ingleside, a retirement community they'd previously visited in Washington DC, to pay the $5,000 deposit. Living in a small town in Connecticut, the organizing of the rehabilitation care that Roger needed proved as difficult as they'd imagined. For months Roger had a hand that did not function properly, and he found it difficult to type and could not drive. They enjoyed one more summer in Connecticut and started sorting and packing over several months ready for their move in the spring.

In 2016 Helen wrote me an email about their move to Ingleside.

'It's a CCRC (Continuing Care Retirement Community), an organization that provides independent apartments (with some extra safety features), assisted living with independent accommodations but staffed 24/7 and full-scale nursing home care.'

Helen said that although the transition was 'pretty difficult'—she missed the shoreline and the beach picnics over the summer—they had now settled and looked forward to an autumn and winter with no worry about snow removal or power outages. They chose this place in part because of the convenience of the subway.

Helen had been to downtown DC regularly to see old friends and do things at her club; she said she felt like a student again, exploring different interests. Pets are allowed, so their dog is with them. Concerts are so regular that they don't get to all of them. Roger found a big band in which to play his ultra-sax.

Helen directed me to a report available on the development of CCRCs in the United States and their strengths and challenges, on the website www.seniorliving.org. Their unit, she explained, was called The Takoma, a one bedroom with a den with 1,024 square feet. The Ingleside website allows you to compare the monthly expenses of living in your own property elsewhere with the cost of living there. Everything has been factored in: rent or mortgage costs, condo fees, property taxes, and insurance policies.

Ingleside, as a CCRC, required a financial down-payment contribution. These financial arrangements vary. Helen wrote:

> Ours is a simple 'declining balance' which means that the amount we could recoup if we left or died goes down every month for two years and finally disappears altogether. That was a bit steep for us—the prices tend to reflect local housing prices which are higher than in Connecticut—and I'm sure that is why we referred to the move as 'expensive.'

For a flat monthly fee of just under $4,500, Helen and Roger get:

- an allowance for meals in a choice of two different dining rooms;
- weekly housekeeping;
- daily 'check in' service (someone would look in on them if they didn't push the button in the morning which indicated they're up and about);
- a pendant which would go off on a fall, and which can be activated if either of them has an emergency other than a fall;
- an excellent exercise program;
- use of a small but well-equipped gym and a pool;
- a shuttle that makes regular trips to local grocery stores and to various museums, etc., on a scheduled basis;
- a rich program of activities including lectures, courses provided by local educational organizations, discussion groups, concerts, movies, and more;
- a well-organized volunteer program of residents which makes it possible to find someone to take on helpful chores such as feeding the cat or walking the dog if you go away for a weekend or so.

Helen considered the $4,500 per month facilities fee as very good value for money.

It would be impossible to rent locally, cook our own food, pay for housekeeping and a gym for this amount.

The outlay was somewhere in the range of $350,000—basically the money we got from the sale of our Old Lyme house. Some of the apartments are significantly more expensive. But what's most important in terms of being accepted as a resident is the outcome of an assessment of your whole financial position. The company doesn't want you to run out of money. You have to lay out the facts of what you're worth—you share with them the information about your financial holdings.

She's aware that if they continued to stay in the apartment at a time when their health deteriorated and they hired aides, the monthly costs would increase. But she says, 'This place promises never to throw you out—unlike the "for profit" ones. In the event of running out of money, they would help you apply for Medicaid which does pay for a lot of long-term care in this country. A lot of middle-class people end up on Medicaid. It's one of the misunderstood issues in our healthcare system.'

Helen's mother was in private nursing care for five years and it ate up a good part of the money she thought her children would inherit. If she had run out of money, Helen would have had to move her to a facility that would accept state payments. Helen and I agreed on the importance of what Helen has just said: that if you're elderly in the United States and not hugely wealthy and you anticipate longevity, you should look for a place that accepts state payments.

Now that they're residents, Helen can see that one of the strengths of the place is the very wide range of choices for coping with the changes that come with aging. This gives Helen a sense of security in light of Roger's stroke. Helen observed that there are lots of couples where one person in the couple clearly has some confusion but who manages in this set up without difficulty. It's also possible for people with disabilities to stay in their apartments with a paid aide in preference to moving into assisted living. They have used their car for grocery shopping and visiting their son and his growing family, but can see that they could manage much the same life if they could no longer drive. They sometimes pick up their grandson from day care and ride with him on the subway to his house.

Helen and Roger were 73 and 68 when we first met in Maputo. Now they're 79 and 74 respectively. They're gleaning the benefits of their thoughtful, thorough, forward planning. They've had so many conversations. They've done their very best to think through scenarios. They chose Ingleside with its continuing care facility as affording them the opportunity of the most joy in their lives, alongside the security of knowing that whoever goes first, the other is well-settled in a safe and social environment.

But even our best plans can be waylaid. Helen and I spoke on November 8, 2016, the day Donald Trump was elected President. Their son, a political appointee in the Obama administration, lost his job the day Trump became president. His professional future is less certain—hopefully he will find new work opportunities in DC, and Roger and

Helen can continue to enjoy the fruits of their planning: leisurely elderliness and grand parenting of family nearby.

My Impaired Judgment

It was thrilling when Joe became the Minister of Housing in Mandela's 1994 cabinet, the first after our democratic elections. It was his opportunity to be creative and build after decades of struggling to bring down a government that disrespected human dignity and had legalized inequality. This pinnacle of Joe's life work was a marvelously fulfilling eight months; then the cancer got the better of him and he died in January 1995, four weeks after a fall that broke his collar bone and signaled the start of the sharp decline towards his end.

Joe's ministerial salary was also a huge boost to our family finances. He'd been earning R4,000 per month when working full-time for the ANC on the negotiated settlement that made the peaceful elections possible in 1994. As a minister his earnings increased fourfold to R16,000 a month plus allowances, which included a very handsome tax-friendly car allowance. He bought a car for me, or rather he signed a loan purchase agreement; the car would be paid off over four years at R4,000 a month.

We chose a Volvo. The company had just started importing to South Africa after many years of boycotting the apartheid-era economy. I was interested in space and reliability after the dodgy second-hand vehicles I'd driven. Kyla wanted to celebrate the new car by going ice skating with friends at the Carlton Centre in downtown Johannesburg, so I chauffeured a car packed with several happy children. I dropped off Tessa at horse-riding lessons, put down the backseat and then filled the trunk, floor to ceiling, with bags of manure to make garden compost. I looked forward to a well-fed garden. I was in love with a car! The last three digits of the license plate were 007—that's what the sales agent ordered.

When Joe died, I was advised, 'Don't make any big decisions, at least not for a year.' So, I kept the car. It was a foolish sentimental decision. Without Joe's salary, I did not have enough monthly earnings to pay the installments of R4,000 per month on top of all my other expenses.

I received a lump sum pension fund pay out, and I used that money to pay the remaining 40 installments of R4,000, that's R160,000 in total. In the South African economy of that time, that sum of money was worth half of a decent middle-class house. What I should have done was invest the money. Now I think it's a no-brainer, so what was I thinking 20 years ago? The truth was, I wasn't. Grief, emotion, and sentimentality impaired my rational thinking.

I had a financial advisor: a gentle guy. He tried to suggest I terminate the car purchase agreement. I wouldn't hear of it. I answered, 'Joe wanted us to have a solid safe car.'

What I really needed was a financial advisor more like Teresa Valdes-Fauli Weintraub, who would have been more insistent and offered me what she calls one of her 'Come to Jesus' moments—those times when she tries to coax an epiphany out of her clients, a wake-up call to help understand the financial implications and arrive at better decision-making.

Teresa is the global president of the International Women's Forum, and she's based in Miami where I'd gone to meet several members of the IWF as part of my research. Teresa mentors women, especially in the field of financial matters.

Interviewed in *The Glasshammer*, an online career resource for professional women, she repeated her personal mantra, 'To whom much is given, much is expected.' She says:

> Many women are savvy investors in their families but many still lack confidence in their own judgment when it comes to making financial decisions. An incredible 90 percent of women will be the sole financial decision-makers for their households at some points in their lives, due to divorce, widowhood, or being the chief or only breadwinner. Women should ask questions to learn what they own, how they own it, and where it is located, in case they have a life-changing event.

I knew what assets Joe and I had. What I didn't understand was the implications of short-term choices on long-term finances. I didn't understand pension savings or endowment policies, which is particularly unwise when choosing to live in a country with such income disparity that only the very poor qualify for what is a very meagre state pension. Rationally, I should have let that Volvo go!

I think if I'd had a Teresa in my life, a certified attorney and financial planner to mentor me with empathy but firmness, explaining the consequences of different options to reach sensible financial decisions, things would have turned out differently.

Teresa greeted me with warmth, as she greets everyone; I'd noticed how she connects so easily when I'd seen her at IWF conferences. Her deep brown eyes brim with emotion when she speaks of something that's pulling her heartstrings, and she's not afraid to be personal—that's part of her magic. But at the very center of her core, she's appropriately tough. She hails from a family that needed grit and determination to re-establish itself. She was born into Cuban aristocracy; the Valdes-Fauli family uprooted itself and migrated to the United States after Fidel Castro seized power.

Teresa became an extraordinarily proficient financial advisor. And she adds a finely tuned psychological reading of her clients to her well-honed technical skills. She dares to venture into the difficult conversations and backs off if the client can't handle it in that moment. She might try again later or she might not, depending on her assessment of the unfolding, fluid, relationship dynamics that she's privy to. She told me:

> People have such different characters. There are those who in their bereavement bury their heads in the ground—they are totally lost. There are those who try and find the papers and say, 'Let's work this out.' I've had women clients who've never written a check, never balanced a checkbook, never paid any bills, and don't know what their assets are. They are just totally unprepared. I have seen it with divorces and seen it with deaths. And sometimes I see an anger that comes from that—from realizing the mess that they have let themselves in for.

Teresa mentioned (not by name—she's careful about confidentiality) a recently widowed client who lives well but is not that wealthy.

> I had to really have a 'Come to Jesus' conversation with her because she wanted to play the game of benevolence by taking the daughter,

son-in-law, and grandkids on these mega trips. I said, 'You know you are going to run out of money. You are trying to do the best you can, but the money will run out if you spend like this.' It took a while, but it was better for me to be upfront in a caring way before it was too late.

Teresa says she coaches clients, doing role plays with them, to prepare for difficult conversations. How does that widow say to her daughter, 'I love you, but I don't think I want to have you take care of me and therefore I can't spend now. This is what I have.'

I shared my Volvo story with Teresa.

Okay, let's start from exactly that point—becoming widowed. Everyone consistently advises, 'Don't do anything for a while, let a year go by.' But, sometimes people want to do something in memory of, and they want to do it immediately, and perhaps they don't realize the consequences of making this donation and taking significant money out of the portfolio. Or maybe they want to take the whole family on a trip that they had always wanted to do. And again, they don't realize the repercussions that once you have diminished the capital it's hard to make it up again.

I think that one of the most important things is communication that's deeply honest. It's rare that people are totally honest with each other about money, including many happily married people.

Teresa mentioned that sometimes superstition is a serious impediment to conversation—the belief that if you talk about dying then you are inviting it to happen. I told her that my late husband Joe only completed his will three days before he died in his fourth year of multiple myeloma. In my recollection, it was the worst moment in all the four years. The room was quiet, the atmosphere leaden; Joe moved his pen over the paper as though he was signing his death sentence, as though this was the ultimate acknowledgment that no miracle was going to happen.

Teresa commented gently but firmly, 'But if people have been doing wills their whole lives, if people talked about it as part of life, it wouldn't be this big thing. I always say the hardest thing is talking about what you want.'

She added that the earlier people have the conversations, the better.

If it's challenging to make good decisions during bereavement, it's also challenging to have good conversations when one person in a couple is close to death.

When Teresa's faced with a situation where one partner is dying, she advises that they consider a transfer of assets, because although there may be insurance policies or endowment policies that may pay out quickly, there is often a hiatus and cash is needed. But sometimes people are in denial when someone is very ill and they just can't hear you and then, said Teresa, 'You just have to hope that there's enough time to be able to solve it.'

She's adamant that whenever a delicate conversation is called for she'll never do it over the phone. That very evening when our meeting ended, she planned to swing by a client who lived in downtown Miami whose partner was close to dying and who was still in denial that this was really happening, refusing to tackle the financial implications.

So, what does Teresa advise people to take care of?

People need to have access to some cash to keep things going because assets get frozen while estates are being wound up. And estates can take years to wind up—if you manage to wind up everything within two years, that's considered very fast. Another thing people need to be careful about is that they don't have to sell things too quickly to liquefy assets for cash flow. A lot of people think jewelry keeps its value. But what happens if you're selling in a fire sale because you need the cash very quickly? It's unlikely you'll get the best deal. The same with art—it doesn't serve you to have to sell under pressure.

It turned out that this is one of Teresa's own worst fears and that close to home she's in the process of getting family members to swallow this medicine. Her soulmate cousin, who is in his 70s, is nine years older than his wife; these are the years when mortality knocks more persistently at the door. When Teresa described her cousin Alfonso* as a 'passionate wine collector' I affectionately thought of my own husband, John, with his dozens of bottles stored on two racks, red and white, and the spreadsheet on his computer tracking what he's bought and when it should be drunk. I was way off and about to reach a new understanding of the term 'wine collector.'

Alfonso's passion is totally different, both in kind and scale. He has bought thousands of bottles of wine as a tradeable investment, they are all of a valuable, collectable grade. Teresa mentions the double-digit figure of exactly how many thousand bottles. They add up to being a very large portion of the couple's retirement investment. But this is Alfonso's passion—not only an investment—so its bound up in identity and Teresa said that means it 'becomes very difficult to undo psychologically.' She coached Alfonso's wife to begin a courageous conversation with him, 'Alfonso, if you have difficulty getting delivery of these wines, bought in from merchants around the world—how do you think I'll be able to deal with them? If we're not careful, I'll be left a mess, such a mess that will hurt me financially.' Alfonso's response was that he wouldn't want his wife to be hurt in any way. He made it clear that he wants to live in their home to the end of his days—no moving to a nursing home. So, he's vested in their working out a plan of how to organize his magnificent wine investment, to be able to get the best sale value, when needed. Alfonso and his wife are lucky to have Teresa looking out for them.

Teresa has consistently tried to get her clients to do the financial planning for their longevity, and to work out for themselves what would happen financially on the death of a spouse or significant other. Her conversations often involve getting clients to realize that there can be more expenses on retirement.

> There are additional costs, you're at home more, heating and other bills go up. And people often opt for supplemental medical insurance. There are also other long-term questions to answer. Do you want to stay at home to the end of your life? If so, can you cover at-home nursing costs or do you want to go into assisted living? You also must think how much it costs to be buried—$10,000? $15,000? Maybe it's better to be cremated? All these costs, and having to think not just about today, but about the fact that you may live way into your 90s. And what, if anything, do you wish to leave behind as an inheritance?

Teresa noted that people reached points in the financial planning process when they made circumspect resolutions, 'I love this home; but I can't afford it longer term.' Or, 'You know; I'm just not going to be able to make that trip every year with my friends.' She's observed that decision-making may be easier when there is a single decision-maker but when it's a couple, going through the numbers, trying to work out what to trim, it can be so hard to fully explore that conversation. It requires a joint acceptance of elderliness en route to mortality.

Teresa told me she has some clients who have a full plan of everything from a list of assets to specifics about what is to happen at their funeral and burial. They update the plan every year or so—and send in their revisions. Teresa's observed that these clients are often the people least worried about dying—often the people most comfortable in their own skin.

I told Teresa about the visit I had made to La Crosse, Wisconsin, where more than 95 percent of adults in the town had completed their Advance Directives. I suspect their preparedness for medical end-of-life choices has spilt over into financial planning. The outcome of the lack of worry, the decisions having been made, the documentation in place, has had an impact on longevity; people in La Crosse live longer than other similar socio-economic strata in the United States and they spend almost 40 percent less on end-of-life healthcare.

I asked Teresa if she thought that she's an exceptional financial advisor in terms of her humanity. She acknowledged that training for financial planners should include more emotional intelligence training on how to have better conversations with clients but that she'd like to think that she's not exceptional. She said that being a financial advisor is not just about the estate planning, but that humanity comes through as part of the offering,

Teresa regularly has financial planning conversations with the bereaved, with clients who are dying, and with the healthy elderly who are mindful of entering the third age. When I asked Teresa the question about emotional intelligence, I had in mind Malcolm Gladwell's *Tipping Point*. I'm adding the category of financial advisors to the list of professions that could make a difference in people becoming more comfortable, engaging more easily in discussion with people, about how they want to live and how they'd prefer to die.

Postscript Seven

Below is the minimalist financial checklist that I drafted for myself. It's very short, but if I carried it out—crossing every t and dotting every i—then the list of action items would be very long indeed. We are all different, so it's best to draw up your own tailor-made checklist. But here's mine:

- **Appoint your power of attorney** in case you're incapacitated and can't make decisions.
- **Work out who needs to know what,** and what you need to know about others.
- **Keep doing the math.** Every so often re-run the numbers.
- **Deal with unfinished bureaucracy.** Avoid leaving loose ends that others might be left to unravel and resolve.

This seems mundane now but once the funeral is over the well-wishers and loved ones leave to get on with their lives, and you have to get on with yours. Tough financial circumstances can cloud grief and spark anger and regrets when this is the last thing you need. The relationship between money and love is complex and powerful and best dealt with when you are in a state of calm and well-being.

PART EIGHT

Winding Up

STORAGE

When I moved from one house to another
there were many things I had no room
for. What does one do? I rented storage
space. And filled it. Years passed.
Occasionally I went there and looked in,
but nothing happened, not a single
twinge of the heart.
As I grew older the things I cared
About grew fewer, but were more
important. So one day I undid the lock
and called the trash man. He took
everything.
I felt like the little donkey when
his burden is finally lifted. Things!
Burn them, burn them. Make a beautiful
fire! More room in your heart for love,
for the trees! For the birds who own
nothing – the reason they can fly.

—Mary Oliver, *Felicity*

Kyla: My Posthumous Voice

So many people don't get around to doing a will, or if they do it does not cover all their assets. They are what's called intestate and, according to the UK's Office of National Statistics, this applies to 60 percent of people in England and Wales. It is astonishing, because when someone dies without a will it is such a rigmarole to get things sorted out; the process can take years. But the hardest part of an imprecise will is the pain involved by those who live on who, in the midst of their grief, must deal with paperwork and complicated legalese. They are often not at their best to tackle the emotional and administrative challenges—especially not in the first few weeks when much of the leg work must be started.

Wills don't need to be complicated. A piece of paper, your wishes written down, signed, dated, and witnessed by two people who don't stand to benefit from the will. That's the bare bones of a will.

You can get more sophisticated. Some wills run to dozens of pages, with many conditional clauses and the anticipation of different scenarios. But however complex it becomes, the legal requirements remain surprisingly simple: wishes, signature, date, and witnesses.

It's hardest to do this when you leave it until the last minute, when you're psychologically and physically absorbed in the immediacy of your dying. At least that's what happened with Joe. He'd fallen on the slope of the sand dunes on the third day of our annual family holiday. You'd think sand would be soft enough to cradle a fall and prevent breakages. But not when you're in your fourth year of multiple myeloma treatments, including cortisone which has brittleness of bones as a possible side effect.

In his last few days, I gently insisted he be explicit about his wishes. He was a public figure. A state funeral was on the cards. I wanted him

219

to protect us as a family by being clear about what he wanted and didn't want. I knew he hated the thought, as I did, of him being placed in an ornate coffin which some people might argue befitted his social standing. I got clarity from him: burial not cremation, and a simple pine coffin. He also spoke about which songs and music he wanted for the memorial service that we would hold for family and friends.

I'd always assumed he had a will, not that there was much to leave. The house we bought together was already in my name, but there was some money and personal items to consider the disposal of.

He did not want to think about it. He said, 'You take care of it.' I refused. Our complex family structure, including his daughters and stepdaughters, required his thinking, his decision-making and accountability. I took notes as he spoke, typed up the one-and-a-half-page document, asked him which two people, non-beneficiaries, should be asked to come and witness him signing. The small gathering to witness his signing was awful. The atmosphere felt close and heavy, almost like the mists of the Pennine wilds of my childhood: so opaque that car headlights can't shine their way through.

Joe used the engraved gold Mont Blanc pen he'd been given as a member of Mandela's cabinet, the first cabinet of the eight-month-old newly democratic South Africa. Joe's fingers moved over the page with the hand of someone who was very ill—a somewhat shaky signature emerged. The bank would challenge the will, despite the confirmed presence of witnesses: the signature did not quite match the signature on file. It would take three months before the bank would accept the will as legitimate.

Why is it that the statistics show that significant numbers of people don't do their wills? Reluctance to engage with mortality? Superstition? Or just never got around to it?

Twenty-one years later, I was visiting Brooklyn. My new granddaughter, the lovely Livia (Hebrew for lioness) was 48 days old. My daughter Kyla, Joe's stepdaughter, asked me to trade some time.

She would look at a work proposal I was drafting, and in exchange I would read and comment on her draft will. Kyla's previous will was now outdated. It didn't anticipate the existence of this precious newborn, who will need at least a couple of decades of love, care, and expenditure on her way to independent adulthood.

I read Kyla's draft and then we sat together and talked about it.

She'd indicated who would have custody of her child if she and her husband were to die at the same time. Good. I asked if she and her husband discussed this with the proposed guardians and if had they agreed? Yes.

She'd laid out in precise detail what was to happen to her property and financial assets. She had allocated some financial resources to her sister to help her take care of their father in his elderliness. My own will at this time had a similar clause to ensure there would be funds for my mum should I predecease her.

Kyla had decided she wanted to donate her organs and written that she'd like to be cremated. She listed the music to be played at her memorial service and the place where her ashes should be dispersed.

I suggested she needed to be more specific about the time frame for the return of the remains of her body, post-organ extraction. Some people donate their bodies to medical institutions and there's a waiting period that can prove difficult for the families who feel they can't complete the rituals they need for their closure.

Kyla's main desire was a simple two-pager that would provide clarity about custody and care of her daughter, but while engaging in the process she had thought through and drawn up a list of bequests. She'd considered each family member and her best friend. Her mother-in-law would receive her two Japanese jewelry boxes; symbolic and so appropriate—if you were to visit Agnes's home you'd notice her love of Japanese objects.

Kyla left me the pair of paintings I sourced for her 30th birthday. I observed that perhaps her husband may want them—they are part of the home they live in together. I wouldn't want to receive something that might make him feel their home was being dismantled.

There were no bequests yet for some family members. She told me she was working out what would be the right something for each of them.

I shared with her the suggestion I'd received from a friend as an additional question for the book I'm writing: 'Is there anything in your list of bequests that may be hurtful to someone you love?'

Kyla responded saying the reason she was being so careful was because of her own experience of seeing the hurt you feel when you've been left out, that you weren't thought about.

I looked at her quizzically.

She told me of her memory of her being 10 years old when Joe died and how he bequeathed to her his collection of ornamental lions —the black ebony one from Mozambique, the soapstone from Kenya, the green malachite from Zambia, the wooden ones with whiskers that always made me smile, that I'd bought for him at Harare's Mbari market. She also remembered how upset Joe's grandchild, 11-year-old Cassie, was at the time.

But Cassie got a handsome allocation of money for her schooling, I interjected. And she got a leather document wallet, made for Joe by the secret service of the old German Democratic Republic, the one with a compartment for hiding things, including his very prized false British passport in the name of Antonio Pinto.

'No, Mama.' Kyla's memory is elephantine. '*You* put together the document wallet for her when you noticed she looked hurt. The fact that her grandfather had left money was of no comfort to her. She wanted something personal.'

She's right. It's true. I have a tendency to reframe facts and emotions as they happened, especially when there's been hurt or deep discomfort. As the neurologist Oliver Sacks wrote in his book *Hallucinations*, 'We now know that memories are not fixed or frozen, like Proust's jar of preserves in a larder, but are transformed, disassembled, reassembled, and recategorized with every act of recollection.'

And 21 years later I am still loyal and defensive of the man I loved. I say to Kyla, 'I think when you're dying there isn't a lot of capacity to be thoughtful about others. That's why it is so useful to do all this stuff when you're healthy and then put it away and get on with living knowing that it's done. It's great you're doing your will now.'

Roz: Your Treasure, My Detritus

My mother moved from her house to an apartment and then to a smaller apartment, and each time she moved she discarded nothing. She has our school reports and every letter written to her by her children and grandchildren. She has every boarding card of every journey she's made. She has brochures from every touristy place she's ever visited, menus and receipts from every special family meal. She has appointment cards, envelopes of x-rays and medical reports from every one of her many visits to innumerable specialists. And she likes what my son-in-law Andrew calls a *tchotchke*; the purchase of an item as a memento. She's always had the need to buy one when she's been on holiday, the statuette of the Holy Infant of Prague, the slate stone bookends from the English Lake District, the African head sculpture from her visit to Victoria Falls. Her apartment is filled with knick-knacks.

To my chagrin, I am cut from the same cloth, a proverbial chip-off-the-old-block. There's some discernible dilution of the disposition to hoard, but it is a strong source of discomfort for me. I envy those friends of mine whose apartments are uncluttered. I'll get there. I have started a scanning project for photos and paperwork. But I'm still finding it hard to shred the photos once they're scanned!

It's little wonder that *New Yorker* cartoonist Roz Chast's book about the decline of her parents appeals to me so strongly. The cover is a cartoon of Chast sitting on a sofa with her parents and with the book title *Can't We Talk About Something More Pleasant?* as the speech bubble of what her father's saying to her.

Chast chronicled the last eight years of her parents' lives. Her account was wry and often funny, because that's what she is, a cartoonist. I laughed a lot but I also found it very thought provoking.

Her parents had lived in the same two-bedroom apartment in Brooklyn for decades—it's where Chast grew up, and they lived there until their 90s, their health in decline. Her father had dementia, her mother fell off a ladder and they had Meals on Wheels after that. By then Chast lived in Connecticut, a two-hour journey away. She described how hard it was to trek backwards and forwards and put support systems in place. Finally, one day when Roz once again asked them if they would consider the assisted living home which was only 10 minutes away from where she lived, they agreed to a 'trial stay.'

Chast wrote, 'I had to move fast before they could change their minds... They packed overnight bags, put on their coats and hats, and locked the door behind them... It was the last time they ever saw their apartment.'

My own mind boggled as I read this, the thought of two 92-year-olds leaving the entire contents of decades of their lives behind them, just like that. But that is what my mother will also do.

Chast had to deal with the apartment, and her memoir is made up of a combination of cartoons and photographs—all with hand-written captions. The photo of the kitchen blender identifies it as vintage 1950s, not its 21st-century retro imitation. There was one photo of a drawer full of jar lids, another of a drawer with dozens of used pencils and crayons. The caption 'I arranged all of my mother's purses on the bed' fell underneath a photo of the purses all laid out—all 33 of them. I counted them in the photograph.

My first reaction was to be astonished, and then I reminded myself, 'Don't point fingers because when you point one finger forward then there are three fingers pointing back at yourself.' I asked myself the question, 'So, how many purses do you own? If something were to happen to you now, and somebody were to open your wardrobe and look at the shelf of purses, how many would they find?' I have at least five or six briefcases, and probably the same number of purses as Roz Chast's mother. I'm in the same league on this score.

Those of us who are older probably grew up with parents who had little when they were younger—those World War II years when so much of the world was impacted, where people and food shortages were part of daily living. When the post-war economy thrived, consumer goods became plentiful but they were purchased by adults who'd known differently. When Scrimp 'n Save meet Abundance, the results can be alarming. And my excuse? Inherited genes? A liking for matching the color of accessories with an outfit? Ten years of living in Mozambique at a time of civil war and scarcity? All of the above!

Chast chose what she most wanted. It was a short list: a few books, a pair of bookends, a picture, a little jewelry, a book of demo embroidery stiches made by her mother, photo albums, and letters. And then? She wrote, 'I left it for the super to deal with. I didn't care whether he kept it, sold it, or threw it out the window.'

Chast's book challenged me. It was a wake-up call to action. Will I make the time to sort and pare down my own accumulation of stuff? My friend Novella recently commented, 'When our parents die, we're horrified at what they leave for us to sort. And then as time goes on, that memory fades, we forget, and leave the same mess for our own children.'

Helen Smit and I agreed to talk about the logistics of her move with Roger from Old Lyme, Connecticut to the Ingleside residence in Washington DC. I had such huge admiration for them. Sorting and packing the family house where they lived for decades would not be left for their son Theo. I asked Helen how she set about the sorting that happened and what afterthoughts she'd had. Perhaps some advice for others?

They'd lived in their Old Lyme house for decades. It's where they carefully chose to settle, a place where they could have both an outdoor life and a modest commute to work. When I visited Boston in 2015 I'd stayed over with them. The kitchen had been extended to create a sitting area overlooking the garden. Helen and Roger strategically placed two comfy armchairs with reading lamps to supplement the overhead lighting. There was a coffee table with coasters and current reading material as well as deep African baskets to catch the overflow of magazines. Many art works hung on the walls, and several wooden sculptures adorned the architrave above the windows. This whole room, as well as every other room in the house, reflected their long and well-traveled lives.

I'd checked in with Helen a few months later when they were getting the house ready for sale. Helen said she was very bored. 'Packing up family pictures, and clearing mouse droppings in the basement isn't exactly intellectually challenging!'

I asked what they did with the things they let go and how made their decisions.

We gave a lot away. We learned a lot. There were things I thought were valuable that you couldn't sell. Everybody who has been through this moving and downsizing says the same thing. Furniture tastes have changed. Silver tableware in this country is now worth only its weight.

One of my sister's grandchildren who lives in the UK wanted to spend time with us before we moved to the city. We offered her the ticket for the trip if she'd help us clean out the basement. Having a cheerful teenager going through boxes of family things proved to be a great help because it would be 'Throw that out! That too, throw it out.' We'd organized a dumpster outside the house to put all the junk in. There were moments that were fun. I'd say, 'Throw it out.' And then she'd say, 'Oh no, don't throw that one out.' And she'd find things that were special for her, 'Wow, this is a picture of my father when he was *thin*!' It was fun having her. We only worked her a few hours a day and she was a great guest. Having someone detached do part of the sorting really helped.

One of the wonderful things about the place we live now is that there are people with all kinds of amazing talents. One of my friends here turns out to have a business restoring old photographs as well as working with new ones. I think I need to digitize some of the family pictures that used to hang in the old house which we couldn't get up in this apartment.

We have a storage unit here chock full of stuff we couldn't deal with at the time of moving. I have some winter projects, particularly in terms of papers, souvenirs, family pictures. It's a question of time or money—making time to do it yourself or paying someone else to do it. But when it comes to papers and family pictures, it's best to do it yourself.

I'm impressed. I couldn't see my mother showing any interest in spending time sorting. I also can't see that I'll be a Roz Chast and take a few items of sentimental value and then ask the superintendent, in our case the caretaker, to deal with the rest. My mum's 'too much stuff' plus my own 'too much stuff' is a future project I'll need to face. I hope I've listened well enough, and that my learning will lead to action.

Dale's List

I sat in the audience watching JR's performance at an arts festival. He was good, very good, at the top of his game. And his boys were grown, now young adults in university, and here he was enjoying himself by getting involved in a lifestyle project that held the promise of living within a community of people with shared values in a rural setting just 90 minutes' drive from Cape Town.

A few weeks later, someone asked, 'Did you hear JR died? He went to hospital for a couple of stents to be inserted. It's such a common operation these days that you don't even stay overnight. You're admitted as a day patient. JR thought it was so routine that he didn't even speak with his sons about it. But there was internal bleeding and that was it.'

I'm told his wife sat in shock, stunned by the news. In her hand, she held his phone; she didn't know the pin code. She couldn't get the numbers of his friends and colleagues. Three days passed before many of them heard the news. As for his funeral wishes, he'd taken care to compose a document but his wife didn't know the password to get into his computer.

When Joe died Tessa had just turned 15 and Kyla was 10. I worried, 'What happens to them if something happens to me?' I made a new will. I opened a bank account in Tessa's name and deposited 'emergency money' into it. Joe's dying taught me that bank accounts get closed on death and that access to money is not that simple or speedy. My daughters knew where to find the file called: 'Mama—in the event of my death.'

Was I unnaturally preoccupied?

Unexpected bad stuff happens all the time. A writing group friend was a passenger in a car. She was the only survivor of the eight people involved in the accident. A father waited in his car for his son to come to the parking lot after he finished football practice. Cell phone thieves left him dead with a bullet in his head. The car hijacking in my driveway: a member of my family listened to the hijackers' discussion, 'He's seen our faces—should we kill him?'

How many of us are truly ready if something were to happen to us today? That we might leave for work expecting to be home for supper but in fact never return: the car accident, the heart attack, the stray bullet caught in the crossfire. Most of us seem to think that we're ring-fenced. It won't happen to us. These things happen to other people.

In my 2013 series for a local newspaper, *Let's Talk about Dying*, I gave one contribution the headline 'Checklist for Checking Out' for readers to consider. My list included:

Conversations. All the people I love must know what they mean to me. Any ongoing unresolved stuff should be receiving my best effort.

My will and financial policies. Is my current will comprehensive? Did I change the beneficiaries of my pension funds? What about my mum's medical costs? Who gets which painting and what about mementos to special friends?

Power of attorney. I'm currently lucid and can write my signature, but what do I need to have drawn up in case of emergency (i.e. the car accident that puts me in a coma)?

A living will. This is the document which indicates what you would want to happen in terms of medical treatment if you are in a coma or on life support.

Advance directives. This document goes further than a living will in that it indicates what's to happen should you become unable to make decisions. I've hit menopause, so I'm now a candidate for dementia. How do I expect to be cared for? An AD includes nominating the person who will make decisions for me when I can't. My doctor needs a copy.

My body. Which, if any, body parts do I want to donate?

My funeral. I have written down how I would like family and friends to mark my exit out of this world.

My remains. I have a plot available in Avalon Cemetery in Soweto alongside Joe. Or have things changed? Would I prefer cremation and for my ashes to be scattered? If so, where?

My numbers. This includes phone numbers, passwords, PIN numbers, policy numbers. Either I need to type up detailed lists and print them out, or I need to make sure that a family member has the information to access them.

That's the practical stuff. You could have all that in place and still not feel ready. Being ready in your head—isn't that the bigger challenge? After that column ran, I received a mail from a client who attended the same church as a woman by the name of Dale, whose relatively young husband, who'd never been ill, had a fatal heart attack. Dale thought they were organized, and that their paperwork was in reasonably good order. She felt confident she could navigate the bureaucracy. She discovered otherwise.

Dale kept track of everything she did after his death to deal with his estate. She circulated her extensive list so that others might be forewarned and forearmed, with the invitation to advise her of anything she'd missed. Following is my edited version of Dale's list.

I anticipate disengagement from some readers. But I'm sharing what myself and others have learned the hard way. In the whirlwind of grief you don't want to have to think and search. So let's get very practical. A couple of these items and terminology will be specific to South Africa only but most are applicable for what everyone has to do the world over when they have to deal with winding up a deceased estate. Dale's missive to friends reads as follows:

Dear friends,

So, you think you are prepared? Think again.

The gift of life is a rare and precious thing, but fragile and fleeting, and can be gone in an instant. Just how equipped are you to deal with that time when your spouse (or a parent) dies?

Here is a list of things that most people will need to facilitate the process of winding up an estate. The things I found I needed or should have had knowledge of:

Existing documents

Be clear where they are—in a safe/bank vault/storage locker—if so, where are the keys and/or what is the combination code?

- Will (current) of the deceased. Who is it lodged with/where is it kept? Hopefully you will be aware of your partner's wishes regarding items of more sentimental value (not specified in the will). Discuss which child should receive what, so that there can be no strife, e.g. Dad's Bible, watch, or tools, Mom's rings, etc.
- Burial policy. If there is one, know where it is kept and with which company, to avoid delays.
- Life policies. Name of company (good to have a contact name) and policy numbers.
- Investments. Know which companies hold which policy and keep a list of all the account/policy numbers. Clarify if they are living life annuities or endowment policies.
- Pension. If there is one, with which company? There could be more than one. If the person is retired it may not necessarily still be held with the company of employment.
- Identity document and passport. Make at least ten copies and get these certified—do this before the ID book front page is stamped 'deceased.'
- Marriage and birth certificates. If applicable, e.g. you will need proof of a legal marriage for pension fund requirements.
- Property title deeds. It would be wise to have access to the title deeds, as this will form part of the estate (if it's in your partner's name it goes into the estate).

- Antenuptial contract. If the deceased is your spouse, have available your antenuptial contract which will indicate the decision you made to marry within or without community of property.

New documents to generate
- A new will. As the surviving spouse or adult child, draw up a new will as soon as possible as your circumstances have changed.
- Original death certificate. The funeral home should be able to supply you with both the original (*do not let this out of your hands*) and numerous certified copies, which you will be need for several entities: bank/pension company/insurance/stop and debit order companies, etc.
- Letter of executorship. Understand that, until the executor has received a letter of executorship from the master of the Supreme Court, any account in your spouse/partner's name will be frozen.

Who is doing what for what purpose?
- Body viewing. Decide who would want to see the body of the deceased before cremation or burial.
- Organs. If the deceased is an organ donor, be clear about who to contact.
- Have a funeral home in mind to assist you with the urgent medical and legal requirements.
- Executor/Executrix: Who is nominated?
- Attorney: If you are the nominated executor, take the will to an attorney to set in motion the issue of the letter of executorship. Dealings with the Master are complex and fiddly, and legally you are not allowed to deal directly with the master of the Supreme Court unless you have the qualifications to do so.
- Financial advisor: Know the name and contact details of the financial broker who dealt with the life insurance and any endowment policies. You may need their assistance in tracing any policies or investments held in your partner's name.

Decisions to be clear about
- Burial (which cemetery) or if cremation then where to scatter the ashes. What were the person's wishes?

Cash flow

- Access to immediate money. Have a bank or savings account of your own where you can immediately access money, and not in a joint account which may be frozen on the death of one partner.
- Budget for two months. Have sufficient money accessible to cover about two months' cost of living—because that is how long it may take for money in joint accounts to become accessible.
- Pension. It is helpful to know what your portion will be, if any, for your financial planning.
- Investments. Know if there are monthly deposits being made into any account and what to do to cancel these.
- Life insurance and endowment policies. Some of these policies will be paid out immediately.
- Insurance policies (house/vehicles). What are the premiums being paid? You must continue to pay to make sure that you continue to be covered while the Estate is being finalized.
- Monthly account payments. Be clear which accounts are paid monthly and how they are paid. This must include any stop/debit orders coming off your partner's current/credit card account (i.e. municipality utility bills/television satellite dish premiums/cell phone/garage card, etc.). All monthly payments/premiums must be paid by you if you are the surviving spouse. This will continue until the account holder's name and banking details are changed, which can only happen when you have the letter of executorship acknowledging who the executor is. If you are not the nominated executor, you must get this letter from that person to enable you to make the necessary changes required.
- Mortgage bond. If the house/flat/any property still has a mortgage bond being paid off, you will need to keep up those payments.
- Foreign income. If the person has any foreign pension monies or income, make sure you know how to get hold of the relevant person/institutions, both to advise of the death of the person concerned, and to find out what you need to do next.
- Diary timelines. Don't let vehicle licenses expire or policy premiums lapse. Get a diary and keep tabs on all upcoming deadlines—it is easy to forget day-to-day stuff when you are preoccupied with all the immediate demands on your time and memory.

Other information needed

- Cell phone. The pin number, PUK number and contract details.
- Internet banking. Discuss with your spouse about your knowing the PIN and passwords, and how to use the facility.
- Vehicle. Make sure you are entitled to drive the motor vehicle if it is licensed in your spouse/partner's name. Remember that any car forms part of the estate, which will take many months to be finalized—you can't sell it in the meantime. Clarify how this impacts insurance and the re-registering of the car into your name if you decide to keep it. Know where spare car keys are kept.
- Security contact details. If the car has an anti-hijacking/theft system, know with which company, and the name and password that you require for their system.
- Health insurance coverage. If you share a joint or family policy, make it your business to understand how it works. Notify them straight away that your partner/spouse has died, and arrange to become the principal member. (In Dale's case, the normal protocols were not followed and she only found out, nearly a month later, that her family's policy had been put into suspension, technically canceled, which left both herself and her family at risk.)
- Tax. Know what is to be done in respect of tax. When was the last return submitted? Which branch did your partner deal with? You will need the account name and tax number.

Dale's checklist was meticulously comprehensive and would take some work to complete. I had two additions. Firstly, another widow advised me that her husband had a debt and that after his death, she was pursued for repayment. They had not planned their finances as to what would happen in the event of his death. The kids moved to less expensive schools—more upheaval at a difficult time—and she moved to a smaller house with more modest running costs. My second addition was the need to name guardians for your children, if you have children who are minors, and make clear any specific wishes that you would want a guardian to know about.

Even when you know all that Dale has so carefully written out, most of us don't keep track and update constantly, even when you've been through the experience of being nominated as the executor of a deceased estate and you've suffered your way through a documentation treasure hunt.

One family I know had parents who once owned a trailer which they then sold. The parents never completed the exchange of ownership paperwork. The elderly parents died, one shortly after the other. The annual license fee for the trailer kept coming to their post box. No one knew who bought the trailer, not the adult children, not the neighbors. For the executor, this was but one item with loose ends in what became a three-year marathon involving dozens of hours to deal with the paperwork so that the attorney could wind up the estate. The executor told me he reported the trailer as stolen—it was the most expedient way he could think of to resolve a bureaucratic daymare.

Dale's final advice: A master file. At the very least, have one master file, in which all relevant documentation is kept.

My neighbor Julie told me that in her family this is known as The Purple File. Whenever she and her husband travel she'd always say to her kids, 'If anything happens, go to the purple file!'

Mohamed: Unnamed Beneficiaries

Mohamed* is a principal of an employee retirement fund in South Africa who I had worked with over the course of my career in agricultural banking. He agreed to share with me some of the problems he'd come across—changing names, of course, to protect identities—his own included. Most cases have been straight forward. People have done the paperwork, filled in the names of the beneficiaries and processing the payment has been unproblematic. But he's had a few surprises and chooses one to tell me about.

He was busy finalizing the payout on a claim from the wife and children of a deceased company employee. He had checked the nomination forms and all the details tallied. The wife was to receive 50 percent of the benefit, and each of the two children, now in their mid-30s, would receive equal shares of the remainder.

At the 11th hour, post-tax and pre-payment into the respective bank accounts, there was a call from two young adults, one still a teenager who'd just completed high school and the other, five years older and married. They informed Mohamed that they were also daughters of the deceased and they had learned about his retirement fund; they wanted to know if they were entitled to receive a share.

Mohamed contacted the wife of the deceased and asked her to come to the office. He wanted to talk to her in person, to break what would be bad news to her as gently as possible, and to inform her that there would be a delay.

Mohamed found himself on the receiving end of a torrent of invective. In the absence of the dead husband, the wife directed her anger at Mohamed.

'She threw tantrums and said they were not going to get a cent,' he told me. 'After we met, she kept calling and repeating, they are not going to get a cent, over her dead body will they get a single cent, and that she will sue if anything is given to these two impostors.'

It turned out to be a messy situation. Mohamed traveled to the small town where the two claimants lived and spent three days interviewing people. The elder sister, in her 20s, was working in a hair salon, and had married. The younger woman, in her late teens, lived with her sister. She had just finished high school and wanted to go on to study further if she could get a bursary or access to other funds. On the birth certificates of the two women, the box indicating paternal identity had been left blank. Mohamed needed evidence to support their claim.

Mohamed interviewed their mother, but she was inebriated and difficult to talk to, putting into question that anything she said could be relied upon. Sadly, she didn't even seem to care.

Mohamed persisted. He knew, from experience, that people talk. What was the talk among family members? What had the neighbors gossiped about all these years? What affidavits, if any, might be drawn up to be placed on legal record as to the paternity of the two young women?

The neighbors confirmed the mother's long-term relationship with the deceased that had ended a couple of years earlier. Other family members vouched that these were indeed the children of the deceased. Mohamed also looked for non-verbal proofs of a relationship. Had the deceased contributed to maintenance?

I couldn't find a paper trail. Nothing in bank accounts to indicate a relationship. Money that changed hands was always cash. And then on the third day I was given a document. It was the letter for a bride price, the marriage agreement, formalized and only put into writing after considerable verbal discussion. When the older daughter was getting married, the deceased man engaged in the deliberations. It was his name on the document; it was he who was present and accepted the bride price for his daughter. This made things clear. No other verification was necessary.

Fifty percent of the funds went to the widow. Then Mohamed and his colleagues considered how to divide the remaining 50 percent. The deceased had five daughters. In his main family home he lived with his wife, two biological daughters and one stepdaughter, and then there were the two newly discovered biological daughters living in the other town where the deceased had frequently traveled for work. Five beneficiaries.

There was a further episode of unpleasantness. The two eldest daughters of the first family considered 25 percent to be their fair share of the pension fund. Now that their mother and five beneficiaries were being considered, they feared they were not going to get the amounts of money they'd banked on. They presented an argument that their half-sister, as having no biological relationship to their father, should be excluded as a beneficiary.

Mohamed informed them that, as their father had always provided for their half-sister, she could not now be excluded. Besides, their father had filled out their half-sister's name on the nomination form, and to exclude her would be inconsistent with the way the deceased had conducted his life.

Mohamed sadly shook his head at how often he has seen how money engenders greed.

I asked Mohamed how often he finds complications in retirement fund payouts.

'Over the past 10 years, there have been plus minus a dozen cases out of 35 that I've handled. Yes, there are issues. Peoples' lives are not straight forward. You wouldn't believe what I come across.'

Gina: Twelve Soups and Eight Questions

My father died in October 1992. My mother, Gina spent that first Christmas as a widow with her sister Inge. Every year after that, except for the year after Joe died, I invited my mum for Christmas Eve dinner where I would try to respect and replicate some of her Czech childhood traditions which she'd tried to infuse into us as her children growing up in England.

One of these was soups. Twelve soups! Mum described how they made them from everything stored on the farm from the summer and autumn harvests: apple, barley, beetroot, carrot, ham, onion, peach, potato, and plum. The root vegetables were stored in pits in the earth, and the fruits were dried or preserved in syrup. She told us about a soup made with carp—a gift fished and distributed from the lake of the largest local land holder. Viennese schnitzel was the other non-negotiable component of the meal, made with veal, not pork. Mum went to a lot of trouble talking to the butcher about his finding her some veal, an uncommon purchase, in the 1960s of my UK childhood.

I've never quite managed 12 soups. The most, with help, was six: three hot, three cold, served in small Chinese tea bowls.

Christmas Eve was a time of marking tradition. But in 2015 it was a moment that marked profound change. On that occasion, Mum, as her 88-year-old self, made a huge effort to dress elegantly, in her dove-blue silk outfit. She dressed while sitting on her bed; Ivy Cele, her patient caregiver, carried everything to her as she made her requests. My mother struggled with the clasps of her jewelry, refusing help, as always making her 'I can do it myself' protest with an edge of irritability in her voice. What she couldn't do easily were her eyebrows—she'd lost them to chemotherapy and they never properly grew back. So, a little makeup, the finishing touches, were my responsibility.

We wheeled Mum down from her apartment on the third floor to ours on the second. She seemed disorientated by the number of people, which included John's family as well as mine. Because December in Johannesburg is a beautiful time weather-wise, we were all seated on the balcony where we'd have the first course of soups. We filled crystal flutes—a gift from Mum—and raised them in a toast. The glassware chinked that special crystal glass sound, but my mother sipped her champagne tentatively, without gusto.

I noticed she had small spoonfuls of each soup; she seemed to have no appetite. When we moved inside to the main dining table, I sat beside her cutting up her tender veal into tiny slivers. It had become difficult for her to chew, she'd lost so much weight, her gums had shrunk and her dentures no longer fitted well. She moved the food around on her plate, and ate hardly anything.

Just then she started to throw up the little she'd eaten. She and I discreetly managed to catch all of it in her napkin and mine—people mostly weren't aware of the mini-drama happening at our end of the long table. Then Mum told me she felt 'woozy' and would like to lie down, so I wheeled her to my study and cleared the chaise for her. She reclined as if she were in a daze. I told her I'd finish my supper quickly and then come back to check in on her.

'Where am I?' she asked me. 'What's this place?'

She didn't recognize my study. She told me she'd like to go home. She asked if John could drive her to her old apartment block a few kilometers away. She'd forgotten that she moved into our building almost five years before.

On Christmas Day, she slept late and the distress and confusion of the night before dissipated. Late morning, John, Tessa and her husband Alex and their 14-month-old son Benjamin and I went upstairs to Mum's place and set the table for brunch: coffee, juice, champagne, fruit, bagels, cream cheese, and smoked salmon. My mother joined us at the table, in her best dressing gown, a creamy satin damask. She enjoyed the little she ate of her favorite food: smoked salmon and cream cheese.

Afterwards, we settled in her lounge and the present-opening began. Mum enjoyed her great-grandson's delight—it was probably the tearing of the paper that Benjamin had most fun with.

From that day on, John and I resolved we'd celebrate Christmas at Mum's place in the coming year. It seemed that the effort of getting dressed and coming downstairs had become huge and seemed to tire her out completely, letting disorientation set in. I surmised her traveling days were now probably over. No more Kruger Park or Cape Town. As for traveling to England to visit her husband's grave, and to see her grandchildren and great-grandchildren there —wish she had mentioned several times—would take Herculean organization and nerves of steel to accomplish, and it was more than I was willing to commit to.

After Christmas, she seemed to find her equilibrium again. She had three, almost four good months, enjoying the world from under the comfort of her floral duvet.

But her affirmation 'Well, at least I've got all my marbles' rang increasingly less true.

'Is my mother still alive?' she asked me. I gently took her back in time 30 years to 1986, the year her mother died. When lucidity returned, she was both a little scared of her mental failing and a little ashamed: 'Don't tell Inge (her sister) that I asked you this question.'

I'd recently watched Alzheimer's capture and decimate a close friend's mental prowess and I was concerned that Mum was taking this same route. I did practical things like phoning the bank to discuss power of attorney. Even though the impending finality of loss stalked me daily, like the pervasive presence of haunting music in the background, it was challenging to face practicalities. Inactivity, avoiding the complex emotion of this kind of bureaucracy, held great appeal.

I went to see Dr. Martin Connell, Mum's doctor, and requested he do a home visit and go over her living will. I wanted to have her wishes on record, and I wanted him and John as witnesses as a support to me should the time come when I might have to act on her behalf.

'Gina, I've come to talk to you about your health,' Dr. Connell said to her as he took her blood pressure. 'I'm concerned you're getting weaker. I'm wondering how to manage your care. You are not wanting to get up and move. How are you feeling generally?'

'Today was cold.'

Dr. Connell took out his stethoscope and asked Mum to breathe in and out, in and out. 'Can I ask you to sit up briefly?'

'The trouble is today I'm stiff.'

Dr. Connell settled back with a single sheet of paper in front of him. I had prepared the one-pager, which included eight questions which were extrapolated from various living wills covering the essential concerns I wanted Mum's decisions on. It's true that people revisit living wills and often change their minds, but at least we would know what she thought now, whilst she still had clarity of mind.

'What I want to talk to you about is how much medical intervention you want. Yesterday you had a bad day and I'm concerned the bad days are becoming more frequent. I want us to think about your care here at home. I understand you don't want us to put you in a hospital.'

'If I get really sick, I'd consider hospital, if there was a chance of a good outcome. I've been in some I didn't like. The nurses were a bit bolshie. I have strong genes. My father lived to nearly 100, my mother was nearly 100, and my aunt also nearly 100. Hospitals are for sick people who have a chance of getting well again. I'd rather die at home. As long as my brain is functioning I want to live.'

'What about CPR, resuscitation?'

My mother answered with her nurse's hat on. 'That's a very big question. It can be successful, but you feel afterwards, was it worthwhile?'

When my father died of a heart attack, my mother tried mouth-to-mouth resuscitation—her family doctor told her that he was pleased she had not succeeded, that the heart attack was so severe that had he lived it would have meant he would not have been able to do most of the things he lived his life for.

'But what would you want for yourself?' he asked.

'You can try, but don't overdo it. If there's a little chance, try. Because I do like life.'

And intravenous feeding?

'It depends if it's feasible that there'll be a good outcome.'

And who should make decisions if you're not capable of making them?

'My daughter,' then she laughed and added, 'I don't think she will try to kill me.'

Dr. Connell then said he'd like to involve hospice as a support to us in managing her frailty. He suggested getting a bed which we would be able to raise and lower. My mum answered that her last 10 years of professional nursing included courses on end-of-life care; she'd welcome having hospice support.

Suddenly Mum was thirsty, and struggled to drink from a glass. Her one eye seemed to become weepy, and she spoke single sentences with pregnant pauses between them.

'If I am ill and showing no improvement in a reasonable amount of time, I am to be let go. If I become a cabbage, I am to be let go. I only want an intervention if a good outcome is feasible. It's no use hanging onto life like a fly for ever and ever.'

They continued talking for a while about hospice care, and then my mum said: 'Well, I still want to go to my relative's weddings. I still want to go to Adolf and Erwin's weddings,' she said, referring to her brothers.

And then the room went quiet. We all looked at Mum, astonished. In that moment she also realized what she had said. Her brothers married long ago. They were also in their 80s.

Dr. Connell, speaking very gently, said, 'Are you aware your memory is becoming unreliable?'

'I'm having very funny sensations, that I'm not in the place where I'm supposed to be... I'd like to have more control of this dipping in and out...'

Eventually, the caring and cautious Dr. Connell took his leave, as did my husband John.

Mum and I sat together companionably. She was tired after the discussion, but said she was glad that her wishes were known. I had one more question that I was curious about; there wouldn't be a better time so I went ahead and asked it: was she was looking forward to meeting her beloved husband, my dad Toni, in heaven?

She surprised me. She told me she didn't think of heaven as a place with people in it. 'It's less about a place,' she said, 'and more about a state of feeling.'

'What does it feel like?'

'Peace. Tranquility. It's a place where you just feel there's peace—you become part of it.'

I asked her what she wanted to be inscribed under her name on the tombstone that she will share with my father. She surprised me again with her answer.

'Shalom,' she said. The Hebrew word for peace.

Postscript Eight

Ever-ready? I learned firsthand how difficult that can be.

I slipped on a paving stone in our garden on a late Sunday afternoon in December 2016, a week before Christmas and the start of our southern hemisphere summer holidays. I'd broken two bones, both the fibula and the tibia. A plate and screws would be needed. They wanted to admit me to the hospital immediately but would operate only when the swelling went down. I pleaded, 'I need to be at the crematorium tomorrow at 9am. There's a service I have to attend.'

The nurse encased my foot, ankle and calf into plaster of Paris and issued a pair of crutches.

'Keep the leg raised,' I was told. 'Come back on Wednesday at 6:30am. The swelling will surely be down, and the orthopedic surgeon will do the operation.'

I had 48 hours' grace. I calmly thought about all the people I knew who'd gone to hospital for operations and died. I mentally trawled my list: my first boss Danilo in Mozambique who had an adverse reaction to the anesthetic; my friend Phyllis's son who went in for a knee operation and got an infection and died; my friend Barney who had a heart bypass, but then a pulmonary embolism ended his life; my friend Margaret who went to have polyps removed, and died in a coma after internal hemorrhaging; and Harold, who came out of surgery on life support because the heart operation was not successful. I was with the family when they were consulted prior to the machines being switched off.

Why should I think it couldn't happen to me? I was not catastrophizing. I didn't feel particularly anxious—simply realistic.

Over the next two days I tidied up outstanding administration. I did my month-end payments early. I took another look at my will and made some adjustments. I discovered loose ends; my husband and I had put money into a shared property and hadn't yet changed title deeds. Affidavits would be an interim solution.

We were to drive to the hospital on Wednesday morning. The evening before John and I sat down and made sure that he knew all the PIN codes and passwords that he might need to access my phone, computer, iPad, as well as passwords for Facebook, Spotify, Apple, and the details of my bank accounts and financial policies. We went over my funeral wishes, the venue, where the ashes should go, the wake, the selection of poems, the speakers, the music. My living will stayed the same; I should remember a copy to take to the hospital in the morning.

I thought we'd finished when I remembered one more thing. What if I am unfortunate? Who would make the request or consent to the life support machine being turned off? I've heard it recommended that it's better to name someone other than your next of kin. It's such a heart-wrenching moment.

I sent a text to my dear close friend Gonda. 'Just updating my living will. Please will you agree to switch off the machines if something goes wrong? It's recommended that you don't ask your spouse to do this. I trust your decision. Love, Helena.'

'Huge responsibility,' she texted back. 'Love you lots and I suppose switching off would be the ultimate expression of love.'

PART NINE

Let's Talk—Towards
the Tipping Point

Ideas and products and messages and behaviors spread just like viruses do. The name given to that one dramatic moment in an epidemic when everything can change all at once is the Tipping Point.

—Malcom Gladwell, *The Tipping Point*

After meeting with so many people, thinkers, scientists, educators, healthcare professionals, social workers, and activists, it is clear that the only way to truly change the world is through teaching compassion. Our society is lacking an adequate sense of compassion, sense of kindness, and genuine regard for others' well-being. So now many, many people who seriously think about humanity all have the same view. We must promote basic human values, the inner values that lie at the heart of who we are as human beings.

—Dalai Lama, *The Book of Joy*, co-authored with Archbishop Desmond Tutu and Douglas Abrams

Let's Talk: In the Media

In January 2011, I was moved to write an article for the South African weekly, the *Mail & Guardian*. Gloom and agitation had swept the country due to the fear of losing of our beloved icon, former President Mandela, who was critically ill. Television cameras zoomed in on reporters who had camped outside Johannesburg's Milpark Hospital, newspapers carried photos of beautiful collages made by children with the message 'Get well soon, Madiba,' and there was a spontaneous Candle of Hope vigil outside his Johannesburg residence. How close were we to the finality of losing our beloved 93-year-old Nelson Rolihlahla Mandela?

I was uncomfortable with the prevailing narrative, and wanted to see if I could write something that would contribute to a shift in the way the media engaged with Mandela's mortality. It seemed to me that people were not yet psychologically prepared for his death. They somehow wanted to him to be immortal.

I decided to write about how Mandela had been so present during the time of Joe's dying days, and how he'd role-modeled empathy and acceptance. The night before Joe died, Madiba had come for a visit. As Joe held his hand in silent acknowledgment, Madiba warmly recounted their student days and told Joe what was discussed that day in cabinet.

Later Madiba ... began to bring the visit to a close. On finishing speaking, he bent over Joe and their heads rested together for a lengthy and poignant moment.

'Good-bye, Joe,' said Madiba as he slowly began to move away. I thought Joe was going to complete the visit without uttering a word, but he decisively took Madiba's hand and said, 'Cheers.'

Joe's doctor was waiting to examine him. He reported that Joe's pulse was now weak and thready, 'I don't think he'll last the night.'

This was good news.

Over the next hours, we sat with him, together, one by one, two by two, in varying harmony of giving each other supportive company while at other times respecting privacy. Hans, (Joe's reflexologist) asked for an oil burner. He blended neroli (ultra-relaxing) with basil (to help release the grief of parting) and bergamot, a combination to create a peaceful atmosphere, making it easier to let go.

Just before 3am ... there was silence, all breathing had stopped ... We each took a glass in our hands and, reiterating Joe's last word to Madiba, we toasted Joe's departure. 'Cheers.'

Now it was Mandela who was ill. But Friday evening's TV news carried footage of him leaving the hospital. Our nation had a reprieve—what might happen in this extra time?

I wrote that I hoped Madiba had returned home to enjoy time with those closest to him, that he relished a sense of a life well-lived and of the country's deep love for him. I noted that Madiba has biological family, his immediate flesh and blood. But then, like Joe but on a much larger scale, he had extended family: us, the whole nation for whom he had lived his life to win our right to democracy. But he was now 93 years old; we needed to be more ready to let him go.

I'd grown up as a Catholic child. Sunday sermons instructed us to pray for the recovery of the likes of Mrs. Wilkinson who was old and sick. I'd been puzzled, 'Why would we pray for her to live longer instead of praying for her to meet St. Peter at the Pearly Gates?' I wrote, 'Would I pray the next time when it's reported that Madiba is very ill?' It seemed to me that the question we needed to engage with was, 'What we might do, as a nation, to be more ready to let Mandela go, and to accept that there comes a time when medical interventions may be considered undesirable?'

I referred readers to the book *Easeful Death* by Mary Warnock and Elizabeth Macdonald, which advocates living well and dying well, and not being kept alive by medical technology when life no longer offers 'critical interest' and present value to the person.

I noted my good fortune. Joe's doctor, Fazel Randera, was the kind of doctor they advocated. He was a doctor who was able to help Joe to die as part of a compassionate, age-old role as an easer of suffering and, at the end, an easer of death.

When Madiba is close to dying, I hope it will not be hooked up to a life support machine that gets switched off. I hope Madiba dies in his own bed or his favorite chair, surrounded by whoever or whatever gives him the deepest feeling of peace: his eyes resting on a favorite painting, his feet being massaged, perhaps the subtle smell of aromatherapy oils.

And when he's this close, I won't be praying for his recovery, my thoughts will be on wishing him the most beautiful, peaceful, loving exit out of this world.

We need to aspire to offer the same composure of farewell that Madiba himself has offered to so many others over the last 20 years. *Hamba Kahle*. Farewell.

The article sparked interest, eventually leading to my column series, *Let's Talk About Dying*. The public response was engaging. People wrote to me with their stories, asked me to come and speak with their congregations. Conversations opened up. My quest to be part of a Tipping Point towards more easeful conversations took off.

The Economist, in their cover story of June 15, 2016, 'A Right to Die,' noted how societies shift their opinions over time. Social behavior judged as morally wrong and illegal in one era becomes accepted in another. Shifts in attitude and legislation on divorce, gay marriage, and termination of pregnancy immediately spring to mind.

Malcolm Gladwell conceptualized how he thinks this shift in social attitude, leading to changed legislation, happens. He opines that it is the simultaneous presence of three groups of social actors: mavens, connectors and salespeople. In a social epidemic, mavens are data banks. They provide the message. Connectors are the social glue: they spread it. But there is also a select group of people—salespeople—with the skills to persuade us when we are unconvinced at what we're hearing, and they are as critical to the word-of-mouth epidemics as the other two groups.

In writing newspaper columns I was trying to be a salesperson. But I also set out to identify the mavens, the connectors, and other salespeople.

Let's Talk: Theology from the Pulpit

Doctor-assisted dying? Critics are dismayed at the gathering momentum in its favor.

'For some,' noted *The Economist* in their story on the subject, 'the argument is moral and absolute. Deliberately ending a human life is wrong, because life is sacred and the endurance of suffering confers its own dignity. For others, the legalization of doctor-assisted dying is the first step on the slippery slope where the vulnerable are threatened and where premature death becomes a cheap alternative to palliative care.'

Nancy Duff is what Gladwell would call a maven. A professor of Christian Ethics at Princeton Theological Seminary in the United States, she wants Christians to contemplate deeply the sanctity of life and God's grace towards the dying. 'No one wants to talk about death—not even the dying. But conversations about death—our own death and the death of people we love—can begin in church. This should be the safest place in the world to express our concerns, our fears, and our hope.'

Professor Duff was invited by Johannesburg's St. Columba's Presbyterian Church to deliver a lecture in October 2015. She named it, 'Death with Dignity: The Ethics of Resisting and Accepting Death.' I sat in a packed church where every pew was filled, 400 people eager to hear what she had to say.

> Knowing when to resist death and when to accept death is a moral and existential dilemma that isn't easily resolved. In the United States, the public and legal debate over the ethics of resisting and accepting death started with cases that involved requests to withdraw life support from patients in a permanent vegetative state: that is a situation where the entire upper brain has ceased to function. You can't come back from it. If the upper brain is damaged, only the lower, the brain stem, continues to function and that oversees basic bodily functions. So, that's how it began. The ethics. When do you withdraw or withhold life support?

The audience around me listened, riveted. Nelson Mandela was top of mind. He'd spent months in a permanent vegetative state. The statistics from two local organizations showed that the number of people who completed their living wills in those months of Madiba's dying increased exponentially.

She ran through some markers of change in public discourse in the United States over the past four decades.

- In 1976, the New Jersey State Supreme Court allowed the respirator to be removed from 21-year-old Karen Quinlan, who was in a permanent vegetative state. Her parents, Roman Catholics who were accompanied by their priest, didn't want the feeding tube removed. She lived for 10 more years.
- In 1983, the US Supreme Court cleared the way for the feeding tube to be removed from 25-year-old Nancy Cruzan who was in a permanent vegetative state.
- In 2005, Terri Schiavo's husband's request to remove her feeding tube was granted.
- In 2014, the body of 33-year-old Marlise Muñoz was kept on what would usually be called 'life support,' except that she had been declared dead at John Peter Smith Hospital in Fort Worth, Texas but was kept on those machines against the family's wishes because she was pregnant. The hospital finally admitted that the baby, who had been deprived of oxygen for over an hour after Marlise died, wasn't viable.

She also mentioned Brittany Maynard's situation as having moved hearts and minds in 2014.

Brittany was a 29-year-old who had moved from California to Oregon to take advantage of that state's death with dignity laws. She had been diagnosed with a type of brain cancer that generally causes death within a relative short period—10 months in her case. She took the prescribed lethal dose of drugs on November 1, 2014.

Pain was the big issue, and Brittany did not want the level of medication required to control her pain that would have resulted in permanent sedation. She collaborated with the organization Compassion and Choices, which ran a media campaign, creating YouTube footage to catalyze public awareness. She became a social media icon and champion for physician-assisted dying.

Brittany had been diagnosed just after she'd married. She'd lived her 20s as a vibrant, full-of-life young woman. She had every reason to want to live, but living was no longer an option. That's why the term *assisted suicide* is so inappropriate for people in this situation—there's a wish to live, but the illness is terminal. As Nancy told the gathering, assisted death gave Brittany one of the few choices she had left to control the situation: the ability to choose when and how she would die instead of allowing the disease to make that choice for her, while robbing her of all the pleasures of daily life.

In the United States, there's no national agreement around withdrawing life support when someone is declared to be in a vegetative state. On support for assisted dying, there is a slow adoption in individual states which may be increasing pace: Oregon (1997), Montana (1998), Washington State (2009), Vermont (2013), California (2015), and Colorado (2016).

Professor Duff is a theologian who supports assisted dying. She noted that concerned evangelical Christians and Roman Catholics have provided vocal opposition to assisted death and her wish was to address some of the issues on which they have based their opposition. She understood their opposition as mainly concerning three issues: the sovereignty of God, the perception of autonomy associated with assisted dying and the belief that suffering should be endured as part of the practice of faith. She set out to allay fears and create dialogue.

She noted that Christians who are against assisted death often base their argument on divine sovereignty, claiming that 'because our lives belong to God, we shouldn't thwart God's purposes by ending life even considering impending death' and 'play God' by helping that person end their life. But Duff doesn't believe that the charge of 'playing God' is useful.

> We could just as easily argue that we are playing God by not letting someone die and by making every effort to keep a person alive, even when medical intervention does nothing but extend dying. Aren't we assuming God-like control by insisting that a terminally ill patient face all the suffering, limitations, pain and indignities that the disease hands out when medical intervention can't control it?

Some Christians, Duff noted, believe that individual autonomy destroys the bonds among people. The argument goes that, as part of the body of Christ, we should not make independent decisions, and we should rather rely on the people around us as we suffer with terminal illness and pain.

While Duff agrees that while autonomy is 'not exactly a Christian virtue … the decisions we make aren't about us alone.' People who go through the process of opting for assisted dying are required and encouraged to have many conversations, and advocates of assisted dying are explicit about the importance of consultation.

Duff also addressed the belief of some Christians that pain also needs to be endured as an affirmation of faith. But she also said she doesn't see why these choices should be imposed on others.

She mentioned the story of Jessica Kelly, an evangelical Christian who lost her son to brain cancer, who had written, 'My son's death was not beautiful. His suffering was great … as the tumor grew, the pain would find a way to exceed the medication's capabilities. He would often wake with a scream, gripping his head as the pressure increased from the fluids trapped within his skull.'

'My question regarding assisted death as a Christian is: when death as the enemy brings intolerable suffering that dying, left to its own time-table, will not soon resolve and medical intervention cannot alleviate, why is choosing to hasten one's death thought to fall outside the will of God?' Duff also said she did not agree with people who thought 'God's grace doesn't meet someone when death is hastened by drugs.'

I don't believe that protecting life means we keep people alive for as long as possible, no matter what their pain or suffering or how meaningless life has become for them. Protecting life can't mean we keep bodies animated. No Christian understanding of what it means to be human reduces our humanity to … permanent sedation at the end of life.

We were created human, not divine, and so we live within the limits of birth and death. We are mortal and have to come to terms with that. We should certainly resist death as long as living is still a genuine possibility, but we shouldn't prolong the agony of dying. We can accept death and even support the hastening of death when such an action is freely chosen by someone who wants to control the final days of life. And we do so knowing with certainty that in life and in death we belong to God.

As I listened to Professor Duff speak to this Christian community, what stayed with me was that her thoughts are non-denominational. Her reflections apply to all of us. What she said was powerful and thought-provoking for every faith and none. As individuals, we are each unique with our own religion or spiritual practices, personally chosen or the outcome of the geography of our birth. But as individuals the world over, we share absolute commonality in the universality of our mortality and the questions and choices that we are challenged to make.

Duff had planned time for a Q&A. But there were no questions. Instead, people took the opportunity to share their stories of relatives dying and families suffering, and the imperative for the law to change to support our dignity as we die.

Let's Talk: Workshops with Parishioners

Rene August is one of the regulars who attends the Friday morning service in the side chapel at St. George's Cathedral, a service which Archbishop Tutu officiates whenever he's in Cape Town and available. We met in 2015 at one of the post-service breakfasts, where Rene August, who had served as a parish priest at St. Aidan's Anglican Church in the Cape Town suburb of Landsdowne, told me about her initiative for parishioners to talk about their mortality.

> I served in this parish and saw generations of families at worship, a patriarch with his children, grandchildren, and great-grandchildren. People were regulars. I'd see them week after week after week. I was on average doing two funerals a week. People would say to me, 'Will you do my funeral one day?' Or, 'I want you to preach at my funeral.' But that's as far as they'd think about it—they wouldn't take it any further. I saw an opportunity to help people think and prepare themselves a little better.

She agreed to talk to me more in-depth about the sermons and workshops she created around issues of elderliness and death. We diarized a date and time and Rene identified a quiet office for us to use nearby the cathedral.

As a reverend, August told me she centered her themes around those issues she found herself regularly having to speak about: Making Plans, Making Time, Making Right, Making Memories, Making Peace and Making Provision. They would all include a passage from the scriptures which supported the points she was trying to emphasize, as well as some questions. She would then invite parishioners to come to the sermons with their extended family, requesting they not make recreational plans for Sunday afternoon but rather have lunch together to further pursue family conversations on the themes.

For Making Plans, she used the story of Jacob at the end of Genesis where he says, 'When I die, please take my bones and bury me with my forefathers.' She also chose the gospel reading which described the Jews bringing Jesus's body down from the cross and laying it in a borrowed grave. There were no plans. She would then ask questions: What are your plans for when you die? Would you like to be buried or cremated? Would you like your organs to be donated? Would you like to die in a hospital, a hospice, or at home? If you were on life support, when would you want the machines to be switched off?

Making Time was about making time for unfinished conversations. Time to say, I'm sorry. Time to say, I forgive you. Time to say, I love you. 'Making Time,' explained August, 'is about being with people who you love, living as though you're going to die, having the conversations, and mending any relationships you need to mend.' She used the story of Isaac and his sons; Isaac knew he was dying so he took time to bless his sons. Making Time also included making time to grieve, and drew upon an Old Testament reading about when Moses died and the Israelites sat for 12 days. Parishioners were provided with details of support groups, relevant books, and contact details for free counseling.

Making Memory drew on Jesus's call, 'Do this in memory of me.' Rene August's view is that the calendar of festivals gets people to gather, and these gatherings are memory markers. 'In the Old Testament, there is Passover and festivals that involve food. All the Jewish festivals, think about them, are meals on certain dates, accompanied by stories. Their purpose is making memory.'

Her sermon on Making Provision covered the need to have a last will and testament and final instructions, while Making Peace focused on conversations about the afterlife. Making Right focused on the need to restore broken relationships, exploring forgiveness and reconciliation.

She also organized Saturday workshops associated with the themes; the Making Plans workshop included different professionals talking about how to make a will, the possibilities and financial consequences of down-sizing, and how pensions and retirement annuities operate, while the workshop on Making Memories included the physical making of memory boxes.

Each Sunday the people attending numbered between 400 and 450 people, and afterwards people left the church to have their intergenerational family lunch and conversations.

The program was so creative and inspirational. My frustration is that it was a one-off.

When I next met Rene she had a new role. She'd just finished running an international workshop on Robben Island, the place of Mandela's incarceration during apartheid. The workshop on justice, transformation, and reconciliation left her brown skin aglow. It was heart-warming to see her so deeply satisfied; at heart she's a connector, but I'd be even happier if there were others taking forward and replicating the series she designed for St. Aidan's. That's the challenge of an individual initiative: how do you give it legs?

Let's Talk: The Global Conversation

In September 2014, I attended the bi-annual conference of the World Federation of Right to Die Societies. There were 47 organizations from 25 countries: 22 from Europe, 9 from North America, 9 from Australia and New Zealand, 3 from Africa, 2 from Latin America—Colombia and Venezuela—just one from Japan, representing Asia, and Israel from the Middle East.

Of all the presentations I attended, three stayed with me the most. The delegation from the Japanese Society for Dying with Dignity gave a comprehensive presentation which included detailed estimates of the consequences of increasing longevity, with regards to the expected increases in the numbers of people with Alzheimer's disease; by 2020, they noted, there would be more than 2 million people living with Alzheimer's in Japan.

The Colombian speaker told the audience that assisted dying was declared legal practice in Colombia by its Constitutional Court as far back as 1997. However, at the time of the conference there was still 'legal limbo' as government stalled implementation by failing to issue the necessary guidelines. Sympathetic doctors were afraid to test a law which had been put in place without the necessary breadth and depth of conversations having taken place in the country. Without these conversations, without a shift in the tipping point of public opinion, the law itself was completely ineffectual.

That 18-year wait would finally end in April 2015 after Oregon's Compassion and Choices, the group who worked with Brittany Maynard to publicize her case, brought success beyond US borders. Maynard's case was followed by a ruling of the Canadian Supreme Court in February 2015, which struck down the federal prohibition on physician-assisted dying, which then renewed Colombian interest. Their Ministry of Health was given 30 days to issue the protocols and on July 3, 2015 Colombia registered its first case of a legally assisted death.

Veronique Hivon, Canadian politician, Minister of Social Services and Youth Protection, described how Quebec had become the first Canadian province to introduce medically assisted dying into its healthcare system. It's now embedded within its end-of-life heath care policy.

Hivon described years of lobbying. A significant group of lobbyists were physicians who had tabled a report saying their patients were facing pain that could not be alleviated, and they felt without tools. They specifically requested Parliament to look at this issue. Hivon tabled a motion at the National Assembly to have a special committee set up to listen to peoples' views. She was surprised when the motion was unanimously consented to. Public hearings were held with expert witnesses, and meetings were organized between commissioners and citizens in eight cities across the province. Commissioners tried to ensure that citizens would hear both the arguments for and against, and that there was also time for ordinary people to share their personal stories of end-of-life care experiences. People appreciated the opportunity to be listened to. Storytelling was a powerful influence—the sharing of heart-felt experiences—and a call to action.

Veronique Hivon, my shero, in her own words: https://www.soundcloud.com/wbez-worldview/Canada-considers-right-to-die-policies.

The legislation known as Bill 52 was implemented. Currently

Quebec politician François Bonnardel has been leading an emotional call for the law to be expanded to include Alzheimer's disease by having the possibility of advance consent.

In a February 2017 interview, Bonnardel described his mother who has had Alzheimer's disease for 15 years. 'For too long I've seen my mother no longer able to recognize me, no longer smile, no longer enjoy life,' he said. 'She has become a prisoner of her own body. Me too. These last three years I have wished that the good Lord would come and take her home.'

His statement came after the arrest of 55-year-old Michel Cadotte, who had just been arrested for second-degree murder after he acquiesced to his wife's request, as an Alzheimer sufferer, to end her life.

Veronique Hivon commented that if this question of including dementia had been included in the initial debates, it's probable that the legislation would not have passed. Bill 52 was not the end of the story; it was the lowest common denominator—time is needed for opinions in society to mature.

South African politicians and advocacy groups have a lot to learn from Quebec. While South Africa has a Constitution which contains clauses protecting the right to dignity in life and the right to decide what's right for one's own body, in late 2016 a judge overturned the ruling which supported Robin Stransham-Ford's request to ask a doctor to give him a lethal injection without the doctor being liable for prosecution.

Eventually the matter of the right to assisted dying will reach South Africa's Constitutional Court, and the manner in which the Constitution is written bodes well for the advocates of assisted dying, But whatever the outcome of judicial opinion, as the Colombian and Quebec experiences have demonstrated, it's people having widespread, community conversations that make the real difference when it comes to qualitative and effective implementation of legislation.

Let's Talk: Over Dinner, Over Coffee

Ray and I are both members of *Time To Think*, a group of coaches and facilitators accredited to use Nancy Kline's Thinking Environment methodology. We see each other at our professional development practice sessions six times a year. At one of these meetings, Ray shared with me that he's part of a small group of individuals who've given themselves the name, Gracious Living and Dying (GLAD). They are eight people who range in age from 50 to 80 who have an evening dinner together half a dozen times a year to discuss how they can live their best lives whilst consciously talking about their inevitable mortality.

Ray invited me to join one of their evening dinners in Johannesburg. I took my mini projector and the worksheets of questions that I'd prepared on my themes. It was good practice. The slides didn't work well enough in a home setting, and I realized I had too many questions for the evening. But people took away the worksheets, and it was later that I reaped my reward.

I received feedback saying that the worksheets with the questions had proved catalytic for the discussions they'd held with spouses or other family members. They wrote the discussions weren't necessarily easy, but that they covered areas which they'd never spoken of and discovered that they were not riding on the same bus after all, at least, not yet.

Next, I was invited by a group of women. Years ago, they'd met one another outside the school gates when picking up and dropping off their young children. They were curious about who they were beyond their commonality of parenting, and had met regularly for years. Most recently, mortality had become a more frequent presence in their lives. One of the women is in the GLAD group, and she suggested I try a different format and no slides. I would introduce the theme and they would talk. I told them the questions I was suggesting, hoping they would talk some more. It worked well, in this lounge setting, with just a dozen people sitting together.

Then I got an invite from Johannesburg's Union of Jewish Women. Elaine, one of their members, is my neighbor. After that, the annual Jewish Think-fest asked me to come along—one of the organizers knew of my writing project. These were large groups of people for the limited amount of time of 45 minutes to one hour. It was challenging. But if I can ignite interest for people to go away and spend more time thinking for themselves afterwards then I won't say no to invitations. But the ripple effect from these evenings will be slow.

In 2004, Bernard Crettaz, a Swiss sociologist and anthropologist, had the idea of launching scheduled, not-for-profit get-togethers where people talk about death, and deepen their understanding of end-of-life issues. In Switzerland and France these discussion groups have called themselves Café Mortel.

Jon Underwood, a former council worker launched the UK's first Death Café meeting in London in 2011, with the aim of providing a 'space where people can discuss death and find meaning and reflect on what's important and ask profound questions.'

Since 2012 Death Cafés have sprung up in 40 cities in the United States. The casual forums meet once a month in coffee shops. Anyone of any age comes in response to Facebook announcements, storefront fliers and 'what's on' listings.

Sixty-year-old Audrey Pellicano, who hosts the New York Café, told *The New York Times* in June 2013, 'Death and grief are topics avoided at all costs in our society. If we talk about them, maybe we won't fear them as much.'

To date, as far as I'm aware of, no one has started a Death Café initiative in South Africa—perhaps our urban planning and fear of night-time driving are not conducive to this. But by word-of-mouth I'm coming across individuals or small groups who are taking initiatives to create conversation opportunities.

How to generate more activity? Would it mean starting up a not-for-profit organization?

In 2014 I'd read about just such an organization in Boston called The Conversation Project. With my travel fund monies, I bought myself a plane ticket and I took myself off to the United States to listen and learn from other experiences.

Let's Talk Everywhere—From Hollywood to the Kitchen Table

Ellen Goodman, co-founder of The Conversation Project (TCP), carries weight. Until 2010 she was an associate editor for *The Boston Globe* and her syndicated columns were also published in the *Washington Post* and almost 400 other newspapers. The *Globe* is the one with a reputation for investigation; it was their sleuthing journalists who meticulously unraveled the story of the Roman Catholic Church in 2002, where the Boston Archdiocese covered up for priests who sexually abused minors; the story which became the subject of the 2016 Oscar-winning film *Spotlight*.

Ellen has accumulated many accolades over the years. She consistently chose to write about edgy subjects that readers might be grappling with, such as termination of pregnancy, seeking to influence their thinking. In 1980 she won the Pulitzer Prize for Commentary.

In 2010, Ellen co-founded TCP, and we met five years later. I asked her about the birth of this project, whose mission it is to get ordinary people to sit around their kitchen table and have end-of-life conversations in the normal course of living, not necessarily because someone in the family is facing a health crisis.

Ellen told me about her father's dying and her parents' denial that his cancer was incurable, something she also wrote about in 2015 for *The New York Times*.

> I was 25 when I flew home for my father's last birthday. His cancer had returned and he would die three months later at the age of 57. What I remember most about that weekend was the large rectangular gift box he opened. My mother had bought him a new suitcase. I don't know if the suitcase qualifies my family for the Denial Hall of Fame. There are so many contenders for that honor. But I've carried the psychic baggage over the years. I have never forgotten that image and how we lost a chance to say goodbye. I still wonder if my father was lonely in the silence that surrounded our inability to talk about what we all knew.

Ellen was close to her widowed mother Edith. Years later, when Edith had dementia, Ellen became her proxy for making decisions. Ellen told me her mom declined to a point where she couldn't decide what to have for lunch, let alone make decisions about her healthcare. So, it was Ellen who found herself facing a cascade of decisions that needed to be made on her mother's behalf. She so wished she could hear her mother's voice in her ear to guide her in the decision-making. What would her mother have wanted? What was important to her? They had talked about so many things, but they had never spoken about this possible decline into ill health, towards dying.

Ellen's interest in the birthing of TCP was born out of this experience of family denialism and her own regret that she did not have certain key conversations with her mother about her end-of-life care and preferences.

Her mother died, and in conversation with her women friends, Ellen found so many of them carrying stories about end-of-life incidents that sometimes had scarred them. Ellen told me she realized that nothing would change until people started having conversations, sharing their stories. She knew this in the very depth of her being from her years of being an activist for women's rights. What became The Conversation Project evolved from there.

Ellen was invited to speak at a Harvard Fellows seminar on gerontology. Afterwards, she and a friend shared their thoughts about how if you open up this terrain of talking about mortality with family, you don't know what you're in for. They convened a discussion group: clergy, journalists, and healthcare professionals. They sat together around a table; everyone took off their professional hats and told their personal stories about dying. The storytelling revealed that people were not only not dying well, but their manner of passing was torturous for their families, and the memories were carried around for decades, an inch below the surface.

In 2011, Ellen convened an 'expert panel' of professionals who assessed their joint experience of trying to improve end-of-life care, and they concluded that after decades of work they had not succeeded in 'moving the needle.' The experience of dying often remained agonizing for the dying person and their family. Ellen told me, 'Systems don't change until the culture changes first, and the bedrock of culture change is peoples' conversations.'

They came up with a three-part strategy: media, tools, and community.

A group of women, led by health professional Jane Roessner, created their first tool: the Conversation Starter Kit. It's a guide for different conversations about dying to have with your family, and your doctor. The women envisioned people having conversations, and that loved ones would share what mattered most to them and that their wishes, spelled out clearly, would have a chance to be respected.

ABC News covered the public launch of this not-for-profit

organization in 2012; now the Starter Kit is available in print and online, and has been translated into French, Hebrew, Mandarin, Portuguese, Spanish, and Hindi will be next. There is also a guide for parents wanting to have conversations with ill children, and another tool is under development for those who have a family member diagnosed with Alzheimer's as well as a guide on How to Choose a Health Care Proxy, as well as be one.

Their media strategy included influencing a public health services campaign. But it also included a Hollywood strategy. Ellen explained they planned to engage scriptwriters on including end-of-life conversations into their story lines on stage, on TV, in the cinema.

Something's happening. Mortality is more frequently the subject matter whether it's the TV series *Breaking Bad*, (2008–2013), the film *Still Alice* (2015) or David Bowie's video released three days before he died of cancer (2016), singing of his death, his faced bandaged, his eyes replaced by buttons, his song 'Lazarus' a parting gift: 'I'll be free/Ain't that just like me.'

The third TCP strategy is community engagement. They hired Kate DeBartolo, a dynamo field worker. By 2015, there were 300 projects in 200 organizations in 40 US states. They found themselves fundraising to hire three more 'Kates.'

Dr. Atul Gawande, the author of *Being Mortal*, the book he worked on during his own Bellagio residency, is an advisor to TCP. The longtime *New Yorker* writer, practicing surgeon and professor at Harvard Medical School, is actively involved in a parallel project called Conversation Ready, which tackles the institutional component: how do we make sure that the conversations families have and the decisions they make will be respected within the healthcare system?

Over my two-day visit at TCP, I heard an often-repeated line from the staff members I met, something which Ellen ended our meeting with: 'It's always too soon until it's too late.'

I'm awed by the breadth and depth of their work. I'm also intimidated. Fund-raising for not-for-profit work is, in my experience, mostly grueling. It requires huge stamina, endless patience, a capacity to write many proposals and then undertake exacting reports to demonstrate accountability on delivery. The TCP advisory board is impressive—they are well-known and respected in their fields. To build something like this in South Africa would take a lot of work, and there is still so much to learn.

I had another destination on my US research itinerary: the Gundersen Health Institute in the small town of La Crosse, Wisconsin, where end-of life conversations are initiated from within the healthcare system itself. This occurrence was and is still extraordinarily unusual. In a UK survey, two-thirds of 971 family doctors said they did not feel comfortable having conversations about dying with their patients.

So, what happened in La Crosse for it to be so different? How did it transpire that by 2016 more than 95% of the residents in the area had their Advance Directives signed off?

Let's Talk: Within the Healthcare System

La Crosse, Wisconsin, is a town of 50,000 people on the Mississippi River, right next to Iowa and Minnesota. That's where the Lutheran doctor Adolf Gundersen set up his medical practice more than a century ago, opening a hospital in 1902 which is now part of the Gundersen Health System. I'd read about their systematic approach to having conversations with patients about their preferred choice of medical interventions throughout their entire lives.

It was Dawn Meyer in the CEO's office who arranged my two-day program in La Crosse. She kindly picked me up at the airport and then swung around to the hotel so I could drop-off my bag, whisking me off to a training workshop that was already underway.

The banners that signposted the way to the huge conference-room-turned-classroom read 'Respecting Choices. Advance Care Planning.' Gundersen was in the process of training facilitators to have specific conversations with patients and I was able to dip in and out of the training a few times during my visit. It was impressive. I considered myself a good facilitator—I've consistently received strong ratings at the business school workshops that I've facilitated—but I was bowled over by the quality of the Gundersen trainers and the quality of their materials. They were remarkable in their engagement with the learners in the room, skilled at drawing out 'teachable moments' from the contributions made by the participating delegates. This was the fruition of more than 30 years of hard work, focus, and iterative improvement.

Then I met the acclaimed Bernard Hammes. Everyone had said to me, 'Oh you *have* to meet Bernie!'

He greeted me warmly, a benign-looking man in his late 50s, dressed smart-casual, nothing sharp about him and the way he presents himself modestly to the world. Over two days, we had several conversations. I could understand why he'd succeeded. He'd had patience, doggedness, persistence, and an unwavering eye on his goal for 30 years. I kept coming back to him saying, 'Sorry, I've thought of another question,' and he'd give me a gentle smile and answer thoughtfully and thoroughly whatever query I threw at him. My first notebook spilled over and I began a second. I felt like the novice, honored to be sitting with someone so experienced in this field.

Being a daily witness to people's pain and suffering was what drove Bernie to start this initiative. He is a pioneering ethicist whose work began as an intervention in the hospital's dialysis unit, and involved assisting nurses to have conversations about end-of-life treatment with their patients. In his book, *Having Your Say: Getting the Right Care When It Matters Most*, he writes about being a young ethics staff member in the 1980s, when he was involved in three difficult cases having excruciating conversations—all the people concerned, himself included, were drowning in emotional and moral distress.

These cases involved patients with end-stage renal disease who had suffered devastating strokes. Healthcare providers expected these patients to survive for some time if dialysis was continued, but they did not expect patients to regain awareness of self, others or their surroundings. In all three situations, the patients would be physically dependent on others for care and required continued dialysis three times a week. Their loving families did not know what to do. When asked what would their parents want in this situation, the families all responded in the same way, 'If only we knew.'

In each case, three things were clear: (1) we did not, and never would, know for certain what the patient wanted; (2) no matter what decision they made, the families and health professionals would live with considerable uncertainty about their decision, resulting in lasting distress; and (3) the uncertainty required incredible amounts of staff time while attempting to sort through the ethical complexities. The outcomes were bad for patients, bad for their families and bad for the healthcare professionals who were caring for them.

At that time the dialysis unit catered for 60 patients. Only two had advance directives when Bernie began his work. He asked the nurses to have conversations like, 'If you have a stroke, do you want to go on a ventilator?' Or, 'If you can't do this or that, do you want to stay on dialysis?' They were reluctant to initiate conversations.

Bernie set up training for all the nurses. Still nothing happened.

Then he tried a different tactic. He honed in on only one nurse and asked her to be the pioneer, to role-model for the other nurses how this could be done. The first time the nurse tried to have a conversation with a dialysis patient, she got the response, 'I don't think I'm ready to have this conversation.' The nurse responded exerting no pressure, just a gentle, 'Let me know if you change your mind.' And eventually it happened, the patient came back to the nurse, and then another patient, then another and the ball started rolling.

Small beginnings. Patience. Determination. Grit. Persistence.

Over 30 years Bernie's pioneering initiative has spread beyond the dialysis unit into the entire Gundersen Health System, developing into something tried and tested, sophisticated and systematic. Patients are engaged in several conversations throughout their lives: First Steps, Next Steps, Final Steps and then grief counseling if needs be.

The First Steps conversation takes place once you've had your 18th birthday—you're no longer a minor, you are now legally responsible for making life choices. The ascribed Gundersen facilitator would go through a set of questions with you, questions like: suppose you're in a car accident and you've got these injuries. Do you want this intervention? Or something else? After the conversation you sign on the dotted line, and it's there on your file which will follow you into the hospital ward, should you be admitted for any reason.

It's sophisticated but not that complicated. As Dr. Gawande wrote in his 2010 *New Yorker* article, 'What should medicine do when it can't save your life?'

Since 1991, it became routine for all patients at Gundersen who were admitted to a hospital, nursing home or assisted-living facility to complete a multiple-choice form that boiled down to four questions. At this moment in your life, the form asked:

1. Do you want to be resuscitated if your heart stops?
2. Do you want aggressive treatments such as intubation and mechanical ventilation?
3. Do you want antibiotics?
4. Do you want tube or intravenous feeding if you can't eat on your own?

The Next Steps conversation? Imagine you've aged a few years. You've started experiencing a chronic condition, say high blood pressure, high cholesterol, or sugar levels indicating that you might be pre-diabetic. At this juncture, the conversation Gundersen would have with you is how can you best live with this, and if possible, how can you manage this chronic condition to stop it from getting any worse?

The Final Steps conversation is when you are diagnosed with a condition that's terminal, or the chronic condition deteriorates to the extent that your quality of life has declined and you are in danger of losing your life. And the consequences are significant. When people talk end-of-life care costs go down and longevity increases. This systematic approach, embedded into ongoing year-in, year-out patient care is the bedrock of an amazing outcome: 96 percent of citizens over the age of 18 in that small town of La Crosse now have advance directives.

The recognition of how important it is to talk is spreading. Author Jo Marchant in her book *Cure* writes that in 2010 Massachusetts General Hospital offered lung cancer patients conversations with palliative care specialists, conversations that supplemented the technical medical conversation conducted by the oncologist. The results: a longer and better quality of life and fewer people opting for more aggressive treatments.

One of the discussion sessions Bernie's office set up for my visit was with the pre-natal palliative care unit. Pre-natal palliative care? Yes, for families where women have pregnancies with a diagnosis where it's probable that the newborn baby will not survive—the scans are showing up as abnormal, but the family feels it's too late or doesn't want to terminate.

Three of the hospital's specialists spoke with me about their program. They showed me a video of a family that prompted tears of gratitude; I appreciated the tenderness the family received from the Gundersen healthcare professionals. The baby died soon after birth, as predicted. The family were supported through the activities they'd decided on. The older siblings helped their parents wash and dress the newborn, who was christened before the funeral took place. Photos were taken, the birth, the washing, the naming: they showed me the template of the memory book that is made for every family in similar situations.

I thought of Cathy Barnett with her quadruplets, and what happened to her and her husband as their dead baby was bundled out of sight with the good intention to protect them. The two experiences could not be more different.

During a tour of the new wing of the hospital, I noticed bright yellow forms on the desks of the administrators of a ward. These were the newest forms being rapidly adopted across the country: Physician Orders for Life-Sustaining Treatment. In different states their names differ but what is consistent is that they are a standardized set of medical orders on a single sheet of brightly colored paper that stays with a patient as she or he moves across healthcare settings.

At the end of my second day, I was still hungry to know more and my questions just kept coming. Replicability? Barriers to entry?

The Conversation Project doesn't have any conditions—its materials are freely accessible online. I liked Bernie's answer. He told me the hospital wanted to feel secure about quality assurance; their conversation guides are being used within a healthcare system. No, they won't make their materials freely available, but they will undertake partnerships. He told me of their current discussions with Kaiser Permanente, a mammoth health insurance company and hospital group, about their use of the Gundersen training materials. That alone would have the power to shift conversations in healthcare facilities across the United States.

Since my visit, I've kept track of ongoing developments. In a *Planet Money* radio interview at the end of 2016, there was mention of the Gundersen program moving to a national initiative called the Coalition to Transform Advanced Care. They also mentioned a study the European Union was funding called The Acton Trial which would test a version of the La Crosse materials in six countries.

The *Planet Money* US radio show team traveled to La Crosse and interviewed several families, including Betty and George Phillips. Betty was healthy, but just in case she was to become sick, she had already specified in her advance directive: No machines. No feeding tubes. No CPR heart resuscitation.

Her husband George also had an advanced directive, 'Yeah, I fixed one up in 2004, that's 12 years ago,' George told the host. 'We don't want to be kept alive just to be a vegetable, you know. She feels a lot like I do. Neither of us wants chemotherapy.'

The host asked, 'Do you guys have cancer?'

'No, we don't. But just in case…'

Because 96 percent of adults have registered their advanced directives, those that haven't yet done them stand out and face peer pressure. Several neighbors talked about the Eriksons, the ones across the street who had yet to complete and submit theirs.

The reporter sought out Catherine and Randy Erikson, who laughed when they heard their neighbor's criticisms, unfazed. Their teenage daughter, Annie, listening in, interjected, 'It's okay. We've talked about all that stuff before. I know what to do. I know for sure that if my mom is ever stuck in a coma and there's no hope for her that she wants me to pull the plug…' She even detailed the plans for her dad's funeral, the Bruce Springsteen song she had in mind.

No one in the Erikson household is the least bit sick; they are in perfect health. The radio host was perturbed by Annie's ease in talking about death.

'Asking strangers questions about death makes me uncomfortable. Because I'm from America where talking about death is like talking about sex, you don't do it—at least not a lot. La Crosse,' he concluded, 'just does death differently.'

At the end of my second day, with no dinner to attend that evening, I was advised to explore the gardens created along the banks of the River Mississippi. I needed to walk to unwind. I needed to come down to earth after being over-stimulated and my head bursting with information, impressions, and ideas.

I left La Crosse, Gundersen, and my discussions with Bernie Hammes feeling inspired. Wouldn't it be amazing if I could be a connector and get South Africans interested? Who exactly? And how to get a foot in someone's door to spark their interest and curiosity?

Let's Talk: Desmond Tutu's Ultimate Leadership Legacy

Archbishop Tutu welcomed me into the visitor's room at his offices in the Clock Tower building overlooking Cape Town's waterfront. We had a follow-up appointment to continue our conversation about dying, which had begun several months before. He directed me where to sit so that he would be able to hear me better with his good ear. We agreed where I should best place the recorder. And as is his customary practice, the Archbishop began our session with a prayer.

Archbishop Tutu's life-long courage to speak out on the issues he is outraged about, or that he feels need urgent attention, is his gift not only to South Africa but also to the world. Tutu is keenly aware of his global standing and wields his influence as a thought leader judiciously, sometimes ferociously, on all issues pertaining to human dignity: apartheid, HIV/Aids policies, homophobia, access to sustainable energy, climate change, the incarceration of black people in the United States, the recognition of gay marriage in the Anglican church. And now, 'closer to my end than my beginning,' as he puts it, he is applying his moral clarity to questions of life and death.

The outcome of our last conversation was an editorial published in *The Guardian*, timed to coincide with the bill for assisted dying that was being heard in the British House of Lords on July 18, 2014. July 18 also happened to be the date of Mandela's birthday—and that specific July 18 was the first since Mandela's death eight months earlier.

In that powerful piece, the Archbishop not only voiced his support for a UK policy change on people having the legal right to choose death accelerated by medical narcotic assistance, but he also spoke about the indignity he felt accompanied Mandela's death. The Archbishop honored his good friend by sharing his heartfelt anger at the manner of his dying and called strongly for new policies that would allow people to die with more dignity.

In our discussion, the Archbishop voiced how appalled he was to hear that politicians arrived, without his wife Graça being informed, at Mandela's private home for a photo shoot when he was very ill. He said as he watched the TV footage he noted his friend Madiba's facial expression was one of threatening thunder and that he was silent throughout.

That was April 2013: a few weeks later Mandela suffered cardiac arrest. Legal documents issued later that year referred to Mandela being in a permanent vegetative state with no chance of return to cognitive engagement. From this time, Mandela's breathing was assisted with an oxygen pipe inserted into the trachea and he was fed intravenously. Mandela officially died eight months later in December 2013.

With our earlier conversation about Mandela on my mind, it took me a while to find the right words to ask:

> Archbishop, in my book I want to write that dying is another area of personal leadership, the ultimate act. And I'd venture to say that Joe and Madiba, for all their inspirational leadership qualities, iconic heroes in the struggle against apartheid, neither prepared well for death.
>
> I don't know how many people I might offend. But my observation is that death is difficult and we who are left behind, we grieve, we suffer. It seems to me that there is even more suffering because of the conversations that people haven't had. But if my book says dying is your final act of personal leadership, and it's one which Madiba didn't get right, will I be on the receiving end of an angry response?

The Archbishop responded:

> You have identified areas that have been taboos for a very long time and I think you will get responses, angry responses, because most of it has been taboo. You must get on your suit of armor, put on your tin hat, your steel helmet, and say, well, yes, and engage. This is the lot of anyone who sticks their neck out. This taboo about not talking about dying, like so many other taboos, it is not rational. It needs to be challenged. It is a heck of a lot better to know, to accept that

269

dying is as natural as growing old. Obviously, the anguish happens when someone dies young or dies violently. But it ought to be the case that, as I have been saying, that dying is part of life.

You know how people look at you and they say 'Oh, you look so young' and imagine that they have given you a compliment. And I say, you know, I have been young, I have been middle-aged, and now I am more old. And that's quite right because if we were to remain young or even middle-aged, our world would not be able to support us. And it's wonderful! How would I have become a grandfather if I remained 17 years of age? But people—look at the trouble they go to!—to hide the fact that they've got wrinkles and gray hair.

The Archbishop had recently been in and out of hospital; through his prostate cancer, this body was voicing its fragility and challenging any denial. I asked how he was feeling about his own dying, considering his own legacy of personal leadership.

He reflected a little and then answered, quizzically at first:

Yes. I've been wondering how I'm feeling. Am I fearful? Is there some element of anxiety about what's next? What happens at the end, before the next beginning? I used to say they must make sure I'm quite dead before they put me in the coffin and in a grave. I don't want to asphyxiate, you know! I do consider it an incredible privilege of having aged. I will be 84 on my next birthday and on at least two occasions the medical prognosis was that I was about to kick the bucket. I think I told you how my father bought the wood for making my coffin and the black cloth for hanging. I ended up with a lame hand—it was polio.

Later, there came a point where I was hemorrhaging and hospitalized. Each time I coughed, a flood of blood would come out. I had noticed—I was about 13 or 14 then—that without exception people who coughed like that ended up being wheeled out of the ward. I expected the same for myself. One time I went into the bathroom and had another coughing attack when it seemed like gallons of blood were coming out. And I sat there and I said to God, 'If it means that I have to die, okay.' And I was surprised at the peace and calm that came over me.

I asked Archbishop Tutu if having been in a state of calm acceptance of the prospect of dying in his early teens did he stay that way? What happened as his life unfolded? He reflected that while he was surprised at his teenage calmness, in adulthood he got a little more anxious. 'Part of it is worry about what's going to happen to your family—your children and your wife.'

The clock moved to 10:30 that Thursday morning, the designated time for the Archbishop to have his weekly tea with all the office staff of the Desmond and Leah Tutu Legacy Foundation. And today one person has a birthday; today there will be cake. We can't delay.

'You know Helena? No? Well she and I are discussing the very important subject of dying,' he told those who had gathered.

I heard some audibly sharp intakes of breath in the room. The Arch had been frail and close to dying a couple of times in the last few months and they wondered how he could be so at ease with talking about this subject matter when they were avoiding speaking of it. But the Archbishop was persistent. He drew people out. Tea with birthday cake became a mini workshop.

One person, Varinia*, spoke of how important it would be to have a book that prompts conversation, how she personally would welcome this in her life. She talked of her grandfather's dying and how her parents were paralyzed by shock and she had to take over all the arrangements. She described her grandfather, a tall, broad-shouldered man of farming stock. She was asked to choose a coffin.

'But they are all too short,' she said.

'No, the size is standard,' replied the owner of the funeral home, 'we just break the legs.'

Varinia began to cry as she said these words out loud. She'd never shared this story with anyone, and the feelings of sadness had continued even with the passage of time.

My friend Gonda, deputy dean at the University of Cape Town Medical School, later confirmed that coffins come in a standard size, and that it was standard practice to break limbs or shoulders. Joe was big, she commented, 'They probably had to break his legs to fit him inside his coffin.'

The legacy of Desmond Tutu, Nobel Peace Prize Laureate, is deep. And he's still adding to it. He is edging down the road towards his life's end, sometimes tapping his way there with his walking stick, other times using a wheelchair.

For the occasion of his 85th birthday in October 2016, he made a video for the US advocacy organization Compassion and Choices—the same group which had helped to spread the Brittany Maynard story, which tipped the scales toward legalizing assisted dying in California, Quebec, and Colombia. At the same time, an article published in *The Washington Post* confirmed his belief that people should have choice about how they die, including medically assisted dying.

> Just as I have argued firmly for compassion and fairness in life, I believe that terminally ill people should be treated with the same fairness when it comes to their deaths. Dying people should have the right to choose how and when they leave Mother Earth. I believe that alongside the wonderful palliative care that exists, their choices should include a dignified assisted death. I have prepared for my death and have made it clear that I do not wish to be kept alive at all costs. I hope I am treated with compassion and allowed to pass on to the next phase of life's journey in the manner of my choice.

The day after the article ran, I opened my emails to find one which had just arrived. The CEO of the Hospice Palliative Care Association of South Africa, Liz Gwyther, had sent out this strongly worded press statement.

> Archbishop Tutu is wrong or misinformed about the life or death issue of euthanasia. The right to live and to die in dignity is one of the basic principles of palliative care... We know that with palliative care people do not have to 'endure terrible pain and suffering.' Palliative care can control pain and enable people to live well, in comfort and dignity until the moment of their natural death... We also know that people who request euthanasia do so because of despair and a gap in the care they are receiving. I would like to have a conversation with Archbishop Tutu to discover his understanding of end-of-life care and what has led him to this philosophy of despair.

Archbishop Tutu? Philosophy of despair? This is the man who cackles with laughter as he drinks his hot chocolate at the Friday morning breakfasts and whose latest publication is called *The Book of Joy*, co-authored with the Dalai Lama and Douglas Abrams?

And the words 'natural death' have no ring of truth for the Archbishop's situation; nothing is natural about his continued living. He's the beneficiary of the finest medical interventions available.

I was saddened by that press statement. Hospice associations in other parts of the world take a different stance. Ann Jackson spent 20 years as CEO of the Oregon Hospice Association. In 1994, she voted against the public initiative which adopted the Death with Dignity Act. Today, she says, she would vote in favor of physician-assisted dying.

> As hospice and palliative care physicians frequently tell their patients, 'I can promise to manage your pain and symptoms, but I can't promise to keep you awake.' Being sedated to the point of a coma is not an acceptable option for most persons whose primary concerns are about losing autonomy, their quality of life, and dignity —as they define dignity.
>
> The major beneficiaries of Oregon's Death with Dignity Act are those who do not use it to hasten their deaths. Of 25 people who talk to their doctor about a request, one will ingest medication to end his or her life. Hospice workers describe patients as making a request on day 1, qualifying for a prescription on day 15, then tucking their prescription, or their medication … into a safe place. That's when they can get on with living. They have a plan, just in case.

A week after the 85th birthday celebration and the release of the thought-provoking video, I sat with Archbishop Tutu in the Wimpy Bar after the cathedral service and asked him how he felt about the negative feedback he'd attracted from some quarters. The Arch laughed, 'I've got my tin hat on. These criticisms don't faze me. People need to learn to respect choices.'

Postscript Nine

Malcolm Gladwell's concept of the tipping point interests me because that's still the question I'm pursuing: what needs to happen for a profound social shift to take place whereupon people worldwide talk more readily and comfortably about dying throughout their entire lives?

I believe we'd live better, more intentional lives if we did this, and I believe we'd possibly suffer less when we encounter loss because some of those conversations will pre-empt possible disappointments or conflicts and oil the wheels of relationships. I certainly wish in my life that there'd been more talking about dying.

Ideas are not static. Social views on child labor, child imprisonment, divorce, adultery, gay marriage, and termination of pregnancy have changed over time. Draft bills legislating the right to die with dignity, including medically assisted dying, are increasing in number in the United States and several countries worldwide.

But my quest covers a wider range of issues beyond the end-of-life preoccupation. I'd like for all the topics covered in this book to be part of comprehensive conversation about how we live and how we die.

I'm optimistic. All the initiatives being undertaken by individuals, community-based organizations, and within the health system and other professional bodies will impact the tipping point and people will talk more comfortably about issues of life, death, and joy the world over.

The process of my research led me to the power of mavens, connectors, and salespersons. Dr. Gawande's *New Yorker* article led me to La Crosse, Wisconsin. Helen Smit, the doctor who I met in Mozambique, knew someone on The Conversation Project advisory board. Archbishop Tutu led me to Reverend Rene August.

I'm comfortable being a maven, but now I need to migrate. More connectors and salespersons are called for if the tipping point is to happen in my life time.

PART TEN

New Beginnings

The end is where we start from.

—T.S. Eliot, *Little Gidding*

Take everything that's bright and beautiful in you and introduce it to the shadow side of yourself. Let your altruism meet your egotism, let your generosity meet your greed, let your joy meet your grief, Everyone has a shadow ... But when you are able to say, 'I am all of the above, my shadow as well as my light,' the shadow's power is put in the service of good. Wholeness is the goal, but wholeness does not mean perfection, it means embracing brokenness as an integral part of your life.

—Parker Palmer, *Let Your Life Speak*

Lost and Found

I was supposed to leave for the airport at midday. Italy for 43 days. I decided on a quick dash to the shopping mall; I needed to stop at the optician and get a new battery for my watch. I had also spotted some travel slippers on sale earlier in the week, and then there was the last food shopping that I wanted to do for my bedridden mother.

It was only when I returned home that I realized I was no longer wearing my necklace. It had unhooked itself, slithered and fallen somewhere in the mall, in one of those shops, along the walkways, or in the parking lot. I started to make phone calls; there was no time for me to go back and retrace my steps. It was a necklace of handmade small silver balls threaded onto a chain—the first gift I remembered receiving from Joe. It was the necklace I wore most often, the one I could wear with any one of my silver earrings. In my will it's bequeathed to Kyla, a recognition of her closeness to Joe.

I choked up a bit. Is this an omen? I was going to spend weeks writing day after day at the Bellagio Center, and some of that writing would be about Joe and his dying. I wanted him to be with me. I wanted the necklace he gave me around my neck as I wrote.

I wanted other people with me on my journey. I wanted their karma. I wanted their goodwill. So I selected jewelry not only for color and variety but for its provenance, as though the objects themselves represented the essence of the associated person and that when I wore that piece they would be with me.

So what to wear instead as I traveled to Bellagio? I decided on a necklace of bluey-green labradorite and the matching earrings; soft shimmering tiles of feldspar arranged in a collar. It's one of John's first gifts to me. You can't easily coil it into an oblong box so I wasn't thinking of traveling with it. But labradorite is the stone of protection, calmness, peace ... and I was feeling a little vulnerable.

This Rockefeller residency was big for me. I hadn't been away from home for so long in recent years; it felt as though I was going on a pilgrimage. There had been weeks of mental preparation and the making of arrangements in order to leave normal life behind.

The creamy pearls and earrings. Nature's Valley: John and I walking to Salt River to cross and hike into the mountains. The river was higher than expected. We stripped down and carried bundles of dry clothing on our heads. I waded chest deep across the river wearing only the pearls. How we laughed when we'd dressed in our dry clothes and then, just a few minutes later, thunder clapped and the skies opened and we were left with the kind of wetness that means that even your ears are filled with rain water.

There was the delicate, silver necklace with the tiny turquoise pre-Christian square cross that my dear friend Gilly brought from Mexico, and the matching earrings. I didn't often wear it, but I wanted Gilly with me. Turquoise, the stone of truth, vision, and creativity. The square cross of a pre-Christian spirituality fitted my awakening from the narrow narrative of my Catholic childhood.

The pink and green watermelon necklace, made of tourmaline, the stone of balance between male and female within oneself. The green is life force; the pink soothes and harmonizes. Another gift from John. I wore this with the filigree pinky-lilac earrings that Marti made, which go so well together. Marti, so present, so there for me, always.

The sparkly blue glass Swarovski earrings that John and I bought together on our honeymoon in Barcelona; the blue accentuating the blue of my eyes. Six days of walking from the Pyrenees to the sea, finding our way down to earth after the intoxicating headiness of our wedding celebration.

The lapis lazuli earrings and ring that I found in a Camden Town market in 1981 was the first significant jewelry I ever bought for myself. The design was a round slice of stone; I loved the matte blue and the flecks. How often these pieces have completed an outfit. They aren't showy. They aren't dangly. They fit my sense of professional self. I often choose to wear them when making a presentation. I would have to present to my fellow residents in Bellagio; I would wear these.

The green glass earrings from Edinburgh that my old friends Pam and Dave gave me last year for my 60th. Pam's work on the emotional labor of nursing and our discussions on end-of-life care are very much with me.

I spent three days in Verona en route to Bellagio with my old friend Novella. She had a tumor on the lung and was scheduled to have an operation in a few days. This was her second brush with cancer; perhaps the tumor was an offshoot of the earlier encounter. I bought small onyx and cornelian earrings as a memento of our time together. Onyx, from the silicate chalcedony, a stone associated with healing and supporting inner strength at a time of physical stress.

I caught the train from Verona to Milan, and would have an hour in Milan before my next train to Varenna Esino, and then there would be the ferry ride across the lake to Bellagio. People rushed to get off the train, but I had no need to. As I got on I left two cases in the luggage area—a large gray one and a small black one—and as I was one of the last to make my way out, those were the only two pieces left, the black and the gray. I hauled them onto the platform and started looking for the platform number of my next train.

We traveled alongside water. My excitement was mounting. On the ferry ride I wanted to cry. Was this really happening? I finally reached Villa Serbelloni. There was warmth in the welcome as I was shown to room V19. It was exquisite, beautiful beyond anything I had ever imagined. A corner bedroom overlooked the lake on two sides and there was an en suite study. Heavenly. A poet would be doing his presentation at 6:15pm, which gave me two hours to unpack and settle. I opened the gray case and began to hang my clothes. Then the black case. The contents were not mine. I had someone else's case; someone else had mine.

The case opened on the parquet floor of my room belonged to a young woman. Where was she on her way to after stepping off the train in Milan? She must be feeling quite upset. She had everything in the case for a few days away from home. Medication, cosmetics, spare contact lenses and solution, an umbrella, a manicure set, nightwear, slippers, lacy underwear, attractive dresses for a slender person. I looked for a name, a telephone number, an email address. But there was no personal identification whatsoever, only an empty spectacles case, brand name Eliza, with the telephone number of an eyewear store in Shensie, Shen Yang Province, mainland China.

I made a list for the police report. I had 28 items in my carry-on bag. One of them was my small red velvet travel box, my box of jewelry— my box of loved ones.

I sat in my room in Villa Serbelloni overlooking the beauty of Lake Como. When I die, I will leave everything behind. Everyone leaves everything. Perhaps in losing the jewelry box I was being offered some small practice in the art of letting go.

I oscillated. Memories drew me to attachment and away from acceptance.

It was the pearls that choked me the most. We'd be getting ready to take a bath together, and John would ask, 'Please put on your pearls. I love to look at you wearing the pearls.' I smiled as I remembered; desiring and being desired.

Ashes to ashes. Dust to dust. No pearls. No attachment. Acceptance.

But I am ambivalent. I love the way that things, anything, a bread board, a tablecloth, a letter opener, offer the pleasure of remembering someone, often unexpectedly. Objects can be such welcome anchors of memory. I treasure their prompts at a time when my memory is beginning to fail me.

Day 12. Afterthoughts
Ambivalence. Oscillation. I am not ready to 'let go.' Twelve days pass. I am failing this test of learning non-attachment. I'd like the red box back.

Day 15. More afterthoughts
Fifteen days. I hear that lost luggage given into a police station is kept for two months and if it is not claimed, it's destroyed. That would be a real pity. I hope my suitcase is opened and that the new owners appreciate the Japanese whiskey, that someone likes the Peony perfume, and that my jewelry gets new owners who enjoy wearing it.

Day 18. Resolution
Eighteen days. My loved ones are with me, jewelry/no jewelry, they are here. They are part of who I've become in my life. This is what matters most. I love myself, I love others, and I am myself loved. From this deep well of loving I draw strength.

Lost Again

My heart is breaking. Tears fill my eyes, spilling over and rolling silently down my cheeks. I breathe, I discreetly wipe the tears away, and recalibrate my composure. My mind is in charge. Keep calm. Exude calm. Don't upset others by letting them see how this is affecting you.

Other times, mostly just after I return home after spending time with Mum, I sob. What comes out of me is those wracking noisy body-shaking sobs, unedited, out of listening range of anyone else, my body telling me the depth of the sorrow I feel. I gulp air between the sobs, the moans, crying as if wounded. I am wounded.

I thought my jewelry story would be the end of this book, but no, life seized me by the scruff of the neck. Just when I thought I was close to done in my work to find my own equilibrium with the acceptance of death, my own and that of others, I discovered otherwise. My mum changed trajectory towards her 90th birthday when, suddenly, she took a dive into dementia and I found myself lost and unraveling.

Grief is cracking my heart and Mum hasn't even died yet. That is, her body hasn't died yet. It's her mind that's giving up on her, and us. It's like Swiss cheese and the holes are getting bigger and bigger. Lucidity has vanished into thin air. And the most recent years of Mum's life have done a disappearing act. She doesn't remember moving from England to Johannesburg 14 years ago. She doesn't remember moving into the same apartment block as me five years ago.

'Why's my linen on this bed?' She thinks she's visiting me on holiday from the UK, and she's puzzled to be recognizing her own damask sheets and duvet cover on this bed.

Sometimes she thinks we're traveling together and that she's in a hotel. 'There's a lot of wardrobe space in this hotel room. Who brought my painting of the Czech farm and hung it on this wall? And the painting of the pink tulips?'

Mum's confusion began more than a year ago, not long after I returned in October of 2015 from Italy. Mum and I had been on regular Skype calls and she'd seen the exquisite bedroom I stayed in with its paneled ceiling, painted furniture and en suite study, as well as the landscapes that John and I walked through for a week as we hiked along the hilltop

281

towns of Tuscany. When I returned, we looked at the dozens of photos together, and in her new state of confusion she began to think she'd actually been with me on this journey. She'd begin a conversation, 'When we were in Italy...' And then there was her disorientation on Christmas eve when she didn't know where she was. In hindsight that was the clearest turning point, the beginning of her decline.

For several days in April she relived my father's death. Her conversations were as if it was 24 years ago and my dad had just died. She spoke as if she was recently widowed, often crying. It was difficult to watch her cry and not easy to comfort her. In the weeks that followed, it was clear she thought she was visiting Johannesburg from England after my father's death, as though she was convalescing with me in her bereavement. Indeed, this is what she did 24 years ago. She stayed for several weeks and every day she'd tire herself out, working in the garden, and eventually went back to England leaving me with a magnificent rockery of orange flowering aloes and gray-green succulents.

Then there was the week in August that Tessa, who was living in Cape Town, phoned to say she was pregnant with her second child and that the due date was my dad's birthday. Mazeltov. Happiness.

Kyla, her New York-based granddaughter, sent photos on WhatsApp of her advancing pregnancy, playfully standing next to a huge watermelon placed on a stool—the round of the melon matching her belly.

The next day, my mum told me, 'I dreamt I was pregnant. I don't want to be pregnant. I can't cope with a baby at my age.' She spoke to me very seriously with anxiety in her voice as though this could be a real possibility. Her logic and memory are completely gone in this moment—there's no man around, she had a hysterectomy 57 years ago, she no longer ovulates.

Ten days ago I listened to my mum's Sunday phone call with Kyla—a 20-minute call with the speaker phone on. Kyla held the conversation thread steady when it would be so easy to let go and give up. It was like listening to a faulty vinyl LP—when the needle keeps jumping back and begins replay with the same repeated lines. I heard my mum ask my heavily pregnant daughter three times, 'How are you feeling?' Each time the question was asked as if for the first time.

I'm trying to enjoy catching glimpses of the mum I knew. Last Monday she was asking what I'd been busy with. I took out my iPad and showed her the pictures I'd taken of fabric samples. We want to re-cover the dining chairs, two sofas and two wing-back armchairs. As we looked at my bad photos, I suddenly said, 'Why don't I go downstairs and bring up the fabric sample books—we still have them on loan from the upholstery shop until tomorrow. I'll be back in five minutes.'

We had a lovely time. My mum, in her day, was such an accomplished seamstress with knowledge of materials and a sense of color. There's a Hertex fabric that's the most expensive; the texture and colors are special but John and I are hesitant about the price. My mum likes it the most.

She advises me, 'Don't go for the cheaper one. You have to buy the best, the most expensive you can possibly afford. You won't be doing this again for a long time.' She's right—it's 25 years since those dining room chairs were last covered!

I'm not sure if there are any of those glimpses still to come.

Yesterday was particularly bad. She was confused, looked anxious and was angry. She's lost her independence. She's not strong enough to get to the toilet. She is still herself enough to feel that diapers are humiliating and strange nurses changing them feels intrusive—an invasion of privacy. She's angry I've hired a night nurse. I try to explain that I'm still working, I need to sleep. Her daytime caregivers—they also have lives and need to sleep. But she's angry. She shouts. She wants the nurse to leave. Or she herself wants to leave. She wants to come downstairs and sleep at our place.

I'm conflicted. It's mid-September and of course I'd love to do what would comfort my mum the most, but next Friday I'll be traveling to attend meetings in Washington and Chicago. I'll have a precious chance to pass through New York and see my daughter in her stage of late pregnancy. I need to set in place care support for my mum that works when I'm not around, and that's sustainable over the months ahead. My mum has been dying slowing. It has been four years since she went to bed, six months now since dementia settled in. Her heart beats strongly. Her pulse is regular. Her kidneys are doing well enough as are her lungs.

But last night she was so unhappy, so confused. I was lying next to her on her bed. I tried everything. We looked at the videos of her great-grandchild Benjamin; up to now her face always lit up as she watched.

Yesterday I did not get that response.

'That person, Nadya*, is she still here?'

'Nadya, the nurse, yes, she's still here. Remember a few weeks ago you slipped and fell in the bathroom and we decided there should always be someone here, just in case you need help.'

'Nurse, my foot. She knows as much about nursing as I do.'

'Mum, that would be a lot. You are a nurse.'

'I don't like this place. It's got bad vibes with her here. I want to go home. Where's my cat. My cat's disappeared.'

'Your cat is in the lounge. She's in front of the fireplace. Let me go take a photo for you. Here she is, you can see on the iPad photo, she's on the carpet in front of the fireplace.'

'I like that carpet; it's got a lovely pattern.'

'Yes, you chose that carpet.'

'I want to go home. Can I take the carpet with me? I want to make a nice place.'

By this time it's 10pm. I've been up since 4am—I was running a workshop all day today and needed to get up early to finish my prep.

'Mum, of course you can take the carpet with you. Can we talk about it tomorrow?' I can hardly keep my eyes open. 'Can I turn your light off?'

'Yes and close the door,' by which she means—keep that nurse out!

I went downstairs and sobbed. I climbed into bed—too tired to undress—seeking respite in the unconscious state of sleep. I cried more, quietly now. I cried myself to sleep.

This feels hard, my mum's slow dying. It hurts so much. It seems to me that it might be easier to be the one who's dying, rather than being the one watching your loved one die. It strikes me how deeply individual, personal and unpredictable our responses are. However much we try to understand death as a common universal experience, part of its universality is how differently we respond as individuals.

Gina's Crossing

I listened to the first birdsong and watch the sky lighten. This time yesterday my mum took her last breath. I was beginning my second motherless day on this earth.

She died just a few days earlier than I'd anticipated. I thought she'd hang in until December 13th when Kyla and her husband, Andrew, would arrive in Johannesburg with newborn Livia. Mum had been hanging in for so long and I truly believed she'd make it.

Our last real conversation was 27 days earlier, the day before I left for New York to be on call for two weeks, to rock and sooth and coo as well as aspire to be the fabulous grandmother that cooks almost every evening, and leaves behind some readymade meals in the freezer — boerewors pasta sauce for Andrew and Ottolenghi fishcakes for Kyla.

The nurse had told me early that morning that Mum had said to her, 'Toni and I just came back from a weekend away.' A weekend away with my long-departed dad! Mum really was time-traveling in her confusion.

That afternoon, I took a long time to bubble wrap the coffee service that Mum wanted me to take to Kyla. I had no reason to hurry; I wanted the slowness. She asked me if there was anything else she should think of for me to pack. And I said, 'No, this is perfect.'

I'd brought a coffee table book with me, hot-off-the press, produced by Adopt-a-School, a school upliftment project, for the occasion of their 10th anniversary. It included profiles of the founding board members, and I'm one of them. A photographer had come to my office and the book includes a photo of me looking very professional, along with a brief profile of my life and how I came to be a board member. Mum couldn't focus easily, even on the full-page photo, and I realized for certain she'd stopped reading. I was already missing her once almost daily tirade about what she'd read in the newspapers, and her customary query, 'When is this President Zuma going? How long is it going to take for him to go? What are your friends doing about him?'

I sat reading the profile out loud in my best reading voice, the one that I have because when I was very young, my mum sent me to elocution lessons along with my brother Roman. There was some snobbery in our mother, the result of her having grown up in the Czech Republic as the daughter of a well-off farmer with good land, livestock, and a tractor. As a post-war refugee immigrant, her birthright snob factor meant she wanted me to learn to speak the 'Queen's English' and not only the vernacular of our working-class Lancashire neighborhood. I fell in love with poetry, and when my parents were short of money and I had to make a choice, I gave up ballet lessons to keep attending those classes.

When I'd finished reading, she said how proud she was of me, that she'd always loved me, and always would. Of course, I began to blubber; crying comes easily to me. The hospice nurse who'd encouraged me to keep to my plan of traveling to Brooklyn also encouraged me to leave having said my goodbyes, telling me it was very possible that Mum would die while I was away.

Mum asked why I was crying. I told her I wasn't sure I'd see her again, that she might die while I was away. She told me she was doing her best, 'battling on' she said, and we talked about Kyla's arrival mid-December.

Two weeks later, my first day back from New York, she said to me, 'I love you. I hope you will be happy with what I've left behind.' But it was slow-motion speaking, like the vinyl that's on the record player at the wrong speed. That first day back coincided with the visit from the hospice nursing sister. She and I sat together at my mum's bedside, all of us looking at Brooklyn photos on my white iPad.

She opened one eye, which is apparently one more than she'd opened for several days, so her caregivers told me. I showed her the photos of her newest great-granddaughter Livia, this chubby little baby girl, gaining weight so wonderfully on breast milk. Then I took out my cell phone and showed her the latest family posting, a video of my two-year-old grandchild, Benjamin, kicking a ball over a line between goal posts, with Alex, his father, shouting goal!

But my mum wasn't herself anymore. She didn't seem to be able to focus to see the photos. There was no brightening of her face. None.

Mum had been bedridden for four and a half years, and moved around in a wheelchair. She chose to go to bed after her hip operation left her feeling traumatized and vulnerable. During these years, I so often climbed into bed with her and showed her photos and little videos on the 'vyte-board,' her name for my white iPad. In that way my mum had traveled the world with me in this last 15 months: Italy, Amsterdam, Blackpool, London, Oxford, Rosslyn Chapel outside Edinburgh, Vienna, Brussels, Cape Town, Chicago, Baltimore, Washington DC, New York, and Weinheim, where her sister lives in Germany.

We'd now reached a crossover point, the change in the color of the litmus paper of the 'joy-test.' Up to now, my mum, however unwell she'd been, had taken huge pleasure in seeing photos of her children, grandchildren, and great-grandchildren. She loved Skype calls when she could see everyone, especially when my niece Stefanie would visit Roman, with her daughter Cerys singing nursery rhymes. If my mum could no longer partake in these pleasures, then what was there left to live for?

The conversation became one way only—they say hearing is the last of our sensory faculties to go, so I always talked with her, even as she lay day after day with her eyes closed, withdrawing from the world. I felt as though I was in Pedro Almodóvar's movie *Talk to Her*, where there's a woman in a coma and the man who loves her sits with her and talks every day, day after day, month after month.

On Friday December 2, I finished my work week of writing. I had been sitting and typing while looking over the banks of the Kruger Park's Crocodile River; typing, tying, and typing some more—my deadline was Kyla's arrival on December 13. I had such a sense of urgency, wanting to finish after almost eight years of part-time writing. John would wake for the early morning game drive at 5am, going off with friends and tea and rusks, and I would stay behind and work on my manuscript.

I knew enough about myself and my ways of grieving to be humbled into accepting that I did not know how I would respond. There have been some deaths, which I've integrated seamlessly like my dad's, and others like Joe's, which have thrown me off-balance for months. A race to the finish. My first complete draft versus my mum's death. Which would happen first?

Returning from the bush I went upstairs to her flat. I greeted her caregivers, Alice and Ivy; it was handover time between them. On hearing my voice, Mum half-opened one eye, the right eye.

Ivy told me, 'Ah, your mum knows you're back. She hasn't opened her eyes all week.'

Alice and Ivy, who did shifts, kept records. I checked the two diaries, one a food diary, the other a diary of Mum's 'state of being'—what she had been saying or doing, if anything. I read she'd eaten very little, drunk very little. Her diaper was mostly dry—her kidneys surely must be struggling.

The next morning, my mum looked even more withdrawn into

herself, not even offering me the one eye, half-open. I decided to sleep in her room that night and in the early evening went upstairs and sat in the wide armchair, slowly sorting out paperwork while watching her caregiver Alice first feed my mum soup, and then crush her medication into berry yogurt. It was like watching Tessa with Benjamin. The two ends of life in my life contrasting so sharply: my daughters Tessa and Kyla both having their babies and my mum's dying. Birth and death happening simultaneously.

Alice and I decided to wash and change my mum and get her ready for the night. That week she had her first ever bedsore in four and a half years, and I'd bought special plasters that morning. We chatted as we washed, wiped, and creamed. My mum's skin was like parchment, so dry, despite the tubs of aqueous cream we'd used. Alice said she hoped my mum would see Christmas—just three weeks away. I told her that I thought differently. Mum was having such a hard time, that I would be glad if she had fewer days ahead of her.

Alice and I were standing, one of us on each side of the bed, talking over my mother lying between us. I said, 'Mum, Can you hear us talking about you? If you can then please know you don't have to stay here longer for anyone. You don't need to wait for Kyla, for Livia, for anyone. They will understand. If you're ready to go, please go. It's okay for you to go.' And I laughed a little because it's strange to have these one-way conversations.

Just when we'd re-arranged the pillows, she began to vomit, brown gluey gooey liquid, spilling out of her mouth. I couldn't catch it fast enough into paper hankies.

Alice and continued talking softly as we worked. It was hard to get a nightdress off over the head of an almost completely limp person. Mum wasn't helping us to move her limbs. Alice and I agreed that the next day she was on duty she would cut the nighties up the middle, hem them and create a row of ties—like the gowns they have at the hospital. Now we understood the reason for that design.

An hour later, we had changed three pillows and pillow cases, the top bedsheet, and Mum's nightdress. She was not swallowing so I swabbed out the brown goo inside her mouth. I then smoothed verbena-infused grapeseed oil into her face, hands, arms, and chest. No trace of vomit. She smelt lovely.

I sat in the big fat chair and watched her breathing through her mouth rather than her nose, a little noisy, but not too labored. She lay on her right side, the pillows propped to support her back so's not to have any pressure on her bedsore. She now looked settled and peaceful, as though she could well have a few more days in her and wait for Livia after all.

I changed my mind about sleeping over. I didn't expect to sleep well enough. And I knew from the long last month of Joe's dying that the caregivers need their sleep, they need stamina. I walked downstairs to my flat. Alice would call me if she had any cause for concern.

The phone rang at dawn, the time of birdsong. Alice. She'd woken early and could hear my mother's breathing when she went to the bathroom. When she returned she realized there was silence in the house.

I was upstairs within minutes. I put my ear to Mum's mouth. I was in a state of disbelief. I imagined that I could see my mum's chest moving ever so slightly. It was my imagination. She'd gone. But I still phoned the hospice nurse and asked her to come and confirm.

I was so sad. I was so happy. I was so relieved and then again so very sad—so many feelings intermingling. I was in a tumble drier of mixed emotions.

My mum's face was calm and her hands relaxed. I've known of people dying in pain, their faces contorted, their hands clenched. My mum's rhythmic breathing had simply stopped. I felt such gratitude.

My last day with her satiated all my needs for love and ritual. Alice and Ivy changed shifts at 6:30am. I asked Ivy to take the time she needed to say her goodbyes and then go home.

Afterwards, alone with my mum, I put on a Bach mass to keep me company as I washed her. I wanted her to have on her day clothes; it seemed inappropriate for her to go to the mortuary in her nightdress. I had a window of just a couple of hours before rigor mortis would set in, after which dressing Mum would be more difficult.

She didn't have last rites. Did it bother her? It struck me that the verbena grapeseed oil was the closest she got, inadvertently, in the absence of a priest, to the sacrament of Extreme Unction, to the anointing of oil that's part of Catholic readiness for dying. The verbena oil would have to be good enough. But I phoned the Jesuit priest, Father Anthony Egan, the only priest she'd ever engaged with in Johannesburg, for reassurance and comfort; it turns out you can give last rites after death or to people in a coma; the timing is more flexible than I thought. After I'd spoken with him I found websites of Catholic prayers for the dead on my iPad, and they became a soothing voice-over on low volume.

Should I have stayed the night? If she was so ready to go, perhaps my sleeping there may have held her back. When we washed her, cradled her gently into her sleeping position, I'd kissed her goodnight. Surely she felt loved and cared for?

I decided I'd trim her hair one last time. We'd had a deal for 12 years that ended a year ago, when she became too unwell to carry out her side of the bargain. I would cut her hair and she would mend my clothes. But the reason I specifically want to do her hair now is because of a friend's story of how the undertakers trimmed his father's unruly eyebrows and moustache and then the family saw a person in the coffin who no longer looked like the man who'd been their father. I would ask the funeral parlor not to do anything cosmetic—just to make sure my mother had her teeth in; she always wanted her teeth in when she went out in public.

I talked to my brother and my daughters. I sent a mail to my book club saying I wouldn't make it for the afternoon's gathering. I sent an e-mail to my Aunt Inge to ask her to let her siblings and my cousins know. Mapi arrived with flowers and cake, and later Audrey also brought cake—African and Jewish customs to arrive with food! And after they left I decided to ignore my phone, I wanted, I needed time, to be quiet.

John, my tender, caring husband, arrived back mid-afternoon from a work event in Mpumalanga for which he had to stay overnight. He, the Jewish person in the family had already sent me a mail when I was in Brooklyn. He'd found and typed up the Catholic prayers to be ready for us just in case my mum died while I was away.

He proposed and set up a three-way call with Tessa, Alex and Benjamin in Cape Town, and Kyla and Andrew in Brooklyn. To my surprise everyone wanted to see Grandma and I clicked the iPad camera button so that they could see Mum lying on her bed, dressed ready to go to the mortuary. Kyla played a favorite piece of music, Bach's Violin Concerto in A minor, the Adante movement. Then we said the prayers, each taking a turn to read aloud. Tessa cried as she spoke and Alex picked up seamlessly. Finally, we each shared a memory. Two-year-old

Benjamin got bored with sitting still and fidgeted! But, all in all, it was wonderful. Later I Skyped with my brother Roman and did the same again.

Finally, in the early evening, Julius Moyo and his wife Catherine Megalane arrived. We'd postponed the mortuary pick up twice, as they were having transport problems. Julius and my mum built a rockery together when my mum worked through her grief over my father's death by redesigning my garden. They'd known each other for 25 years.

It was great to see Julius, the gardener, step confidently into his Sunday role of lay pastor. He praised my mother's spirit eloquently, loudly, sincerely intoning prayers that wished Mrs. Dolny, Granny, a good passage into her afterlife.

The undertakers rang the doorbell. They unfolded the gurney and unrolled a blue-patterned Basotho blanket. They carefully lifted Mum into place, and we accompanied her to the van downstairs. Now almost eight in the evening, John and I returned to my mother's apartment. We cut some bread and cheese, poured out two glasses of red wine and made a toast to her. Long life.

Post-mortem

Two days later, after many flower deliveries and visits, after setting up a memory table with photos and objects that people tell me they associate with my mum when they think of her, I sat quietly and thought about Mum's dying. What had gone well? What would I do differently if I could rewind the tape and rescript our movie?

My thoughts were that with my mother being so very ill physically, I became so preoccupied with the medical physicality of dying that I neglected the spiritual. I spoke earlier about the two diaries that were kept, recording details of both food eaten or not and my mother's state of being. When I came back after my two weeks of being a mother to Kyla and grandmother to newborn Livia, I had read the two diaries and saw that in the state of being book my Mum asked two days after I left, 'When is the Catholic priest coming?'

My friend Pam, who is a professor of nursing, had told me a year earlier that in her long experience when people are getting themselves ready to die, they often want a visit from a spiritual person; it doesn't have to be an officiant of their own religion, but someone whose spiritual stature they acknowledge and respect. Ivy had written in the diary that my mum called out, 'Mother Mary, come help me. I can't carry this pain anymore.' The diary entries recorded that when my brother Roman telephoned, she was too tired to speak. It was also written that she had begun to sporadically call out the names of her five siblings dead and alive, and my grandmother's sister, her beloved aunt, Tante Dolfi. I had been told some time ago that the calling out of names also often happens in the days and hours preceding death. But I did not read the signals of how close Mum was to her dying, I never followed up by calling the priest for last rites.

After my mother died I read both diaries again. I think, in retrospect, I didn't pay enough attention to the entries made whilst I was in Brooklyn that spoke to her state of mind because I was so convinced that my mum was hanging in, 'battling on' as she'd herself called it, clearly waiting for her granddaughter, Kyla, and newest great-grandchild, baby Livia, to arrive. And perhaps she would have battled on for nine more days if I had not told her that it was okay to go, that we'd understand her choice that battling on had become too hard. It is still amazing to me that she died that very night.

I was comforted by Getti's assertion that my mum died in a state of grace, and Father Egan's information on last rites. But my reflection and my learning is about the challenge of keeping a balance, about not getting so consumed by the immediacy of the physicality of dying: the preoccupation with mouth comfort, moving body position to prevent bedsores, creaming skin, inserting suppositories, changing diapers. Somehow, amidst all of this, you want to keep your eye on the spiritual ambience: loving words, the murmur of prayers, poems, psalms, low lighting, soft singing, gentle music might be what's most important for all of you.

My mother's compassionate family doctor, Dr. Connell, telephoned and we talked about the how of my mum's passing. He was complimentary of our having managed the home care to the very end. I told him of my missing a beat on getting a priest to come.

Two days later he sent me a mail in which he introduced me to the concept of the 'royal priesthood:'

The basic message is that we are all members of the royal priesthood and therefore can act as spiritual persons and agents of God, which I think you consistently did. You could not know the time she would die. You companioned her through her journey to death and saved her from loneliness. Your goings and comings, and confidence that she would understand and cope, asserted her essential dignity and autonomy from you. I think you did great!

I googled 'royal priesthood' and read more. I was not aware of Martin Luther's offering a religious view of a unitary world of human beings— not a world divided into the 'extraordinary' of those who are the officiant members of a spiritual ministry, and us 'ordinary' beings. The concept asserts that 'no believer has greater access to the Creator than any other.' Luther's doctrine of the universal priesthood of all believers gave equal rights and responsibilities to both laypersons and clergy.

John, with deep kindness, reminded me of his mantra, the one he made up and offered to me at the time of our preparing for our wedding. As we discussed flowers and music and I agonized over not being able to find 144 matching napkins, he said, 'Not everything has to be perfect in order for it to be perfect.' I need to accept that we did more than okay. I have enough to be proud of—we're allowed, in life, to drop a stitch or two.

New Beginnings

This morning, *eight* weeks ago, I sat with my mother who'd just taken her last breath. Today, *six* weeks ago, we'd gone for a celebratory Sunday lunch with my brother and my daughters. My mother had come home for her wake on Friday night, a wonderfully inclusive occasion, and her Saturday afternoon funeral was splendid. Our halcyon Sunday summer afternoon drew to a close. My daughters, my brother, all started packing—their departures were imminent and my daughter Kyla asked, 'Mama, can you just take Livia for a while.'

With much heart-gladness I took my lovely grand-daughter in my arms, now eleven weeks old. There's something about the vulnerability of such small babies that is heart-melting and so affirming of new life. And with Livia, I'd been startled by feeling an almost electrical connection.

I carried her outside and stepped down into the garden. Lizards, flowers, butterflies, there was a lot to show her and talk to her about. And then I slipped, there was sand on a paving slab and my legs shot out from under me. I held on to Livia as tightly as I could. Thankfully, she was unhurt. I wasn't so lucky.

My x-rays later that evening showed two broken bones, the fibula and tibia on either side of the ankle, and three days later I had a sophisticated carpentry operation. The orthopedic surgeon fixed a plate and eight screws into the one bone and inserted two long screws into the other. She commented later, 'Your bones are good and hard, I had to drill. Sometimes people your age have bones like cheese.' Livia's four-year-old cousin Simon looked at my x-ray and said, 'She's a little bit robot.' I appreciated his humor, because my own was at a low ebb.

The combination of grief and physical pain was itself an unspeakable cocktail exacerbated by sleep deprivation. For 30 days I had first a cast and then a 'moonboot' to be worn 24/7 which disturbed me when I moved at night. Drugs? I left hospital with dozens of painkillers. They messed with my brain and bunged up my bowels; I stopped taking them. I swallowed Traumeel and tissue salts—they smoothed only the sharpest edge of my pain, but at least I had my mind, and felt like me.

It proved important over the next weeks to create and hold onto lighter moments as a counterweight to the heaviness of pain, grief, and tiredness. I had one magical interlude with my grandson, Benjamin. He'd become a 27-month-old toddler learning to talk at a gallop. We were on holiday and sat overlooking the garden at the edge of the Tsitsikamma Mountains. Two turacos—beautiful birds with vivid coloring—had built a nest in the tall milkwood tree right next to the window. We were both spellbound, watching for movement.

His mother Tessa passed to and fro behind us several times, and couldn't believe it was her fiddly toddler sitting so quietly beside me. The turacos were mostly very still, and we watched them carefully, and they in turn seemed to watch us. Stationary, they are a silken green around the head and upper back, a coloring which changes to a sheen of blue-purple on their lower body. They have a white ring around their red eyes and a white crenulation along the crown of the head. Our bird book showed us what would be on show if we got lucky and saw them fly.

We sat patiently in our magical bubble. Suddenly one turaco flew up and swooped across to land in the neighboring tree, revealing the dramatic, exotic crimson feathers of its underwings. As it swooped, Benjamin's face lit up and his eyes shone, as he whooped, 'Bird! Flying! Ings. Whed!' (His word for wings, his pronunciation of red.) It was our shared moment of pure joy, our catching of happiness.

We sat still some more, and other birds flew back and forth in the garden. I showed Benjamin the brown long-tailed mouse bird, the Cape robin, the yellow weaver. Then suddenly it was me that exclaimed with excitement. My face became one huge smile. There was a hovering, a sudden flash of emerald iridescence, the greater double-collared sunbird, the closest African evocation of my totem, the hummingbird.

Colibri, hummingbird, spirit-guide confirming my calling.

The slow healing of my broken ankle, my compromised mobility, created confinement. But I had 18 readers lined up who'd offered to give me feedback in a tight turnaround time—a gift I did not want to squander. I felt urgency to use whatever energy I had to finish the first complete draft of this book. And with my totem rooting for me, I pressed the send button on my laptop.

While my readers read, so did I. I re-read all the stories I'd written and thought about what meaning they held for me in their totality. It seemed to me that the most difficult challenge is the dance of life between the now and the future. We're always making decisions, especially about health, time, and money. When I turned 30 and my father was 60 he said to me, 'Be careful with your timing. When I was young I didn't have money; when I was old I didn't have health.' I listened and have heeded his advice.

I chose to walk the Inca trail and the Camino when my knees still had cartilage. Now I consistently create time for my adult children and grandchildren in a busy working life because the future is undependable. I fell in love with a sculpture which was way beyond my budget, and cashed in a pension policy to buy it. My argument—I may not reach that pensionable age.

When John and I married in 2008, we each wrote our vows and mine included, 'I aspire to live with and love you with no deferment, that there should be no unfinished business, no regrets of how we share our time together. I pledge to love you fully in the present, in the knowledge that this life is transient, that every day is precious.'

PING. An incoming text message. Several days after sending out the draft manuscript my computer and phone began to receive responses from the readers of my draft manuscript.

The text message: 'Enjoying reading the stories. The ones on relationships challenged me. I'd had a serious blow up with a very good friend several years ago and we've never spoken since. Just want to tell you, I phoned him. I have nothing to lose, but possibly something to regain. We'll be meeting next week. Thank you.'

I got an email from 'heartsease'—that's the mail address Dr. Connell chose for himself. He wrote, 'You bring wisdom and beauty to a subject that is shunned with fear and distaste. You model taking control from the professionals and putting it where it belongs, in the hands of the dying person and their loved ones.'

An e-mail came in from the United States, one of my readers visited parents over a weekend and used the draft worksheets with the questions as a guide for their decision-making conversation, 'Thank you for the questions. Going through them with my father was a gift to him, to me, to my entire family. The questions are a wonderful resource, which will make a difference to so many.'

And in conversation readers told me of what the stories had prompted them to do.

One said, 'I realize I have to have a conversation about my mother's wedding ring. I'm the youngest of the sisters, but I want her ring. Why should it come to me? When I was a kid my mom came to watch me play sport at school, and she noticed the diamond had dropped out of its setting. She and I spent hours and hours looking for it. I need to have the conversations now.'

Over a coffee one of my earliest readers told me that she'd first read the drafts of the stories on secrets a year ago and these stories had haunted her for several months. Why? Because she herself had a secret concerning the circumstances of her child's conception. Now she'd taken the plunge to tell her child, an undertaking she had spoken about with her therapists over many years, but she'd never acted before. The risk proved worthwhile. Her child, now a young adult, had thanked her for her courage and a renewed closeness emerged between them.

Yes. Yes. Yes! This is exciting for me!

This is what I wanted. This was the whole *why* of my writing. This was worth the eight-year commitment. People having conversations. We suffer when death draws near but we suffer much more when we don't talk. More talking, less suffering. That's the why of what I've done.

My experience of writing the book, of listening to peoples' stories has shaped me, taught me so much. Now I was getting a sense from my first readers of its impact on them.

And you? What have the stories illuminated for you? Will you be having conversations, tending to certain relationships that could benefit from your tending? Will you make sure that those dear to you know of the special place you have for them in your heart? Will you consider how your secrets might be handled to create less harm to those you love? Will you write out your end-of-life wishes and specify your rituals? Will you think a little more about ordering your affairs and your adminstration and keep in mind Mary Oliver's poem 'Storage' as encouragement to deal with your clutter? And most importantly what does Oliver's 'The Summer Day' poem mean for you? How might you now shape what remains to you of this earthly life you've been offered?

The hummingbird in me imagined flying, riding the aircurrents far and wide across continents over several days as hummingbirds are apt to do, glancing down and taking note of all the conversations taking place that I've had a hand in prompting. An imagined possibility, becoming a reality, answering Wangari Maathai's invitation, 'Be a hummingbird in your community, wherever you are. It's all we're called to do—the best we can.'

I truly believe that a significant step towards change in the 21st century would be peoples' reconnection with ritual and their willing engagement to talk about mortality as part of living well. I want to be part of making this happen.

When drafting the 'Let's Talk' stories in chapter nine, I'd revisited Malcolm Gladwell's *The Tipping Point* yet again. Gladwell wrote, 'If you want to bring about a fundamental change in people's belief and behavior ... you need to create a community around them, where those new beliefs can be practiced and expressed and nurtured.'

There is a need for change in the training curriculum of several professions: doctors, nurses, lawyers, religious ministers, shamans, social workers, and politicians. These professionals all touch and influence our end-of-life decision-making.

We have midwives and doulas who assist with birth. It's time now to support an emerging midwifery, doulas for dying.

I will discern my ongoing role in being part of this change I want to see; there are many opportunities ahead. But whichever way I find to engage, wherever I choose to be, and whoever I'm with, I'll be mindful that joy is the elixir of life that makes us want to wake up every morning and engage with the world, whatever our age, our mobility, our general state of health. And I'll keep the words of the 12th-century mystic Rumi close to my heart: 'Let the beauty of what you love, be what you do.'

I plan to revisit these conversations about living and dying, asking myself if, before forever after, am I really living wildly, as best as I can, the one precious life I have been offered?

And you? Since we all die, what will you do with your life?

Ah, there I go again, falling into the trap of the focus on *doing*, not paying enough attention to the importance of the way of *being*. Wasn't that the key lesson for me to have learned from my journey with my mother—the need to balance the being and the doing, the material and the spiritual?

At the core of our impermanent existence, surely the reframed question for us to keep asking ourselves is: Since we all die, what will you *do* with your life and how will you *be*?

PART ELEVEN

Live the Questions

This is now. Now is. Don't postpone
till then. Spend the spark of iron
on stone. Sit at the head of the table.
Dip your spoon in the bowl. Seat yourself
Next to your joy and have your awakened soul
pour wine . . .

—Rumi

Conversations with Ourselves

The questions. The questions pertaining to each of the nine parts of this book are offered in the spirit of Mary Oliver's poems: 'Invitation,' 'The Journey,' and 'The Summer Day.' Find them online. Enjoy the read.

Reflection time. Create some time and a place for reflection, with as little chance of being disturbed as possible.

Review and select. Review the series of questions. Which ones resonate with you? Which ones, if any, do you feel it would be relevant to work with?

Write by hand. I urge you to write by hand rather than typing on a keyboard. Writing on an electronic device would be better than the keyboard. The hand–mind connection is said to be more powerful. For myself, seeing my own thoughts written out in my own handwriting has had more impact in the longer term. 'Ah, so this is what I thought. Here it is, in my own hand-writing. This was my truth at that moment.'

I'm trying to store less paper in my life—what's working for me is to initially write on paper and then scan and store electronically.

I want to beg you, as much as I can, to be patient toward all that is unresolved in your heart and to try to love the questions themselves like locked rooms and like books that are written in a very foreign tongue. Do not now seek the answers, which cannot be given to you, because you cannot live them. And the point is, to live everything. Live the questions now. Perhaps you will then gradually, without noticing it, live along some distant day into the answer. Resolve to be always beginning – to be a beginner.'

—Rainer Maria Rilke

*Which is worth more, a crowd of thousands,
or your own genuine solitude?*
...
*A little while alone in your room
Will prove more valuable than anything else
That could ever be given to you.*

—Rumi

1. Living Life Alive

SCENARIOS

- A 23-year-old woman is given six months to live; she deliberates on how she wants to spend this time doing what with whom.
- A 50-year-old man reviews his life. He concludes he does not feel joy in his work and plans change.
- An 88-year-old bedridden woman contemplates her ebbing life force. What she appreciates is that she has joy and treasures every day.
- A child dies. It changes how the mother thinks about love and work and how to parent her other children.
- A 40-year-old hiker begins to suffer with a physical disability. He makes a plan of the hikes he most wants to do whilst he still can.

QUESTIONS FOR CONVERSATIONS

1.1 What, if anything, would you do differently, if you were to truly embrace the possibility that you could die unexpectedly, even tomorrow?

1.2 Living life alive: if you engaged with the possibility of finite time periods, say one or two or five years, to live—what activities would you bring forward in your life?

1.3 Living life with intention: what more, if anything, do you want to achieve emotionally, spiritually, physically, materially, or in terms of accomplishments?

1.4 What could you discard from your life to make it easier or happier? What do you consider to be a burden in your current life that you could handle differently?

1.5 What life habits do you want to change?

1.6 What are you grateful for and at peace with in the life you have lived so far?

1.7 What would you like to be remembered for?

2. Relationships

QUESTIONS FOR CONVERSATIONS

2.1 Do those you love know this for certain? Is there someone who needs (or that you would like him/her) to know you love him/her?

2.2 Are there people who have greatly influenced you in a positive way, or people you admire or respect, who have no idea how you feel about them and that you may want to tell?

2.3 In the event of your death, is there a message you want someone who is close to you to receive either after your death, or on the occasion of a significant event in their future?

2.4 If there are relationships in your life that matter to you, but which you are not completely at ease with, what actions might you consider taking?

2.5 Is there someone you want to forgive?

2.6 Is there someone you wish to ask forgiveness from?

2.7 Is there anything you want to forgive in yourself, something you are not proud about?

2.8 If you knew you were to die sooner than you anticipate, what actions would you take to make changes in any of your relationships?

3. Secrets

SCENARIOS

- A pension fund administrator at a company is handling the administration of a deceased employee. The administrator is dealing with the family that everyone at work knew of; one day a second family turns up.
- At a funeral people notice a woman who has no connection with the family circle, sitting at the back crying. It is the deceased's mistress of many years.
- A surviving spouse opens the deceased's bank statements and discovers significant expenditures on pornography sites.

QUESTIONS FOR CONVERSATIONS

3.1   If the reason people keep secrets is to prevent the breaking down of relationships when those secrets are revealed, why risk this before you die?

3.2   Are you sure you don't have papers (letters, pictures, documents) that will be an unpleasant surprise for your loved ones once you are gone?

3.3   If you leave something to someone in your will who your family is not aware of, what measures can you take so that your wish will not be contested or become a source of pain?

3.4   Is there anything that you want to consider disclosing about yourself to others to feel more complete about yourself?

3.5   Do you have a private, virtual, 'online' engagement, perhaps under another name, that you would want to be closed off, which needs a password? How would this be done posthumously?

3.6   If you have a secret you're not prepared to risk disclosing, that you expect to be hurtful for your loved ones on discovery, what might you consider doing to lessen that hurt? Is there any trusted person to whom you could delegate the task of delivering a disclosure letter after your death that might soften the blow?

4. Respecting Choices

SCENARIOS

- A man is supplied with oxygen intubation after heart failure. Weeks later, he says, 'Doctor, don't ever do that to me again. I'd rather go.' Months later, his heart fails again. He is unconscious and cannot speak. His daughter insists on 'full code'. Weeks pass on life support before the family agrees to switch off.
- Suzanne, a 32-year-old, decides to be an organ donor but does not tell her family. When she dies in a car crash her parents are shocked to see her in the mortuary with no eyes.
- A couple differ in their preferences about how much medical intervention they are each comfortable with. They realize they are both right, and love means they must accept and respect their differences.

QUESTIONS FOR CONVERSATIONS

4.1   If you knew that end-of-life decision-making could be a source of conflict for both family members and physicians, what decisions and preferences can you make explicit and write down to pre-empt such difficulties?

4.2   If you knew that people are different—some want to be surrounded by nearest and dearest while others want their private space—what care might you take to clarify this with someone when they are dying?

4.3   What would you like for yourself spiritually, if anything, at the time of your dying, and are others aware of your wishes?

4.4   If you could choose, where would you like to end your life? Home? Hospice? Hospital? What environment would you like? Quietness or music? If you want music, then what kind? Lighting? Candlelight? Scents? What aromatherapy oil do you most like? Who, if anyone, would you like to be there with you?

5. Ritual

SCENARIOS

- An ailing 85-year-old atheist woman is adamant that she does not want any fuss made when she dies. He daughter recognizes her own need for ritual and organizes a church service and boat trip to scatter the ashes at sea.
- A mother died. The elder son began to put in place the funeral arrangements. The elder daughters have some different views but feel their voices are not being heard. The youngest daughter arrives with the notes her mom has made during a conversation they had weeks ago. Peace reigns.
- A family quarrels about what to do with a loved one's ashes.

QUESTIONS FOR CONVERSATIONS

5.1 If you acknowledge the importance of ritual as enabling acceptance for those who live on after your death, what attention might you give to indicating what rituals you would like to happen when you die?

5.2 If you knew that being as explicit as possible about your wishes could help avoid conflict at a time when people are often not at their best, what can you take care to be specific about? Consider: burial versus cremation; cloth, cardboard or casket; songs or readings; ashes kept in an urn or dispersed, and if to be dispersed, where?

5.3 As your ritual requirements may not match everyone's preference or beliefs, would you consider explaining why you have made those choices to make those staying behind comfortable with your wishes, and so that they might better know and understand your choices?

6. Bereavement

SCENARIOS

- J. is incapacitated on the death of her husband. She is depressed, unable to work effectively. She is angry that society has forgotten how to offer condolences.
- P. simply says he cannot live without a woman, that there are some men like that. He remarries a few months after burying his wife.
- M. is devastated by the sequential death of her parents in their 80s. As the months go by, she feels worse not better. 'Time heals' is not happening for her. She cannot recognize any stages of grief in the passage of time; nothing helps.
- A teenager learns her father has been killed in a shoot-out. She is sent for bereavement counseling. Her relationship with her father was not good. She expresses relief that her father died. It is her grandfather who is her mainstay.

QUESTIONS FOR CONVERSATIONS

6.1 If you knew that acknowledgment, compassion, and non-judgment are the three most important things to offer a bereaved friend, colleague, acquaintance, or neighbor, how might you greet them when you meet them just after their loss, and in the months that follow?

6.2 If you knew that we all grieve differently and over different time periods, how would you support someone you care for whose bereavement is extended?

6.3 Different deaths elicit different responses at different times of our lives. Do you have a sense of your own strengths and weaknesses in coping with grief? How you are likely to be affected physically, mentally and spiritually? What can you do to prepare yourself and those around you, in so far as it is possible?"

7. Money. Planning. Emotions

SCENARIOS

- When M. does her calculations for a traditional burial, she realizes how expensive it is. She decides this money could go to educating the younger generation in her family. She decides to convince her family that she wants a cremation.
- Carl and Imelda have been married for 50 years, and have lived in the same family home all their married lives. Now the staircases are difficult to manage. And spreading their money between running the house and healthcare is getting tighter. All their children live in different cities.

QUESTIONS FOR CONVERSATIONS

7.1   We are living in a world where families separate, and where there may be no one who can move in to live and care for you in your elder years; what decisions might you consider making earlier in your life to support your lifestyle in your longevity?

7.2   Who, if anyone, do you feel a responsibility to make a financial provision for and, if so, what can you put in place to take care of this concern?

7.3   A time might come when you are not able to administer your own financial affairs. Have you put measures in place to deal with this eventuality?

7.4   What is the budget that's needed for you to have the send-off that you'd like to have, including any wish for a wake, the funeral, the after-ceremony, a tombstone?

7.5   If you knew that you do not want your family to incur funeral debts when you die, what decisions would you make, and what savings or policies would you put in place?

8.   Winding Up

SCENARIOS

- A man goes for an operation. He dies. His funeral wishes are on his computer. Neither his wife nor anyone else has any passwords.
- A mother with an adopted two-year-old goes for an operation. Her sister enquires about her will and guardianship. Other family members weigh in to silence her on raising these issues. The next day, after a post-op embolism, the mother dies intestate.
- It takes M. three years to wind up his parents' estate. There are so many missing documents.
- In his will a father leaves his four children unequal shares to his estate: 50%, 30% 15% and 5%. On his death bed he has regrets and says, 'Make it right.' The siblings first agree then one reneges. Relationships deteriorate.
- A woman is diagnosed with dementia. With her family present she drafts her living will. She gives advance consent for decisions to be made when she is unable.

QUESTIONS FOR CONVERSATIONS

8.1   In a time of bereavement, people are expected to deal with a challenging paper trail of administrative issues. Who knows where to find your passwords, your bank account information, your financial policies, your last will and testament, all essential for the process of bringing closure in terms of winding up your estate. What access to information can you organize?

8.2   Many people have an online life. Are there aspects of your virtual life that should be closed off when you die? If so, is there someone who will do this for you who knows the passwords?

8.3   Would you consider being specific about your wishes about who inherits what—particularly regarding personal items—

so that potential disagreements and misunderstandings are avoided?

8.4   The emotional and other consequences of bequests can be disturbing; would you consider disclosing the contents of your will with the beneficiaries in advance so that there are no surprises?

8.5   What's treasure for you may be junk for someone else to sort out. What can you do now that will make it easier for the loved ones you're leaving behind?

8.6   If you wish to donate any of your organs, what formalities need to be put in place and who of your loved ones, if indeed anyone, do you want/need to tell?

8.7   What are your guidelines for how you would like to live should you become mentally incapacitated?

9.   Let's Talk—Towards the Tipping Point

- E. was so close to her mother. She thought they talked about everything. Then dementia happened and conversations were no longer possible. 'I was asked to make decisions on my mom's behalf, how I wished I could hear her voice, how I wished I knew her preferences.'
- Dr. D.: 'I knew my patient's preferences. He'd talked to me about them. But he didn't write anything down, he didn't tell his family. He was hospitalized with a stroke. They put him on full code. There was nothing I could do to say otherwise. I needed the paperwork to support me.'
- A terminally ill UK woman wanted to end her life. She'd illegally obtained the lethal phenobarbital and stored it in her fridge. She'd discussed her choice with friends but never with family members who now looked after her as she reached her point of intractable suffering. She became too weak to go downstairs to get her drugs. Her family did not agree with her choice and would not help. Her last two weeks were not as she'd wished.

QUESTIONS FOR CONVERSATIONS

9.1   If you knew that having the conversations about your mortality, and end-of-life preferences is important for the people who will be there with you at this juncture in your life, who do you still want to have such conversations with? Who else needs to be in the know? Are there people you love who you feel you should not have this conversation with for whatever reason?

9.2   What conversations can you start within your family to help others deal with all these issues while they are alive and healthy?

9.3   What else, if anything, do you need to do to feel at ease with the life you are living and your choices about dying? Confucius said your second life begins when you face the fact that you only have one and will die: are there changes you wish to consider making about the way you are living the next part of your life?

9.4   What other questions can you think of, if any, that you want to address for yourself or discuss with other people?

Acknowledgments

The author and publisher gratefully acknowledge permission to reprint:
'The Summer Day'
By Mary Oliver
From *House of Light* by Mary Oliver, Published by Beacon Press Boston
Copyright © 1990 by Mary Oliver
Reprinted by permission of The Charlotte Sheedy Literary Agency Inc.
'Storage'
By Mary Oliver
From *Felicity* by Mary Oliver, Published by The Penguin Press New York
Copyright © 2015 by Mary Oliver
Reprinted by permission of The Charlotte Sheedy Literary Agency Inc.

Writing this book has been a gift, enriched and encouraged by people's generosity and support. I have been enormously privileged to listen. I have many to thank for their different contributions in bringing this book to fruition over a period of eight years. I wish to acknowledge:

'The Arch,' who, on my visits to Cape Town, kept asking, 'Is the book finished yet?' I'm grateful for Archbishop Emeritus Tutu's financial contribution to my research which meant so much more to me than the money; it felt like a vote of confidence. His sponsorship of my Bellagio application, as well as the warm support received at the congregation's Friday morning after-service breakfast were hugely appreciated.

Joel Joffe, Baron Joffe of Liddington, defense attorney during the Rivonia trial, later a member of the UK House of Lords proposed a Private Members Bill, Assisted Dying for the Terminally Ill, and contributed financially towards my travel and stood as a referee for my Bellagio application.

Those who participated in the creating of this book, people who offered stories, conversations, shared experiences, gave me technical support, reviewed my questions, agreed to be interviewed, invited me to discussions, or to give presentations including: Agira*, Amelia* Archbishop Emeritus Desmond Tutu, Reverend Rene August, Althea Banda Hansman, Steve Barak, Brenda Barbour, Cathy Barnett, Gillian Beeton, Emily Berlin, Carol Berra, George Bizos, Claire Bless, Pumla Bolani, Caterina Borelli, Selma Browde, Linda Buckley, Stephen Burrow, Graeme Butchart, Diana Callear, Kate Callahan, Malcolm Campbell, Dale Carolin, Julie Cliff, Audrey Coleman, Louise Colvin, Sean Davison, Colleen Dawson, Kate DeBartolo, Roman Dolny, Anne Doyle, Jim Eitel, Renée Ephron (nee Slovo), Scott Erbele, Jenny Evans, Bianca Fauble, Amanda Ferguson, Nomboniso Gasa, Polly Gaster, Elaine Gavshon, Dale Gaudie, Cheryl Goldstone, Ellen Goodman, Callum Grieve, A. Erik Gundersen, Ferial Haffajee, Bernie Hammes, Elysa Hammond, Derek Hannekom, Trish Hanekom, Ruth Holmes, Suzanne Hotz, Cas Human, Panie Human, Atrayah Janye, Gail Jammy, Jill Joubert, Rob Katz, Ho Siu Kee, Florrie Kerschbaumer, Hans Kerschbaumer, Gunilla Kercher, Alan Kirschner, Rachel Kyte, Carrie Lapham, Caroline Lambert, Willem Landman, Lee Last, Lucille*, Lumimbe*, Roger Le Compte, Joann Ledderman, Kyla Lee, Rana Limbo, Meredith Little, Janet Love, Ezekiel Lothlare, Oscar Marleyn, Eusebius McKaiser, Angela Melamed, Totsie Memela, Getti Mercorio, Dawn Meyer, Mapi Mhlangu, Mish Middelmann, Banyana Mohajane, Rob Moore, Mary Morris, Thenjiwe Mtintso, Ruth Muller, Ondine Norman, Bridget O'Laughlin, Pulane*, Sam Peinado, Radha Pillay, Novella Palombo, Jonathan Foster-Pedley, Harriet Perlman, Ina Perlman, Vincent Pinkster, Richard*, Cyril Ramaphosa, Joyce Sikhakane Rankin, Danielle Rathke, Vasu Reddy, Aura Reinhardt, Melissa Revels, Anton Richman, Brendan Robinson, Helen Rudham, Ken Rudham, Khatija Saley, Mohammed Saley*, Diane Salters, Neville Schonegevel, Patsy Schonegevel, Lali and Ray Sher, Kwanele Asante-Shongwe, Julie Schroeder, Mike Scott, Zukie Siyotula, Pulane Sibeko*, Helen Smit, Dave Smith, Stefanie Smith, Pam Smith, Epiphany Stransham-Ford, Penelope Stransham-Ford, Robin Stransham-Ford, Irene Staunton, Nokuzola Patricia Tebeka, Rosanne

Trollope, Terence Tryon, Margaret Urban, Marie Walter, Monika Weber-Fahr, Michael Weeder, Ed Wethli, Teresa Valdes-Fauli Weintraub, David Wield, Jill Wilke, Julie Wilson, Frances Wilson, Gary Wolman, Janine Wolman, Ilundi Wuyts, Marc Wuyts, and Solomon Zwane*.

My Bellagio community: Pilar Palacio, Caterina Borelli, Maria Cardines, Shoma Chaudhury, Stephen Coit, James Cronin, Denise Fairchild, Laura Frader, Katherine Geurts, Elysa Hammond, Peter McCarey, Susan Napier, Loyisa Nongxa, Angela and Ken Ofori-Atta, Chuck Peters, Jonathan and Tina Quick, Jesus Ramirez-Valles, Stephen Rapp, Ruta Sepetys, John Skrenty and Michael Smith. I'd like to especially acknowledge Pilar and Ruta who actively continued their support beyond our shared residency, and Caterina, filmmaker, who went the extra mile in redoing the images for my presentation.

Those who offered quiet space for writing, hand-in-hand with friendship: in London, Gill Walt and Isky Gordon; in Maputo, Margarida (Guida) Marques and José Forjaz; in New York, Kyla Wethli and Andrew Por; in Miami, Emily Berlin; in Rome, Novella Palombo; and Pam Smith in Edinburgh.

My Time To Think professional community led by Nancy Kline. Their premise that questions are generative shaped my approach. Nancy consistently affirmed with me that writing is our soul food, requiring we make the time for it in our lives. Maryse Barak led me to the School of Lost Borders, brought ritual to our work together, and encouraged me to read more of Rumi. Trisha Lord beamed encouragement as did Sunny Stout Roston who also offered advice on editing. I've continued to benefit from the encouragement of colleagues I've met at the Annual Global Faculty Meetings: Stephanie Archer, Linda Aspey, Catherine Duvel, Ruth McCarthy, Sarah Hartman, Monica Schuldt, Susan Schuurmans, and Candice Smith.

My fellow students of Ontological Coaching, pioneered by Alan Sieler, an approach which emphasizes the interrelationship of body, language, and emotion as the expression of our way of being in the world. Special thanks to Stephen Beukes, Vicky Coates, Julia Bonadei-Thorns, Laura Malan, Erma Steyn and Karen White, for their engagement as I danced between studies, coaching work, writing, and family responsibilities. Yasmin Lambat coached me for 10 sessions in how to soften my core which made it physically easier to be in the world. Karen White for introducing me to Leadership Embodiment work with herself and Wendy Palmer.

The Sunday Afternoon Bookclubbers who read the first draft are an amazing group of human beings; dynamic, independent thinkers who bring passion and integrity to any discussion. And to think I was afraid they'd be too reticent and not give me the robust feedback I so wanted! Well, they spoke out loud and clear: Marina Appelbaum, Astrid Fleming, Pulane Kingston, Catherine Koffman, Silindile Kubheka, Wacango Limani, Nomsa Mbere, Mapi Mhlangu, and Alessandra Pardini.

Others who read the manuscript and gave supportive, insightful, critical feedback: Daniel Barnett, Charlotte Bauer, Howard Drakes, Angelo Fick, Steven Goldblatt, Marti Janse van Rensburg, Daniel Musiitwa, Gonda Perez, Sue Rabkin, Alexia Walker, and Des Williams.

I had the good fortune of engaging with two extraordinary doctors, Fazel Randera and Martin Connell, as well as Hospice nursing sister, Frances Hoziak, who brought competence underpinned by compassion to every one of her home visits.

My editor, Tanya Pampalone, proved to be an engaged professional with clarity on boundaries, respect for deadlines, and appetite for the subject matter. Farida de Villiers patiently undertook many hours of transcribing interviews.

Monika Weber-Fahr not only gave feedback on the worksheets but also proposed the title *Before Forever After*.

Marina Appelbaum, who has boundless energy, a capacity for caring deeply, and an entrepreneurial eye for business. She made me do the math and escorted me to meet Klara Skinner at Staging Post whose ease and helpfulness made contracting an enjoyable experience.

On the home front Ivy Fikile Cele, Alice Ntombizodwa Maphosa, Julius Moyo, Catherine Megalane, and Refiloe Ramaisa worked beyond the call of duty, and offered compassion and patience when it was most needed.

My daughters, Tessa Josina and Ruth Kyla, offered me the gift of their confidence in me in trusting that I'd be respectful when I wrote about them.

John Perlman lived with me during the eight years it took to complete this manuscript. His experience as a journalist, his eye for the pace of story, as well as grammar were invaluable. He engaged in many hours of rich conversation as well as partnering with me on the journey of accompanying my mother to her end.

And last, but not least, my mum, who was proud of me, believed in what I was doing, who sadly wasn't able to read to the end, as her dying became the unplanned—for lived experience of all that I'd been writing about.

Notes on Sources

These books are either directly referred to or have formed part of my background reading and influenced my thoughts as I selected the stories and wrote on each of the nine themes.

INTRODUCTION: **The Hummingbird**

Andrews, Ted. *Animal Speak: The Spiritual and Magical Powers of Creatures Big and Small*. Woodbury. Minnesota. Llewellyn Publications. 1993.

Compte-Sponville, Andre. *The Book of Atheist Spirituality: An Elegant Argument for Spirituality without God*. Great Britain. Bantam Books. 2008.

Frankl, Viktor E. *Man's Search for Meaning*. London. Rider. 2004.

Gladwell, Malcom. *The Tipping Point*. Great Britain. Little Brown and Company. 2000.

Maathai, Wangari. *I Will be a Hummingbird*, www.youtube.com.

Peat, F. David. *Blackfoot Physics: A Journey into the Native American Universe*. Great Britain. Fourth Estate. 1994.

School of Lost Borders—offers vision fast and rites of passage training, located in the wilderness, that cultivates self-trust, responsibility and understanding. See website www.schooloflostborders.org.

Simmons, Robert and Niasha Ahsian. *The Book of Stones: Who They are and What They Teach*. Berkeley, California. North Atlantic Books. 2005.

Tutu, Desmond Mpilo. *God is Not a Christian*. London. Rider. 2011.

PART ONE: **Living Life Alive**

Oliver, Mary. Red Bird Poems. I considered three of Oliver's poems as openings: 'The Invitation,' 'The Journey,' and 'The Summer Day.' 'The Journey' leads the reader pointedly to reflect on the purpose of their life. 'The Summer Day' asks the reader what will they do with the opportunity of their one earthly life. I chose 'The Invitation' for its light, gentle but powerful tenor which Oliver chooses to close with a quote from Rilke, 'You must change your life.'

Albom, Mitch. *Tuesdays With Morrie*. United States. Doubleday. 1997.

319

Arrien, Angeles. *The Second Half of Life: Opening the Eight Gates of Wisdom.* Boulder, Colorado. Sounds True, Inc. 2005.

Bastian, Edward W. and Tina L. Staley. *Living Fully Dying Well: Reflecting on Death to Find Your Life's Meaning.* Boulder Colorado. Sounds True, Inc. 2009.

Beck, Martha. *Expecting Adam.* New York. Three Rivers Press. 1999.

Beck, Martha. *Finding Your Own North Star: Claiming the Life You Were Meant to Live.* London. Piatkus. 2001.

Capra, Fritjof. *The Tao of Physics: An Exploration of the Parallels between Modern Physics and Eastern Mysticism.* Great Britain. Flamingo. 1982.

Dolny, Helena. *Banking on Change.* South Africa. Penguin Books. 2001

Dolny, Helena. 'The Challenge of Agriculture' in Saul, John S. (ed) *A Difficult Road: The Transition to Socialism.* USA Monthly Review Press. 1985.

Grof, Stanislav. *Books of the Dead: Manuals for Living and Dying.* UK. Thames and Hudson. 1994.

Heidegger, Martin. *Being and Time.* New York. HarperCollins. 1962.

Ho Siu-Kee. *The Constrained Body.* Hong Kong. Hong Kong Arts Center. 2010.

Kalanithi, Paul. *When Breath Becomes Air.* New York. Random House. 2016.

Kline, Nancy. *Time To Think: Listening to Ignite the Human Mind.* UK. Cassell Illustrated. 1999.

Langer, Ellen J. *Mindfulness.* 25th Anniversary Edition. USA. Da Capo Press. 2014.

Mandela, Nelson. *An ideal for which I am prepared to die.* Speech delivered from the dock. April 1964. www.guardian.com.great speeches. Also video footage available online. The Nelson Mandela Foundation Archive has an online archive with background documents from the Rivonia Trial.

Moore, Thomas. *Care of the Soul: How to add Depth and Meaning to your Everyday Life.* Great Britain. Piatkus Books.1994.

Moore, Thomas. *A Life at Work.* Great Britain. Piatkus Books. 2008.

Murphy, N. Michael. *The Wisdom of Dying: Practices for Living.* UK. Element Books Limited. 1999.

O'Kelly, Eugene. *Chasing Daylight: How My Forthcoming Death Transformed My Life.* New York. McGraw-Hill. 2008.

Pausch, Randy. *The Last Lecture.* New York. Hachette Books. 2008.

Rehm, Robert. *People in Charge.* Great Britain. Hawthorn Press, 1999.

Tutu, Desmond and the Dalai Lama with Douglas Abrams. *The Book of Joy.* New York. AVERY, Penguin Random House. 2016.

www.ancient-origins.net Pan Gu. *The Chinese Creation Story.*

Wesker, Arnold. *The Wesker Trilogy, Chicken Soup with Barley, Roots, I'm Talking about Jerusalem.* England. Penguin,1964. As a teenager I acted the role of Beatie in Roots which shaped my after-high school decision to take a gap year.

Whyte, David. *The Three Marriages: Reimagining Work, Self and Relationship.*

New York. Riverhead Books. 2009.

Part Two: Relationships

Ditzler, Jinny. *Your Best Year Yet*. London. Harper Element. 2006. This is the book which has the wheel of life on which to plot your relationships and choose what it is that you want to plan for the next year or two.

Keen, Sam. *Fire in the Belly: On Being a Man*. New York. Bantam Books. 1991.

Hausner, Stephan. *Even If It Costs Me My Life: Systemic Constellation and Serious Illness*. USA. Gestalt Press. 2011.

Leader, Darrian. *The New Black: Mourning, Melancholia, and Depression*. London. Hamish Hamilton. 2008.

Madanes, Cloe. *Relationship Breakthrough: How to create outstanding relationships in every area of your life*. New York. Rodale. 2009.

Rosenberg, Marshall B. *Nonviolent Communication: A Language of Life*. USA. PuddleDancer Press. 2003.

Servan-Schreiber, David, *Healing without Freud or Prozac: Natural Approaches to Curing Stress, Anxiety and Depression*. UK. Rodale. 2005. Chapter 12. Enhancing Emotional Communication describes a tool, STABEN, to be used for preparation for a challenging conversation that my coaching clients have found especially useful.

Some, Sobonfu. *The Spirit of Intimacy: Ancient African Teachings in the Ways of Relationships*. New York. Quill, HarperCollins. 2000.

Tannen, Deborah. *You Just Don't Understand: Women and Men in Conversation*. New York. HarperCollins. 2007.

Tutu, Desmond Mpilo, and Mpho A Tutu. *The Book of Forgiving. The fourfold path for healing ourselves and the world*. London. William Collins. 2014.

Part Three: Secrets

Paul, Caroline. *The Lost Cat*. New York. Bloomsbury. 2013

Part Four: Respecting Choices

Byock M.D., Ira. *The Best Care Possible: A Physician's Quest to Transform Care through the End of Life*. New York. Avery. 2013.

Callanan, Maggie. *Final Journeys: A Practical Guide for Bringing Care and Comfort at the End of Life*. New York. Bantam Books. 2008.

Chabot MD PhD, Boudewijn. *Taking Control of Your Own Death by Stopping Eating and Drinking*. Amsterdam. Foundation Dignified Dying. 2014.

Davison, Sean. *Before We Say Goodbye: Helping My Mother Die*. South Africa. Penguin Books. 2012.

Doyle, Derek and David Jeffrey. *Palliative Care in the Home*. Oxford. Oxford

University Press. 2000.

Fitzpatrick, Jeanne, M.D. and Eileen M. Fitzpatrick, J.D. *A Better Way of Dying: How to Make the Best Choices at the End of Life.* USA. Penguin. 2010.

Gawande, Atul. *Being Mortal: Illness, Medicine, and What Matters in the End.* London: Profile Books Ltd. 2014.

Kaur Khalsa, Guru Terath. *Dying into Life: The Yoga of Death, Loss and Transformation.* Illinois. Versa Press. 2006.

Kessler, David. *The Needs of the Dying: A Guide for Bringing Hope, Comfort, and Love to Life's Final Chapter.* Tenth Anniversary Edition. New York. Harper. 2007.

Hookham, Lama Shenpen. *There's More to Dying than Death: A Buddhist Perspective.* UK. Windhorse Publications. Ltd. 2006.

Humphry, Derek. *Final Exit: The Practicalities of Self-Deliverance and Assisted Suicide for the Dying.* USA. Delta Trade Paperback. 2010. This book encourages conversations, provides technical information about self-help assisted dying. Appendix D provides a template for a Living Will and Durable Power of Attorney for Health Care for North America.

Lawton, Julia. *The Dying Process: Patient's Experience of Palliative Care.* London: Routledge. 2000.

Maturana Romesin, Humberto and Gerda Verden-Zoller. *The Origin of Humanness in the Biology of Love.* Exeter UK. Imprint Academic. 2008.

McCullough M.D., Dennis. *My Mother, Your Mother: Embracing 'Slow Medicine', The Compassionate Approach to Caring for Your Aging Loved Ones.* USA. Harper. 2008. This book provides a comprehensive overview indicating milestones in the decline of health and increased fragility in the elderly, which is helpful for those who find themselves as the caregivers.

Morhaim M.D., Dan. *The Better End: Surviving (and Dying) on Your Own Terms in Today's Modern Medical World.* Baltimore. The John Hopkins University Press. 2012. This book has a comprehensive Resources Section providing websites on specific topics covered as well as USA State-by-state listings of advance directive websites.

National Audit Office. 'Survey to Doctors in England – End of Life Care.' UK. medeConnect. 2008.

Nitschke Dr., Philip. *The Peaceful Pill Handbook.* USA. Exit International. 2012.

Palmer, Wendy and Janet Crawford. *Leadership Embodiment: How the Way We Sit and Stand Can Change the Way We Think and Speak.* Printed by CreateSpace, An Amazon.com Company. 2013.

Periyakoil, Vejeyatni S, and *Do Unto Others: Doctor's Personal End-of-Life Resuscitation* – Their Attitudes toward Advance Directives. DOI: 10.1371/journal.pone.0098246. May 2014.

Rumi, Jalaluddin. *Rumi the Book of Love: Poems of Ecstasy and Longing*. Translation and Commentary Coleman Barks. San Francisco. HarperCollins 2005.

Scholz, Fridolin E. *Kuhlandchen. Alte Heimat*. Germany Rautenberg Druck. 1998.

Sheehy, Gail. *Passages in Caregiving: Turning Chaos into Confidence*. New York. Harper. 2010.

Simmons, Robert and Niasha Ahsian. *The Book of Stones: Who They are and What They Teach*. Berkeley, California. North Atlantic Books. 2005.

Thamm, Marianne. *The Last Right: Craig Schonegevel's Struggle to Live and Die with Dignity*. South Africa. Jacana. 2013.

Volandes, M.D. Angelo E. *The Conversation: A Revolutionary Plan for End-of-Life Care*. New York. Bloomsbury. 2015.

Wanzer, Sidney and Joseph Glenmullen. *To Die Well: Your Right to Comfort, Calm and Choice in the Last Days of Life*. USA. Da Capo Press. 2007.

Warner, Felicity. *Gentle Dying: The Simple Guide to Achieving a Peaceful Death*. United Kingdom. Hay House. 2008.

Warnock, Mary and Elisabeth Macdonald. *Easeful Death: Is there a Case for Assisted Dying*. New York. Oxford University Press. 2008.

www.mylivingwill.org.uk. This is a comprehensive website for UK residents. It provides for you to complete online a Living Will consisting of two parts. The ADVANCE STATEMENT of preferences and wishes (e.g. Wash my hair once per week) is not legally binding. THE ADVANCE DECISION which indicates which medical treatment is acceptable and what's to be refused is legally binding.

Williams-Murphy, Monica and Kristian A. Murphy. *It's OK to Die*. USA: "Author's Draft" published by the Authors and MKN and LLC. 2011.

www.agingwithdignity.org/5wishes.html. Five Wishes is an advance directive that looks more holistically at a person's needs: medical, personal, emotional and spiritual. It was written with the help of the American Bar Association's Commission on Law and Aging and is valid under the laws of forty US states and the District of Columbia. Copies available online, by phone or by mail.

Yalom, Irvin D. *Staring at the Sun: Overcoming the Terror of Death*. San Francisco. Jossey Bass. 2008.

PART FIVE: Ritual

Anderson, Megory. *Sacred Dying: Creating Rituals for Embracing the End of Life*. New York. Marlowe & Company. 2001. This is the book in which I found the opening Hildegard of Bingen quote whose music I've long enjoyed and who stands out for me as a female, multi-talented, spiritual leader.

Anderson, Megory. *Sacred Dying: Creating Rituals for Embracing the End of Life*. New York. Marlowe & Company. 2001.

Andrade, Mary J. *Through the Eyes of the Soul, Day of the Dead in Mexico*. San Jose. La Oferta Review Newspaper, Inc. 1996

Arrien, Angeles. *The Four-Fold Way: Walking the Path of the Warrior, Teacher, Healer and Visionary*. New York. HarperCollins.1993.

Beck, Renée and Sydney Barbara Metrick. *The Art of Ritual: Creating and Performing Ceremonies for Growth and Change*. Berkeley. Celestial Arts. 1990.

Campbell, Joseph with Bill Moyers. *The Power of Myth*. USA. Anchor Books. 1991.

Jensen, Derrick. *A Language Older than Words*. USA. Chelsea Green Publishing Company. 2004.

Krige, Eileen Jensen. *The Social System of the Zulus*. Pietermaritzburg. Longmans Green & Co. Ltd. 1936.

Lamm, Maurice. *The Jewish Way in Death and Mourning*. New York. Jonathan David Publishers. 1969.

Lewis-Williams, J.D. and D. G. Pearce. *San Spirituality: Roots, Expressions, and Social Consciousness*. Cape Town. Double Storey Books. 2004.

Mahdi, Louise Carus, Nancy Geyer Christopher and Michael Meade. *Crossroads: The Quest for Contemporary Rites of Passage*. USA. Open Court. 1996.

Orr, Emma Restall. *Ritual: A Guide to Life, Love and Inspiration*. London. Thorsons. 2000. See pages 66-68 on 'power objects' such as the items requested by Robin Stransham-Ford for the room in which he died.

Ryman, Anders. *Rites of Life*. Koln. Evergreen GmbH. 2010.

Rinpoche, Sogyal. *The Tibetan Book of Living and Dying*. London. Rider. 2002.

Slovo, Joe. *The Unfinished Autobiography*. Johannesburg. Ravan Press. 1995.

Some, Malidoma Patrice. *Ritual: Power, Healing and Community*. USA. Swan Raven & Company. 1993.

Starhawk. *The Pagan Book of Living and Dying: Practical Rituals, Prayers, Blessings and Meditations on Crossing Over*. New York. HarperOne. 1997. This book may be particularly useful to people who do not have access to the rituals provided by a formal religion but who want the supportive role of ritual during dying, then death and bereavement.

Van Gennep, Arnold. *The Rites of Passage: A Classic Study of Cultural Celebrations*. Chicago. The University of Chicago Press. 1960.

Xinran. *Sky Burial: An Epic Love story of Tibet*. New York. Anchor Books. 2006.

PART SIX: **Bereavement**

Abrams, Rebecca. *When Parents Die: Learning to Live with the Loss of a Parent*. Great Britain: Routledge. 1992.

Alexander, Elizabeth. *The Light of the World: A Memoir*. New York. Grand Central Publishing. 2015.

Barker, Elspeth. *Loss: An Anthology.* Great Britain. J.M.Dent. 1997.

Bonnano, George A. *The Other Side of Sadness: What the New Science of Bereavement Tells Us About Life After Loss.* New York. Perseus Books. 2009.

Didion, Joan. *The Year of Magical Thinking.* London: Harper Perennial. 2006.

Grollman, Rabbi Earl A. *Living with Loss, Healing with Hope: A Jewish Perspective.* Boston. Beacon Press. 2000.

Ironside, Virgina. *You'll Get Over It: The Rage of Bereavement.* London. Penguin. 1997.

James, John W. and Russell Friedman. *The Grief Recovery Handbook.* New York. HarperCollins. 2009.

Konigsberg, Ruth David. *The Truth About Grief: The Myth of Its Five Stages and the New Science of Loss.* New York. Simon & Schuster. 2011.

Kubler-Ross, Elisabeth. *On Death and Dying.* Great Britain. Routledge. 2007.

Kubler-Ross, Elisabeth and David Kessler. *On Grief and Grieving: Finding the Meaning of Grief Through the Five Stages of Loss.* Great Britain. Schuster and Schuster Inc., 2005.

Lewis, C.S. *A Grief Observed.* London. Faber & Faber. 1961.

Mishkan T'Filah *Meditations before Kaddish – A progressive Siddur.*

O'Rourke, Meghan. *The Long Goodbye: A Memoir of Grief.* Great Britain. Virago. 2011.

Parkes, Colin Murray and Holly G. Prigerson. *Bereavement: Studies of Grief in Adult Life.* London. Penguin. 2010.

Pogrebin, Letty Cottin. *How to be a Friend to a Friend Who's Sick.* USA. Public Affairs. 2014.

Worden, J. William. *Grief Counselling and Grief Therapy: A Handbook for the Mental Health Practitioner.* New York. Springer Publishing Company, LLC. 2009.

Part Seven: Money. Planning. Emotions

Aries, Philippe. *The Hour of Our Death: The Classic History of Western Attitudes Toward Death Over the Last One Thousand Years.* Oxford. Oxford University Press. 1991.

Damasio, Antonio. *Descartes' Error: Emotion, Reason and the Human Brain.* New York. HarperCollins. 1994.

Doughty, Caitlin. *Smoke Gets in Your Eyes: & Other Lessons from the Crematory.* New York. W.W. Norton & Company, Inc. 2014.

Samuel, Lawrence R. *Death, American Style: A Cultural History of Dying in America.* USA. Rowman and Littlefield Publishers, Inc. 2013.

PART EIGHT: Winding Up

Chast, Roz. *Can't We Talk About Something More Pleasant?* New York. Bloomsbury. 2014.

PART NINE: Let's Talk—Towards the Tipping Point

Dolny Helena. 'Praying for Madiba.' *Mail & Guardian*. South Africa. 2011.

Dolny, Helena. 'Let's Talk About Dying.' *City Press* Sunday column series. South Africa. 2013.

Duff, Nancy. *Death with Dignity: The Ethics of Resisting and Accepting Death.* Public Lecture. Johannesburg. 2015.

Hammes PhD., Bernard J. (Editor) *Having Your Own Say: Getting the Right Care When It Matters Most.* Washington. CHT Press (Center for Health Transformation). 2012.

La Grange, Zelda. *Good Morning, Mr. Mandela*. South Africa. Allen Lane. 2014.

Limbo, Rana and Kathie Kobler. *Meaningful Moments: Ritual and Reflection When a Child Dies*. La Crosse. Gundersen Medical Foundation. 2013

Marchant, Jo. *Cure: A Journey into the Science of Mind over Body*. Edinburgh. Canongate. 2017

Slovo, Joe. *Slovo: The Unfinished Autobiography*. Johannesburg. Ravan Press. 1995.

Tutu, Desmond. 'Desmond Tutu: A dignified death is our right – I am in favour of assisted dying.' *The Guardian*. July 2014.

Tutu, Desmond. 'Archbishop Desmond Tutu: When my time comes, I want the option of an assisted death.' *The Washington Post*. Washington. USA. October 2016

PART TEN: New Beginnings

Eliot, T.S. *Collected Poems 1909–1962*. London. Faber and Faber Limited.1963. The title of this section of this book is taken from the Four Quartets. Little Gidding. written in 1942.

Oliver, Mary. *New and Selected Poems. Volume One*. Boston, Massachusetts. Beacon Press. 1992. The tile of Ten: Four, 'A Bride Married to Amazement' comes from the poem, '*When Death Comes*.'

Palmer, Parker J. *Let Your Life Speak: Listening for the Voice of Vocation*. San Francisco. Jossey Bass. 2000

PART ELEVEN: Live the Questions

Rilke, Rainer Maria. *Rilke of Love and Other Difficulties*. I.Mood.John L., ed. New York. W.W.Norton & Company Ltd.

All the books from Part One are relevant to this section. I would add:

Sieler, Alan. *Coaching to the Human Soul.* Volumes I, II and III. This trilogy is about ontology, our way of being in the world. The first volume covers language, 'The words we choose to use to create the reality we live in.' The second volume covers emotions, how these impact on our choice of language and also their impact on our body posture and health which is the subject matter of volume three.

Sieler, Alan. Coaching to the Human Soul, ontological coaching and deep change, volume 1. Victoria, Australia. Newfield Institute Pty. 2003.

Sieler, Alan. Coaching to the Human Soul, ontological coaching and deep change, volume 2: Emotional Learning and Ontological Coaching. Victoria, Australia. Newfield Institute Pty. 2007.

Sieler, Alan. Coaching to the Human Soul, ontological coaching and deep change, volume 3: the biological and somatic basis of ontological coaching. Victoria, Australia. Newfield Institute Pty. 2012.

Made in the USA
Middletown, DE
07 November 2017